My Valley • the Kananaskis

Ruth Oltmann

Rocky
Mountain Books

Front cover: The Fortress from the Kananaskis Valley before the golf course was built. Photo: Gillean Daffern.
Back cover photo: Gerald VanderPyl, Rocky Mountain Express, Jan. '96.
Map on page 4 by Roger Peterson, Boulder, Colorado.

**Published by
Rocky Mountain Books
#4 Spruce Centre SW
Calgary, Alberta T3C 3B3**

The publisher gratefully acknowledges the assistance provided by the Alberta Foundation for the Arts and by the federal Department of Canadian Heritage.

COMMITTED TO THE DEVELOPMENT OF CULTURE AND THE ARTS

Canadian Cataloguing in Publication Data

Oltmann, C. Ruth (Charlotte Ruth)
  My valley

  Includes bibliographic references.
  Previous ed. has title: The valley of rumours.
  ISBN 0-921102-40-2

  1. Kananaskis Country (Alta.)--History. I. Title.
FC3695.K36O58 1997   971.23'32   C97-910014-3
F1079.K34O58 1997

Contents

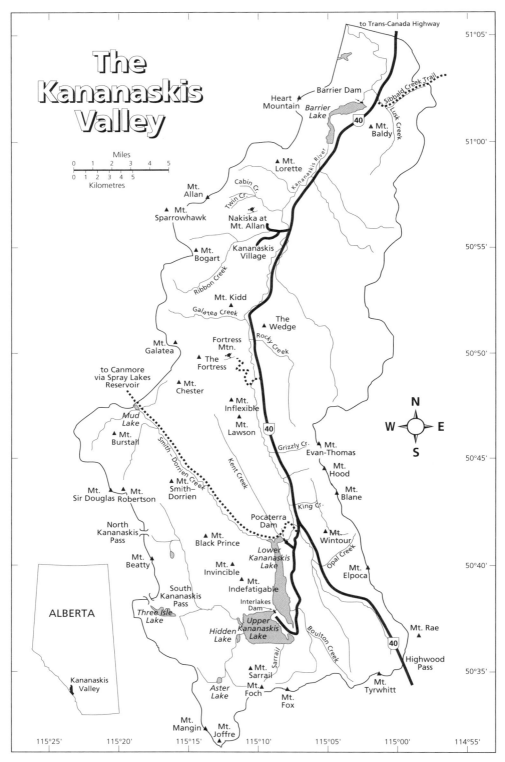

The Kananaskis Valley

Miles
0 1 2 3 4 5

Kilometres
0 1 2 3 4 5

to Trans-Canada Highway

51°05'

Barrier Dam

Heart Mountain

Barrier Lake

▲ Mt. Baldy

Sibbald Creek Trail

Lusk Creek

51°00'

▲ Mt. Lorette

Kananaskis River

Mt. Allan

Cabin Cr.

Twin Cr.

▲ Mt. Sparrowhawk

Nakiska at Mt. Allan

50°55'

▲ Mt. Bogart

Kananaskis Village

Ribbon Creek

Mt. Kidd ▲

Galatea Creek

The ▲ Wedge

50°50'

Mt. ▲ Galatea

Fortress Mtn.

Rocky Creek

▲ The Fortress

to Canmore via Spray Lakes Reservoir

▲ Mt. Chester

Mud Lake

▲ Mt. Inflexible

▲ Mt. Lawson

40

N

W — E

S

▲ Mt. Burstall

50°45'

Smith–Dorrien Creek

Kent Creek

Grizzly Cr.

▲ Mt. Evan-Thomas

Mt. ▲ Hood

Mt. ▲ Blane

Mt. ▲ Mt. Sir Douglas Robertson

▲ Mt. Smith–Dorrien

Pocaterra Dam

King Cr.

North Kananaskis Pass

▲ Mt. Black Prince

Lower Kananaskis Lake

▲ Mt. Wintour

Opal Creek

Mt. Beatty

Mt. ▲ Invincible

Mt. ▲ Elpoca

50°40'

South Kananaskis Pass

▲ Mt. Indefatigable

Interlakes Dam

ALBERTA

Three Isle Lake

Hidden Lake

Upper Kananaskis Lake

Boulton Creek

Mt. Rae ▲

40

Kananaskis Valley

▲ Mt. Sarrail

Sarrail

Highwood Pass

50°35'

Aster Lake

Mt.▲ Foch

Mt. Fox

Mt. Tyrwhitt ▲

Mt. Mangin

Mt. Joffre

115°25'   115°20'   115°15'   115°10'   115°05'   115°00'   114°55'

4

Preface

The Kananaskis Valley is a unique mountain valley situated in the eastern slopes of the Canadian Rocky Mountains and is approximately 90 kilometres long and six kilometres wide. It extends from the North Kananaskis Pass on the Continental Divide to Morley Flats at the Trans-Canada Highway. Near its source at the Haig Glacier and the North Kananaskis Pass the river tumbles down the narrow Turbine Canyon as Maude Creek, becoming the Upper Kananaskis River before it reaches the Kananaskis Lakes. Along its way north it passes spectacular rocky peaks and mountain meadows, swirls by the Kananaskis Country Golf Course, becomes the waters of Barrier Lake before crashing through the Widowmaker and the kayak slalom course at Canoe Meadows, and ends its journey at the Bow River.

The valley is becoming well known to Canadians for its spectacular beauty and recreational benefits. As one of the most accessible valleys in the Canadian Rockies, thousands of people visit it each year and enjoy its wonderful scenery.

The story of the valley starts with the Neolithic native peoples and continues beyond our lifetimes. Long after we are gone it will still be here, casting its special charm on visitors.

When I first began researching the story of the Kananaskis Valley in the 1970s for my book *The Valley of Rumours … the Kananaskis*, I encountered almost insurmountable obstacles; there was so little written information. After digging in archives and libraries, I discovered some of the best sources elsewhere. These sources were not dusty old records, but living human beings. It was through the people who have lived and worked in the valley that the missing links in its story finally came together. Without exception, fond memories remain in the hearts of these people.

I am particularly indebted to the people who contributed to my first book. Many of these people have now died, but their memories still live, and they create a picture of a beautiful and fascinating mountain valley.

Stories about the Kananaskis Valley are everywhere. During these last years of research I have listened to stories about the valley while sitting on the edge of Georgia Strait with Lynne and Dick Bowen, on the top of the smallest island in Vancouver with Pat Duffy, with Dennis and Ginny Jaques in their home in Vancouver, in my own home in Exshaw with my cousin John Johnsrud, and with Bruce and Christine Ernst who were visiting the valley from Quesnel, B.C. I have sat overlooking the city of Kelowna with Bud and Verna Smithers, across the snowy expanses of Chestermere Lake with Art Longair, in the city of Medicine Hat with my long time friends Pete and Marcia Wallis and Cynthia, Bob and Cathlin Mutch, and in the heart of Calgary with Param Sekhon, Lionel Jackson, Allan Legge, Tessy Bray, John Dupuis, Floyd Snyder, Gordon Hodgson, Lucille and Pete Roxburgh, Barney Reeves and Alf Skrastins. In Canmore I heard stories from Verda McAffer, Bob and Joanna Swanson and Bob Reynolds, and in Bow Valley Provincial Park from Jim Stomp and Dave Hanna. Ian Getty and I sat in Nakoda Lodge on the edge of Hector Lake and talked about the Stoney Indian's relationship to the valley.

Thank you to Glen Boles and Gordon Matthews of Cochrane for their stories. It was wonderful to see Gordon, still active at 86, and Ida after many years. And thanks to Ingrid Von Darl for sharing her life on the Kananaskis Lookout. A special thanks to Steve Donelon of Kananaskis Country for taking time on his day off to tell me about the wolf, bear and moose research in Peter Lougheed Provincial Park.

These fine people have not only enthralled me with their stories, but have enriched my life immeasurably. I have thoroughly enjoyed meeting the ones I didn't know and talking with old friends.

As always, the Glenbow-Alberta Institute is a great source of information. The story of the Kananaskis Valley would not be complete without the help of the people who have been in the background. Some have given me leads to other stories and some have contributed in small ways that were invaluable. Several of my storytellers came to the Barrier Lake Information Centre for other reasons. When our conversations revealed their background in the valley I asked them for an interview. They were like a gift from heaven. Thank you for your help and for sharing your stories. You are all part of the rich mosaic of the Kananaskis Valley.

A special thank you to everyone who contributed photographs and to Roger Peterson for the map.

My special thanks also to Tony and Gillean Daffern, my publishers, and their very able editor Janice Redlin, who taught me much about editing.

And to the One who created this valley and led me here, I will always be grateful.

Ruthie, 1997

Introduction

The car bumped and rattled over the dirt road at a speed far too fast for the potholes. I barely had time to look at the scenery while I held onto my seat. I wasn't sure I wanted to be here with this mad driver, and anyway, what was a hostel work party?

The crazy driver and I were going to Ribbon Creek Hostel in the Kananaskis Valley for a hostel work party, and would be meeting up with a group of seasoned Calgary hostellers. The hostel was the old A-frame building at the time and it was my first hostel experience. As it turned out, it was fortunate I was a heavy sleeper and never noticed the infamous pack rats.

We arrived on a Friday night in May of 1967. The next day everyone got involved in various projects. There were still some bits and pieces of the old mining village around and I remember going with Don Gowans to salvage some of the lumber to add to the hostel. While we were wandering through the site I stepped on a nail that went right into my foot. While I managed to extricate my foot, it eventually became infected, so I spent the weekend nursing it, and the next week soaking it in the kitchen sink! Since I wasn't much help after that Geoff Spedding amused me by taking me out in his four-wheel drive Landrover. We bumped and lunged over the rocks of Evan-Thomas Creek, but all I remember is the big boulders and a hazy glimpse of Mount Kidd while I hung on for yet another crazy driver.

No one told me what kind of food hostellers took to eat when at a hostel, and my boyfriend didn't tell me either, so on Saturday night when we brought out the strawberries, shortcake and whipped cream everyone made fun of us and I was too inexperienced to get the drift. I expect there is a lot more strawberry shortcake eaten today than in those days. People were pretty basic with the food they brought.

Following this adventure I became actively involved in the hostel association and went hiking, climbing, ski touring, downhill skiing and the whole bit for the next several years.

Being involved in the hostel association means you participate in more hostel work parties. That is what brought me to the Kananaskis Valley the second time—to help work on the foundation for the new Ribbon Creek Hostel. I can't remember much, except that it was in the fall of 1969 and I had my arm in a cast after having broken it in the Bugaboos, and that I was carrying rocks for the foundation with one hand.

In May of 1970 I moved to the mountains for the summer to manage the Spray River Hostel near Banff. That was the beginning, as I spent the next eight-and-a-half years running hostels and never left the mountains.

The third time I went to the Kananaskis Valley was for the opening of the new Ribbon Creek Hostel in 1970. I was still hostel manager at Spray River Hostel, but I didn't have a car. Rini Boers said he would come with me and we got a ride from one of his friends and were dropped off at Dead Man's Flats, across from the Grizzly Bar. We started hiking at six in the morning and planned to be at the hostel in time for the opening festivities and free dinner at supper time.

Canmore Mines was still operating and we managed to hitch a ride for about three kilometres on the back of one of their pickup trucks. It was a wild and hairy ride; hanging on to oil drums as we careened around sharp, rising corners on a narrow, rough road. We were unceremoniously dumped at the actual trail, not very far from treeline, at which point we were on our own. We didn't know much about the trail. I had asked a lot of people for information, but the most I found out was that it was 18 miles long and where to start it. We discovered the actual mileage when we got to the summit of the mountain as there was a big sign stuck in a cairn, although it was partially eaten by chipmunks, we could still read that it was eight miles to Dead Man's Flats and five miles to Ribbon Creek.

Because of our early start and the shorter mileage, we reached the summit with plenty of time to lay on the rocks and look at the view, take pictures and eat the last of our food.

The hike down the mountain to the hostel did not take long and we arrived around four in the afternoon. Pip and Alex Buchanan were the hostel managers at the time and were more famous for owning a monkey than Pip's bike ride from Spray River Hostel to the Banff hospital to have a baby. While waiting for the hostel people to arrive from Calgary with the free dinner we had a great visit, unfortunately, the free dinner never did arrive as the official opening had been postponed. Neither the Buchanans nor I had a phone in our respective hostels, so we could not be notified. Pip and Alex fed us and after all these years I still owe them a dinner in return! This may never happen as the last I heard they went back to Tasmania.

At one point in the evening I laid down in the dorm for a few minutes, but when I heard Marion Elliott arrive I got up and walked into the kitchen and promptly passed out! I'd gotten sunstroke. That taught me to wear a hat when I'm hiking.

At the time Rini was a university student working for the summer at the Bank of Montreal in Banff. We met when his friend Marilyn MacKay told him about me at Spray River Hostel where I had made it a habit to give away tea to whoever came by. Rini's banking career eventually took him to Toronto where he is now vice-president of human resources for the Bank of Montreal; and I, within two years of our hike, found myself back in the Kananaskis Valley commencing a long career of Kananaskis adventures. I didn't plan it that way, but I wouldn't have missed it for the world!

The Kananaskis Valley

1

Native Peoples

The sun rose and set on the Kananaskis Valley for thousands of years before I set foot within its portals. The glacial ice that stretched from the Great Divide along the Bow Valley advanced and receded at least four times, carving the spectacular mountain peaks and cirques, and forming the contours of the Kananaskis Valley today.

The people who first found the valley, as long ago as 8,000 years, had no concept of the role the glaciers played in forming the river and the mountains. They just enjoyed the beautiful environment, and the opportunities for hunting and the collection of medicinal herbs.

Knowledge of the Neolithic native peoples who first came into the valley stems from archaeological work that was primarily carried out by Dr. B. O. K. Reeves of the University of Calgary's Department of Archaeology. The Alberta government commissioned Dr. Reeves to make an archaeological reconnaissance of the Kananaskis Valley while a right-of-way for Highway #40 was being cleared in the early 1970s. This reconnaissance revealed 11 prehistoric sites; thus discovering the valley's rich prehistoric past.

Dr. Barney O. K. Reeves
The first time I did any archaeology work in the valley was probably around '66/67. I was in graduate school then. We went up and looked around the creek south of King Creek. We looked in some road cuts and found some flakes and then we went up the Smith-Dorrien Valley and back down through the gap to Canmore. It was an interesting road at that time.

Those are the early memories I have of the valley before we did the archaeology work on the highway in 1972 and 1973.

This was when the government of Alberta had passed the Alberta Heritage Act, which was changed to the Historical Resources Act in '74. The Department of Highways and Transport, whose minister was Clarence Copithorne, was reasonably proactive. In fact, the only environmental impact study they ever did was of Highway #940. As part of that they had an archaeological study done—we did the study for them—and found one very good site and did the excavations on that site the next year. We took a sample. Instead of excavating the whole area that was going to be destroyed, we excavated about five per cent. We laid out an excavation grid and systematically excavated each square—2x2 metre square—and recorded all the information, retrieved the artifacts, took them back, catalogued them and analyzed them. Those artifacts are still at the University of Calgary in the Archaeology Museum collection.

That was the Wasootch Creek site. There were four people working on the dig for three or four weeks. There is still a lot of the site left. It's on the forested side of the valley, and the artifacts we got out of it indicated it was occupied, probably at a time when the valley was quite a bit more open—during the time we call the mid-Holecene drought. That's the period since the last glaciation, the last 10,000 years. At that time there was a reasonable amount of information from the Rockies and now we have a lot more in the last 25 years that indicates the valleys were much more open than they have been in the last 3,000-5,000 years.

When we did our work at Wasootch Creek we found one particular type of chert, but I didn't know where it was coming from. I knew it was coming out of one of the Mississippian formations most likely, and that it was similar to stuff we'd seen in Banff, but it was a little bit different, in terms of specific mineralogy and micropaleontology. In the Lower Kananaskis reservoir area they found tremendous workshops composed of all kinds of waste material of the same rock type, indicating that somewhere close to that reservoir, or the original lake, there is a very large quarry. They did a bit of work when they built the new Smith-Dorrien Road and did an excavation on a very large workshop and again it was all this material. So there was a very large quarry up there, and someday when I have the time and energy I'll go find it.

According to the archaeological data prepared by Dr. Reeves, the earliest known occupants of the valley were representatives of what has been called the Mummy Cave Complex, present on the east slopes of the Rocky Mountains between 5500 and 1500 BC. This culture occupied sites (such as one excavated near Wasootch Creek) during the Atlantic Climatic Sub-Episode, a period of optimum climatic conditions for man in the northern Rockies. Interpretation of the information available for this period indicates the valley could have supported large native populations.

Of these 11 locations, the Wasootch Creek site, which was contained wholly within the highway right-of-way, was judged to be of considerable value. This campsite is dated ca. 4500 BC (+/- 500 years), and was probably occupied during the winter months. A large number of artifacts were collected from the site during the salvage excavations carried out in late May and June of 1973 by a crew of four field archaeologists. The sites were dated according to relative dating techniques.

Although charcoal was fairly common in the area, it could not be used for radio carbon dating as it was thought to represent burnt root systems and charcoal scattered over the site in pre- and post-occupation forest fires. The Wasootch Creek site had the largest artifact yield per unit of surface site area (some 50 times greater than the other locations in the lower valley), suggesting it represented a major base campsite occupied by a large group for a long period of time within the year, and/or occupied for several years. The site was probably occupied during a time when its forest cover was not so great and the ground water table was lower. Such conditions would occur only if mean precipitation values were lower and mean temperatures higher than those of today. Precipitation, particularly in the winter, was less by 25 per cent during the time of occupation and temperatures were higher by 2-3°C, the latter caused by a decrease in cloud cover in the northern Rocky Mountains. These changes reflect a climatic pattern characterized by a mild winter with frequent chinooks. Snow storms and outbreaks of cold arctic air were not common.

The native people in the valley probably had a seasonal resource utilization pattern consisting of small family bands who engaged in hunting bison and other ungulates during the spring and summer, in areas such as the Kananaskis Lakes and upper Ribbon Creek. In the fall the bands would disperse to follow the migrating ungulates back to the lower Kananaskis Valley and adjacent foothills. During the winter the bands likely recongregated at such places as the Wasootch Creek site.

While this was probably the general pattern, the Kananaskis Valley was not necessarily used by only one group. There was undoubtedly much travel, of both a socio-religious and a commercial nature. There is evidence, particularly in the type of stone used by the native occupants, that considerable trade took place between the Kananaskis and the southern Rocky Mountain Trench-Kootenay Lakes area people in British Columbia.

In prehistory terms, the use of the valley's minerals and rocks was extensive. Coarse-grained quartzites, sandstones, and soft limestones and dolomites were obtained from nearby till or gravel outcrops. The harder of these rocks were used in making large butchering tools and the softer were used extensively in working the hides of the animals. Fine-grained cherts suitable for manufacturing a variety of implements—projectile points, knives, scrapers, perforators, and engraving and cutting implements—were obtained from nearby riverbeds and outcrops. Blocks, cores and flakes were produced at the quarry and carried back to the campsite for further working.

Schooner Island on Upper Kananaskis Lake. Photo NA-695-39 courtesy: Glenbow-Alberta Institute.

The 5,000 artifacts recovered from the Wasootch site consisted of a variety of tools, debitage and core fragments manufactured largely from cryptocrystalline cherts, chalcedonies and microcrystalline quartzites, sandstones, limestones and dolomites. This archaeological data gives a picture of a highly developed, albeit primitive economy and society, based upon a variety of resources: bison and other ungulates, minerals for tools and trade, and manufactured goods.

Other archaeological work has been done in the valley: at the Upper Kananaskis Lake, at the junction of Smith-Dorrien Creek with the Kananaskis River, near the present Kananaskis Emergency Services Centre, at the junction of Fortress Mountain Road with Highway #40, near Elbow Pass and on the Stoney Indian Reserve along the Kananaskis River. The Reeves' data gives a good picture of the Neolithic native peoples and their activities.

Unfortunately, archaeological data can only give us an idea of how the native people lived with their environment. Because they kept no written record, how they felt about the land they roamed, and the customs and beliefs that they held, are difficult to ascertain. Our knowledge of the native people, beyond the archaeological field, is derived from white man's records.

Early in the eighteenth century, the Kananaskis Valley was under the control of the Blackfoot Confederacy tribes (Blackfoot and Peigan) and cohabited by the Sarcee. The most recent native people to use and occupy the valley are the Stoney Indians, a mountain Sioux band who have resided in the area since the mid-nineteenth century.

Irene M. Spry, in her book, *The Papers of the Palliser Expedition 1857-1860*, reveals to us the native people of the 1800s and their way of life as described by explorers, who recorded their observations and opinions in daily journals during the Palliser expedition. John W. Sullivan, an astronomer and secretary to the expedition during 1858, described the Stoney Indians as:

> ... a tribe of Thickwood Indians, whose hunting grounds lie along the base and in the valley of the Rocky Mountains. They are very poor, and go about almost naked, and suffer great misery through want of food. Occasionally they make excursions into the plains after the moose, elk, long-tail and short-tail deer, the big-horned sheep, and bears. They are very expert hunters. They are sprung from the same stock as the Plains Stoneys, and their language differs only as a provincial dialect from that of their kinsfolk of the plains. Unlike that nation, however, who possess all the vices common to the prairie tribes, the Rocky Mountain Stoneys are peaceful and inoffensive. They have been converted to the Christian religion, and are unusually attentive to the truths which have been taught them by the missionaries. Every morning and evening they devote a short space of time to religious duties, and make it a rule to rest from the labours of the chase and travel on Sunday. The sacred music which has been taught them is most characteristic, and when singing in one of the solitary valleys of the Rocky Mountains, their chant sounds intensely wild. In former years they numbered far more tents than at present: now we believe there are only 35, or about 250 souls....

James Hector, on a branch expedition in 1858-59, and Captain John Palliser, noted the religious activities of the Stoney Indians. Palliser felt their good Christian behaviour was because of the lack of the corrupting influence of the white population. Hector observed their hunting prowess and was pleased to see they had not yet lost the art of the bow and arrow, their ancient weapon. He was concerned with their fate, as well as other tribes, and made the following comments in his journal in 1859:

> I had a long talk with the chiefs about what was likely to become of them and the other Indian tribes. They said that every year they find it more difficult to keep from starving, and that even the buffalo cannot be depended upon as before, because being now only in large bands, when one tribe of Indians are hunting them the other tribes have to go without until the band migrates into their country. The Stoneys are all Christians, and some of them can read and write in their own language, using the Cree syllabic characters, which were invented by the Wesleyan missionaries. They are very desirous of having tools and a few simple agricultural implements; and, as they are very steady, I have no doubt that if they were supplied with these, and direction given to their efforts, the best part of them would soon settle down, and leave their vagrant mode of life. Their chiefs at least seem to be quite in earnest about the matter.

Captain Blakiston was also greatly concerned about the native tribes and he, too, noted the religious aspect of the Stoney Indian life and their desire to learn to farm. In 1858 he met some Thickwood Stoney Indians at Trap Creek, just above the junction of the Highwood River, and entered this account in his journal:

> During the afternoon I held a talk with these Indians. I told them plainly for what reason we had been sent to the country; that Her Majesty was always glad to hear of their welfare, and that any message which they might have for Her I would take down in writing. 'We are glad,' said an old man, 'that the great woman Chief of the Whites takes compassion upon us, we think she is ignorant of the way in which the traders treat us; they give us very little goods and ammunition for our furs and skins, and if this continues our children cannot live. We are poor, but we work well for the whites. The Indians of the plains treat us badly and steal our horses, but we do nothing to them, for the minister tells us so.' In answer to questions from myself, they said that they would wish white people to come and live among them and teach them to farm, make clothes, etc., so that 'their children might live,' for the animals are getting every year more scarce. I may here state, that I have been fortunate enough this year to fall in with many camps of the different tribes of Indians inhabiting this country, from whom I always obtained as much information as possible on their present state, and their wishes as to the future; and I hope to draw up a report on the same for the information of Her Majesty's Government; for without doubt, when deciding on the future of this country, some provision should be made for the poor uncivilized beings to whom by right the soil belongs.

Grant MacEwan records that by 1877 many changes were taking place in the West and… "The uncertainty of Indian temper in the southwestern section of the prairies was enough to discourage traders and settlers from going there. Members of the Blackfoot, Blood, Peigan, Sarcee and Stoney tribes were known to be cranky and tough. Naturally, they resented the new order and did not hesitate to display their anger. As a result, the acceptance of a settlement treaty on September 22, 1877, was seen as a major triumph in taming the West."[1]

The Stoney Indian's relationship to the valley today has also changed, as they seek to show their relationship to the valley to the white man. For example, when Kan Alta Golf Management Ltd., who operate the Kananaskis Country Golf Course, wished to expand and build another golf course on the east side of High-

Stoneys–cutting buggy trail, 1912. Photo NA-695-19 courtesy: Glenbow-Alberta Institute.

way #40, adjacent to Evan-Thomas Creek, the Stoneys entered a submission at the Natural Resources Conservation Board hearing on June 5, 1992.

Peter Wesley made the following comments regarding the Stoney's relationship to the land in the Evan-Thomas Creek area:

> … when you talk about land and the Indians, all you hear is hunting. So I'm going to share with you a bit of the magnitude of the relationship the Stoney Indians have with the land. Not only do we use the area for hunting, but for fishing and trapping in the Evan-Thomas area. My father, Lazarus Wesley, has a trapline that goes from the Stoney Reserve to Galatea and Canmore. The area has been a traditional camping area. It's a relay area, homing area, rendezvous territory. It has spiritual and medicinal use, and it's an area of worship.
>
> Gathering takes place there; herbs, plants, berries, rocks, minerals, moss. The Evan-Thomas area and south is popular with the Stoneys for porcupines. It is called the Trail of Many Porcupines. Porcupine quills are used for ceremonial regalia for gatherings, powwows, religious and other events and purposes.
>
> Porcupine hair is used for headgear that is native—which the native grass dancers wear in preparing the grass for their religious sun dance ceremonies. Bear claw necklaces are worn as a sign of strength during times of negotiations, both in the past and present.
>
> Not only do the Stoneys still hunt for food, but the furs are still used for hair ties for little girls at naming ceremonies and rights of passage ceremonies. So, it's used as a trapline, not only in the Hudson's Bay sense, but you know, it's before them and after and now and in the future.

Vision Quest site, King Creek. Photo: Gillean Daffern.

The Evan-Thomas area has been used for initiation ceremonies, rites, birthing areas, rites of passage, relationships, objects and symbols, friendships, as well as an area used by newlyweds in the same manner as what is known today as a honeymoon. Also a final resting place or burial site.

... I myself was raised on game, fish, berries and plants of the Kananaskis region. I am an Indian and I choose to continue any Indianness in my closeness and continuity with the land. Because of the solitude and the closeness with God through the creation, holistic wellness takes place. This region is an outdoor classroom in which to study life, weather patterns for forecasting, growth of the forest and foliage, fowl, animals, tracks, wisdom and lessons from nature. I will be taking my 13 year-old son into the Evan-Thomas area for his initiation, his rite of passage into manhood. This is the same location that I had my initiation. The Evan-Thomas area provides the location for teaching legends, ideals, philosophy, virtues, values, traditions, customs, history, lessons, survival skills and the traditional ways of the Stoneys.

The Stoney name for the Evan-Thomas Creek area is 'Chase Tida.' Chase means a burnt timber. Tida means a flat. The general area is Chase Tida ... meaning Many Porcupines Creek. And Indian Trail is Ozada Chagu, meaning Many Porcupines Trails that goes to Eden Valley from the confluence there.

Obviously, the Stoney people still use the valley as part of their way of life, and they still come to enjoy the valley's awesome beauty. In past years they travelled through the Kananaskis Valley to the Palliser River canyon where they believed the spirits of their dead animals went to live.

Today, scattered throughout the Kananaskis Valley, Stoney people have set up a number of vision quest sites. These sites change every year since they are dependent on wherever the person is drawn. The native person leaves brightly coloured pieces of cloth with tobacco (or kinnikinnick) knotted on the ends. These pieces of cloth are then tied to a number of trees in a remote area. They are left to naturally disintegrate. Typically five or more of these vision quest sites are found each year in Kananaskis Country. The tobacco is a gift to the Great Spirit. King Creek, Barrier Lake and Ribbon Creek are places where hikers have reported seeing vision quest sites.

There is also a large gathering, held annually, called Tai Jurabi Chubi, or the Sun Dance. These gatherings involve a central tree, or trees, and the use of sweat lodges (formed like a log tipi). Gatherings have been held in the Sibbald Lake area—off Highway #68, and also at Morley Flats, at the entrance to the valley. The Stoney people prefer to keep the rituals of their sun dances private.

Today we have many white man's names for the features in the valley, but the Stoneys had their own names. The Stoney name for Mount Baldy was Sleeping Buffalo. On the east side of this mountain, in the early white man's days, Indian women camped to await the return of the men from the hunt, keeping a lookout in order to have a meal ready upon their arrival in camp. The Stoneys called the Kananaskis River Mînîthnî-ozada, that is, tributary of the Cold Water (Bow) River. The Kananaskis Lakes were simply called Ozada Imnî—Valley Lakes.

Thus, the Stoney people have left their mark on the valley, not only in the past, but also in the present.

Early Explorers

By the time the first white man set foot in the valley, the native people were no longer using it in the same way. The trails had been obstructed by deadfall, and the numbers of wild animals had dwindled. This phase of the valley history was one of transition from independence in the hands of the Stoney native people, to dependence upon the growing urban influence of the white man as he moved west across the prairies and into the mountains.

James Sinclair

In 1841 settlers were few in the Canadian west, although there was a sprinkling of courageous settlers and missionaries, forerunners of more to come. It was in this year that James Sinclair, "son of a Scottish father, and partly Cree mother, graduate of the University of Edinburgh, challenger of the Hudson's Bay Company monopoly and a leader among the native-born Red River settlers,"[2] took a company of Red River settlers to Oregon, through what is now the Canadian Rocky Mountains, via White Man Pass in the Spray Lakes valley. While this proved to be a good route, Sinclair had also heard about another route reputed to be shorter. When he brought more settlers from Red River in 1854, he chose this new route.

B.C. Archives.

Sinclair had met the native chief named Mackipictoon at Fort Edmonton in 1841 and heard about the shorter route from him. Mackipictoon belonged to the Wetaskiwin band of Cree. This most unusual person was also known as Broken Arm from a conspicuous infirmity. During his 1854 expedition Sinclair met up with Mackipictoon and secured him as a guide over this recommended shorter route. Although the presence of Mackipictoon and his Cree followers was an asset while on the prairies, he proved to be a great disappointment in the mountains.

Mackipictoon's idea was to take the Sinclair party up the Strong Current (Kananaskis) River and over a pass that had never seen a white man. Things did not go well from the beginning. The party of settlers was large; the total number of people being 100, which included Sinclair's own family, and there were 250 head of cattle. While at the Bow camp (the confluence of the Kananaskis and Bow rivers), they were delayed for two weeks by the birth of a baby.

The carts had to be abandoned at the Bow camp and from there the people made a pack train with the horses and oxen. Whatever animals could be spared from packing were ridden by the women and children, and the mothers carried their babies papoose-fashion on their backs. The party thus proceeded up the Strong Current River. The route became more difficult with each passing day and the people and animals became more weary. Because of the difficult "terrain it was necessary to have an advance party of men proceed ahead of the main party, scouting for the best route and clearing the way for the others." Mackipictoon eventually admitted to being lost and the party had to travel by compass. Although they had secured two Stoney guides, no mention of their help has been recorded.

Turbine Canyon, 1937.
Photo NA-33-512 courtesy:
Whyte Museum of the
Canadian Rockies.

Upper Kananaskis, 1937,
North Kananaskis Pass.
Photo NA-33-528:
R. M. Patterson.
Courtesy: Whyte Museum
of the Canadian Rockies.

At this point in their journey there appears to be some discrepancy in the story John V. Campbell, Sinclair's brother-in-law, mentions in his log of the journey.

> At one place we came to a place that had to be bridged; a most fearful spot. Small trees were thrown across a narrow chasm that seemed almost bottomless…

D. Geneva Lent states that after this narrow chasm the Sinclair party came to the Lower and Upper Kananaskis lakes country. However, it is possible that the record of events in the John V. Campbell narrative, from which Lent frequently quotes, is out of order. There are no chasms along the Kananaskis River between the Bow River and the Lower Kananaskis Lake narrow enough to make a bridge of small trees or so deep that they would seem almost bottomless; but what is now known as Turbine Canyon on Maude Creek, which drains into the Upper Kananaskis River from North Kananaskis Pass, would fit this description.

Lent assumes the party went over the South Kananaskis Pass by way of Three Isle Creek; this was a debatable question to Lent. We now know there is a small cliff band below Three Isle Lake, which is impossible to scale with horses and cattle. The North Kananaskis Pass is the more likely route. While the North Kananaskis Pass is higher than the South Kananaskis Pass, it is still possible, with much hardship, to take horses and cattle. Turbine Canyon would fit Campbell's aforementioned description. The shale and boulders referred to by Lent are, today, prevalent on the North Kananaskis Pass route, while the South Kananaskis Pass summit area is an alpine meadow.

South Kananaskis Pass, 1937. Photo NA-33-563: R. M. Patterson.
Courtesy: Whyte Museum of the Canadian Rockies.

Irene M. Spry, editor of *The Papers of the Palliser Expedition, 1857-1860*, thinks it is probable that Sinclair did not take either of the Kananaskis passes, but rather Elk Pass. This would be possible, although there are no masses of shale or boulders on this pass; the pass remains in the trees, and would not take them to the Kootenays, their final destination. There is no doubt Sinclair's route was extremely difficult. Whereas the White Man Pass route had taken him 10 days, the Kananaskis Pass route took 30 days. It is the measure of the man that he did not give up.

John Palliser

In 1841, when Sinclair took his first party of settlers over the mountains, Ontario and Quebec were joined under the Act of Union; Canada was just beginning to experiment with confederation. This spirit of confederation continued to grow until the drive to annex the west and form one country from sea to sea began to be expressed publicly. With the election of the Grits in 1856 this desire became government policy. This new Government of Canada had its eye on the west, especially as the Hudson's Bay Company licence was due to expire in 1859. The year 1857 saw both Canada and the British government decide to investigate the company's claim and its record.

Photo NA-588-1 courtesy: Glenbow-Alberta Institute.

To this end, they sought an impartial opinion of the country. In May of that year the British government commissioned John Palliser to lead an expedition to gather detailed information on the nature and resources of the prairie west. Palliser's expedition encompassed the years 1857 to 1860, and during this time his party was the second European group ever recorded to see the Kananaskis Valley, to follow the river to its source and cross the Continental Divide.

In 1848 James Sinclair had told Palliser of the pass he heard about from Mackipictoon. Palliser never forgot about Mackipictoon's pass and on August 18th, 1858, accompanied by his secretary Mr. Sullivan, and with nine horses, he left the ruins of Old Bow Fort with the intention of crossing the Kananaskis Pass.

Prior to Palliser's arrival in the Kananaskis Valley, no white man's name had been applied to its features. Hence, the day before his departure from Old Bow Fort, Palliser named the pass he intended to cross:

> ... Kananaskis Pass, after the name of an Indian, of whom there is a legend, giving an account of his most wonderful recovery from the blow of an axe, which had stunned but had failed to kill him, and the river which flows through this gorge also bears his name.

In Palliser's printed report, and the Hector papers, the name is spelled Kananaskis. However, various spellings occur, not only in Palliser's papers and report, but also in Blakiston's papers. Kananaskis, Kannenaskis, Kannanaskis, Kinnonaskis, Kananaskasis and Kananaski's all appear. Blakiston also uses Kananaski or Lake River, or Emigrant Pass.

On the 19th of August Palliser reached the Kananaskis Prairie, where it was rumoured the legendary Kananaskis was hit by the axe. (This area is located

Maude Lake, 1937. Photo NA-33-547: R. M. Patterson.
Courtesy: Whyte Museum of the Canadian Rockies.

between the Kananaskis Country Golf Course and the Kananaskis Emergency Services Centre, and has more recently been known as Brule Flats.)

Palliser was very impressed with the valley as he progressed along its course and described it as magnificent. Both Palliser and Sinclair found the obstructions of fallen timber the biggest hazard in their journeys. Wind was not the only cause of fallen timber. During their second day of travel from Old Bow Fort Palliser noted in his diary:

> ... all forests are not destroyed by the hand of man, for we saw whole masses of forest, isolated in mountain cliffs, fallen by fire, the mountain trees burnt in places so precipitous that no human hand could ever have reached them.

He also noted a large number of bears and commented on how they stripped the bark off the trees to get at the turpentine.

When Palliser's party reached Kananaskis Lakes they set up camp. It is possible, while his men were busy preparing the meat of two elk they had killed, Palliser had time to go over Elk Pass to the Lower Elk Lake. While this is not the route over the Divide that he took, he does describe the area accurately in his journal.

The expedition noted the presence of mountain goats and caught two fish in Lower Kananaskis Lake, which was later to become famous as a fisherman's paradise. They crossed the Kananaskis River above Lower Kananaskis Lake and came upon Upper Kananaskis Lake, which impressed Palliser so much he wrote:

…we came on a magnificent lake, hemmed in by mountains, and studded by numerous islets, very thickly wooded. This lake, about four miles long and 1-1/2 miles wide, receives the waters from the glacier above, and is a favourite place of resort to the Kootanie Indians.

Before the construction of the power dams, the Kananaskis River ran between the two lakes for about a kilometre, connecting the two lakes. It had a 2.5 metre-high waterfall at the outlet of the lake and a 12.3 metre-high waterfall about 100 rods downstream. There was a trail on each side of Lower Kananaskis Lake, but the east side was swampy and the native people mainly used the one on the west side.

Following the Upper Kananaskis River, the party arrived at Lawson Lake and proceeded on to Maude Lake at the summit of the North Kananaskis Pass. Maude Lake drains to the Pacific Ocean via an underground stream and then surfaces, joining LeRoy Creek. On the east side it flows to the Saskatchewan River, and the Atlantic Ocean, via Maude Creek and the Upper Kananaskis River. Palliser gauged the summit level of the pass to be 5,985 feet above sea level. The pass is actually 2363.6 metres (7,682 feet).

Palliser's party camped at Maude Lake, where he observed the siffleur (marmot) and noted in his journal the Shuswap Indians made clothes of the siffleur skins. The party arrived at the summit of the pass on August 22nd, five days after their departure from Old Bow Fort.

The following morning the descent of the pass began, following LeRoy Creek to the river below, "which the men ever afterwards called Palliser's River, to distinguish it from the other branch of the Kootanie River." In his general report Palliser states:

Our journey across the Kananaskis Pass, although arduous, was not formidable, on account of abrupt ascents and descents on the eastern slope of the mountains, and the principal difficulty to be overcome was the amount of timber to be cut in order to allow the horses to force their way through. On the western slope we found the descent very steep, and the obstructions from fallen timber so thick and so severe that on the 24th of August we were occupied 14 hours in accomplishing six miles, and hard work it was.

Thus they left the Kananaskis Valley, later to return to Edmonton House via the Kootenai Pass. Palliser felt a road from the "Kananaskis Pass to the Columbia River, in the neighbourhood of the 49th degree, would not be a very arduous undertaking," therefore, in 1859, he sent Sullivan, his secretary, from Fort Shepherd back to the Kananaskis Pass in order to see if it was possible to establish a line of communication across the Rocky Mountains to the Pacific without crossing the boundary of the United States. Sullivan's journey from Fort Shepherd was so difficult, because of obstructions, he had to leave his horses and continue on foot to the Kananaskis Pass. Sullivan's account of the trip evidently discouraged Palliser from considering this route. At the end of his famous expedition Palliser stated:

Of all the passes traversed by our Expedition, the most favourable and inexpensive to render available for wheel conveyances would appear to be Vermillion Pass….

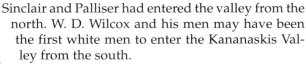

W. D. Wilcox

Sinclair and Palliser had entered the valley from the north. W. D. Wilcox and his men may have been the first white men to enter the Kananaskis Valley from the south.

Wilcox was accompanied by Henry G. Bryant, James Wood, Tom Lusk and Ben Woodworth. They left Banff in August 1901 for Spray Lakes with the intention of visiting the Kananaskis Lakes. They had started out with two Swiss guides, but Wilcox sent them back at the forks of the Spray River, 20 miles south of Banff. Their plan was "to proceed directly south from White Man's pass (above the present-day town of Canmore) and make the Kananaskis Lakes their headquarters, and then to follow the Elk River southwards" for further exploration.

Wilcox had Dawson's map, which led him to believe the Spray Valley lead directly to the Kananaskis Lakes. However, because they mistakenly followed the upper Spray River beyond the Spray Lakes, and not Smuts Creek over the pass at Mud Lake, they went over Palliser Pass and ended up in the Palliser River valley. This resulted in the party becoming totally lost and only with great difficulty did they find a very high pass that took them into the Elk River valley. (This is the pass R. M. Patterson called The Pass in the Clouds in his book *The Buffalo Head*.) From the Elk Valley they headed north, eventually reaching the Kananaskis Lakes by crossing Elk Pass. It took them 15 days to get to the Kananaskis Lakes.

It is unclear from Wilcox's writings if he was looking for the pass up Smuts Creek, which the Smith-Dorrien/Spray Trail road goes over today, or if he was looking for the North Kananaskis Pass that Palliser and Sinclair had used. If he was looking for the latter, it is understandable why he couldn't locate it. It cannot be seen from the Palliser River valley as it is approached from Palliser Pass. A person would have to be up high on LeRoy Creek to see the pass, and even then it just looks like a high ridge between mountains.

Arriving at Kananaskis Lakes, Wilcox and his party camped beside the river between the two lakes. They had brought a folding boat with them and were successful in catching trout, and they saw many wild ducks and geese. They used the river between the lakes as their access to explore the area.

Wilcox observed, "The bottom of the lake near the shore is covered by several species of water plants, whose long stems wave gently in the current of the inlet stream, and the surface of the water is constantly ringed by trout rising to flies. We were startled at evening and after nightfall by the melancholy cry of the loon, the hooting of owls and other mysterious sounds made possible by lynx or mountain lions."

The group spent a week at the Kananaskis Lakes doing "survey work and exploration of the surrounding region." On the second day they moved camp to Upper Kananaskis Lake. "From our tent we looked out on a revelation of beauty hardly equalled anywhere in the mountains. This lake is pear shaped and about two miles in diameter. It is circled by very high mountains of the

Opposite. Photo NA-529-3, c. 1920,
courtest: Glenbow- Alberta Institute.

Hidden Lake and Upper Kananaskis Lake before hydro.
Photo NA-695-38 courtesy: Glenbow-Alberta Institute.

main range of the Rockies, and has four large islands and several small islets, all densely wooded, which give an endless variety of view from various points.... No fish were ever seen or caught in this lake, while the lower lake abounds in them."

While at Upper Kananaskis Lake Wilcox took James Wood with him to look for the North Kananaskis Pass. Shortly before reaching a lake he left Wood and on finding the lake he named it Lawson Lake. As he walked, he kept discarding items he was carrying so as to lighten his load and go faster. Rushing along he thought the pass had to be on the other side of Lawson Lake, only to discover he had to go farther and farther. It was late in the day, but he was so anxious to find the pass he kept rushing on. He eventually came upon Maude Lake, "a desolate lake," and arrived at the pass (now called North Kananaskis Pass) at four in the afternoon, and calculated it to be 7,805 feet. He could see down the valley to the Palliser River and where one of their camps had been.

Back at Kananaskis Lakes, the expedition met an old Indian who called the lower lake Stony Lake. There were 20 to 30 men, women and children, plus 50 horses in the native group. Wilcox noted that the Indian women drove their horses by speaking quietly or "making a gentle hissing noise ... entirely different from the vociferous shouts and curses of the average white packer."

Wilcox and his party explored the area further and they found what we now call Hidden Lake, Fossil Falls and Aster Lake, the latter of which was at the base of a long glacier. They also found many fossils, as well as the spring where Hidden Lake's stream gushes out near Upper Kananaskis Lake (it now gushes up into the lake since the lake has been enlarged). From Wilcox's writings it appears he

25

climbed to the top of Mount Indefatigable as well. Wilcox and his party left the Kananaskis Lakes on August 24th and followed the Kananaskis River to the railroad. "The last 20 miles were easier because of the now disused lumber road."

George W. Pocaterra

The most colourful individual, and one of the few men, besides Palliser, to leave his mark indelibly on the valley, was George W. Pocaterra. Much had happened before George Pocaterra arrived on the scene in 1905, but his name and spirit will endure throughout history. Born in Rocchette, Italy, Pocaterra, whose father ran a textile factory, came from an ancient aristocratic family. He had attended the University of Berne, Switzerland, and when he arrived in Canada in 1903 he was fluent in German, Spanish, Italian and English. He was to become fluent in Stoney as well. He started work in Winnipeg, but soon came west to High River where he worked for the Bar D Ranch. In 1905 he and a cousin, who had lived in Brazil and Argentina, homesteaded the Buffalo Head Ranch in the Eden Valley. This ranch later became one of the first dude ranches in Canada. (The ranch is still in existence and is located on the north side of Highway #541, between the town of Longview and the Kananaskis Country boundary.)

Pocaterra made friends with both white men and Indians. He eventually became a blood brother to Paul Amos, a Stoney Indian, and a great friend to Three Buffalo Bulls with whom he saw the Kananaskis Lakes from the summit of the Great Divide for the first time. (Most of the Amos families live today on the Stoney Reserve just west of Highway #40, near the Trans-Canada Highway.) Pocaterra describes his initial trip to the Kananaskis Valley as …

> A fairly quick trip over Alridge Pass, over the second range of the Rockies, then down the long, steep slope to Elk River, up the beautiful valley of that large stream to the Elk Lakes, the headwaters of the main tributary of the Kootenay, and over the Elk River Pass to the Kananaskis Lakes. The most beautiful mountain scenery in the world, as far as I am concerned, was at these lakes but now is completely spoiled by the power dams, the drowning of the marvelously beautiful islands and exquisitely curved beaches, the cutting down of the centuries old trees, and the drying up of the twin falls between the two lakes, and the falls below the lower lake. From the Kananaskis Lakes we moved up a tributary from the east over a pass (the Highwood), down the Highwood River to my old Buffalo Head Ranch.

Pocaterra became involved in fur trapping in the Kananaskis Valley. Fur trapping went back hundreds of years to the time when the native people trapped animals in order to clothe themselves. Later, during fur trading days in Canada, the valley was, no doubt, a source of income to the native people, who sold their furs to the Hudson's Bay Company factor at Morley.

George W. Pocaterra. Photo NA-695-2 courtesy: Glenbow-Alberta Institute.

Opposite. Photo NA-695-17 courtesy: Glenbow-Alberta Institute.

Pocaterra's camp, Lawson Lake. Photo NA-695-18 courtesy: Glenbow-Alberta Institute.

The winter of 1906/07 was spent trapping in the upper Kananaskis Valley with Paul Amos and another Stoney friend. The previous summer the three men had built a cabin and stocked it with dried venison and pemmican. Sometime after Christmas they left Morley, travelling by horseback as far as the Eau Claire logging camp, where they switched to snowshoes and toboggans. The toboggans were made out of empty coal oil tins. While they were at the Eau Claire camp, Pocaterra found a newspaper dated 1898, which carried news about the Spanish-American war.

Upon settling themselves into the cabin at the Kananaskis Lakes, they divided up the area for trapping. Pocaterra took the area around the two Kananaskis Lakes, up the creek that was later named after him, and over the Highwood Pass to Storm Creek. His two partners took Elk River Pass and the headwaters of the Kananaskis, and over North Kananaskis Pass to the headwaters of the Palliser River (Palliser Pass).

The winter proved to be a memorable one and was later known as the year of the blue snow. The snow was so deep the men had to strap on their snowshoes before leaving the cabin. The fur-bearing animals travelled under the snow, thus making trapping impossible. Pocaterra estimated approximately 75 per cent of the animals died that winter, and they once found two dead goats beside the Kananaskis River.

Because of the tremendous amount of snow, avalanches fell where none had fallen before. Pocaterra witnessed one of these, marvelling at the speed with which it moved and noting the partial vacuum it created, which made it appear to roll backwards. He watched trees being snapped like dry twigs and others being sucked in like matches. (The years 1977 and 1991 were similar winters, with over a metre of snow falling in one snowfall at Upper Kananaskis Lake.) Pocaterra found it impossible to cross the ice of Upper Kananaskis Lake; which he believed to be weakened by hot springs. (Ted Schulte, formerly of Calgary Power Ltd., claimed the weakness was caused by snow cover that insulates the ice and keeps it thin.) The six islands on Upper Kananaskis Lake were named Hawke, Hogue, Cressy, Pegasus, Schooner and Aboukir during Pocaterra's time.

Pocaterra and his friends remained at the Kananaskis Lakes until the end of March when their supplies ran out. One of their caches had been raided by butcher birds and they were very hungry. On their way back to Morley they encountered friends coming to meet them with more supplies.

Trapping was not Pocaterra's only activity in the Kananaskis Valley. He was also involved in mining exploration. In 1910 he was prospecting for coal in the Evan-Thomas Creek valley and also for the MacKay and Dippie Coal Syndicate on the slopes of Elpoca Mountain, near Highwood Pass. He placed stakes to mark off this latter area and years after his work a Dominion land surveyor saw one of the stakes with Pocaterra's name on it and named the creek nearby Pocaterra Creek. It was about two years before Pocaterra knew his name was on the map of Alberta. He also built a cabin along Pocaterra Creek that still exists in a decrepit state.

Not only did Pocaterra's name grace a beautiful, crystal clear stream, but in 1955 Calgary Power Ltd. built a dam on Lower Kananaskis Lake and named it the Pocaterra Dam. R. M. Patterson, in his book *The Buffalo Head*, writes of Mount George and Mount Paul in his tale of adventures. The topographical maps of today do not show these names on any mountains, but from Patterson's description they appear to be peaks at the most northerly end of the Elk Range.

Pocaterra sold The Buffalo Head Ranch to R. M. Patterson in 1933, and returned to Italy to settle the affairs of his father's estate. While abroad he met Canadian coloratura soprano Norma Piper who was studying in Milan and in need of someone with an aggressive nature to take charge of her career. It was just the sort of thing that appealed to Pocaterra. Conquering the wilderness or conquering the operatic world, a challenge was something to be met. They were married on June 18, 1936, just as Piper's singing career was blossoming. In July 1939 she had engagements for the next opera season in France, Austria, Romania and Italy, and was to go to Manila to sing at the opening of a large opera house when World War II broke out. They returned to Canada and settled down on a ranch along the Ghost River in 1941.

Pocaterra returned to the life he had led before, but the Kananaskis Valley was, for him, never the same again. By that time Calgary Power Ltd. had enlarged Upper Kananaskis Lake for use in water storage, and because of the road that was built in 1936, civilization was entering the valley.

The Pocaterras moved to Calgary in 1955 where George died on March 13, 1972, at the age of 89. However, his spirit lives on in the valley he loved so much and in which he spent so many happy times. Pocaterra Creek and Pocaterra Dam remind us of this colourful man, and he is also remembered by Pocaterra Trail, Pocaterra Hut and Pocaterra Group Camp, all in Peter Lougheed Provincial Park and close to the creek that bears his name.

Left to right: Paul Amos, George Pocaterra, Elijah Hunter, 1907. Photo NA-695-13 courtesy: Glenbow-Alberta Institute.

Pocaterra, 1906. Photo NA-695-12 courtesy: Glenbow-Alberta Institute.

Lawson Lake, 1937. Photo NA-33-543: R. M. Patterson.
Courtesy: Whyte Museum of the Canadian Rockies.

ree Isle Lake, 1937. Photo NA-33-544: R. M. Patterson. Courtesy: Whyte Museum of the Canadian Rockies.

Raymond Patterson

Raymond Patterson, who bought the Buffalo Head Ranch from George Pocaterra in 1933, was a great friend of Pocaterra, and together they travelled throughout the Highwood district of the present Kananaskis Country, and to the Kananaskis Lakes and over Elk Pass into British Columbia. Patterson became well known for his books of adventure. In his book *The Buffalo Head*, he outlines some of his adventures in the Kananaskis Valley. Several times he went over the North Kananaskis Pass and then back into Alberta over the South Kananaskis Pass to Three Isle Lake to fish. The cliff on Three Isle Creek did not allow horses to ascend by that route.

It was reading Patterson's book about this roundabout way to Three Isle Lake, and subsequently hiking there myself, that helped me to understand why Sinclair and Palliser would have had to go over the North Kananaskis Pass, rather than the south pass. In 1975 when I did the loop hike from the north to the south pass with five friends, we sat on the edge of the scree just below the north pass and could see a trail going around the shoulder of Mount Beatty toward the south pass. We followed this trail, and found the switchback corners overgrown, but the traverses distinct. Some time later someone told me about a map of the Kananaskis area in the first-aid room of the Lafarge cement plant in Exshaw. I checked it out and saw the trail we had hiked shown on that map, which was dated 1937.

Gold Seekers and Surveyors

*A*s Palliser's expedition was progressing across the prairies, news that gold was discovered at Lytton in the Fraser Canyon, in what is now British Columbia, reached Victoria. By 1858 thousands of miners were pouring into central British Columbia, and the following year Dr. (Sir) James Hector found a party of nine American argonauts on the Blackfoot Trail, planning to cross North Kananaskis Pass.

At the junction of King Creek and the Kananaskis River, close to where the park offices and staff housing for Peter Lougheed Provincial Park are located, there is a flat area the Mountain Stoneys called the-place-where-many-whitemen-came-to-us. This is thought to refer to Sinclair's party, but could possibly refer to these American miners.

The Lost Lemon Mine, mentioned on an interpretive sign on Highway #40, south of Highwood Pass, leads one to believe this mine was in Kananaskis Country. Although many people associate the legendary mine with the Kananaskis Valley, the facts as outlined in *Frontier book No. 4* on the Lost Lemon Mine indicate the mine was thought to be located in or around the headwaters of the Highwood and Oldman rivers, if it existed at all.

Dr. Lionel Jackson
There is a bit of silver that has been found in the Rockies, but no one has ever found gold. Gold is never associated with basalt. There have been silver showings in the headwaters of the Old Man River and certainly there were silver

mines in the Field area, but there's never been any indication of gold at all. That Lost Lemon Mine gold, if it existed, probably came from a stagecoach hold up.

While people conjecture about whether or not gold is in the valley, real gold was found in a different form. In 1883 and 1884, George Mercer Dawson and Louis B. Stewart, who were probably the first surveyors in the Kananaskis Valley, surveyed the valleys of the Bow, Kananaskis and Spray rivers and the Smith-Dorrien Creek for timber. They divided the Kananaskis into five timber berths. They recorded an area of good growth in the south, but the rest had either been destroyed by fire or consisted of small second-growth timber. Around the shore of Lower Kananaskis Lake there was a second growth of jack pine. The Upper Kananaskis Lake had very little green timber. A timber berth located in the Smith-Dorrien Creek valley had large- to medium-sized spruce that may have escaped fires owing to its isolated position. On the whole the country appeared very desolate to the surveyors. Dawson comments on the same situation that had faced Palliser in 1858: Owing to comparatively recent fires, the trail is in some places much encumbered with fallen trees, and it had lost much of its old importance as an Indian route across the mountains.

A. O. Wheeler

A. O. Wheeler was the next notable person to reach the Kananaskis Lakes, in 1916. Wheeler spent the years 1913-1923 surveying the boundary between Alberta and British Columbia, from the American border to the 120° Meridian. It was a phenomenal undertaking, considering the times and the heavy equipment in use at the time. Wheeler was also one of the co-founders of the Alpine Club of Canada and was responsible for many achievements in Canadian mountaineering over three decades.

Photo P-5263 courtesy:
Provincial Archives of Alberta.

There are 44 peaks in Peter Lougheed Provincial Park and 38 of them were named by Wheeler. The names are largely grouped by nationality. There are four British generals grouped together: French, Haig, Smith-Dorrien and Robertson; and two admirals: Jellicoe and Beatty. Mount Maude and Maude Lake were named after General Maude who defeated the Turks at Baghdad. Field Marshall Putnik (Mount Putnik) was from Serbia.

> Tracing the Divide to Elk Pass, Wheeler saw the 'striking peaks ... dominated by Mount Joffre,' which he named for 'distinguished generals who have rendered such names immortal through their splendid service to France in the great world war now in progress.'[3]

Most of the peaks named after French military leaders are south and west of the Kananaskis Lakes—Joffre (the highest peak in Kananaskis Country, at 3450 metres), Foch, Cordonnier, Mangin, Lyautey and Sarrail. "Foch and Joffre helped to halt the German offensive of 1914 at the Marne, preventing the fall of Paris."[4]

Wheeler named the mountains in what is now the centre of Peter Lougheed Provincial Park after "British ships in the Battle of Jutland... Black Prince,

Warspite, Invincible, Indefatigable, Kent, Chester, Inflexible, Warrior and Marlborough."[5] Mount Galatea, just north of the provincial park, was also named for a battleship. The names of more British admirals were chosen for mountains in 1922, probably by Wheeler when he was doing some trail clearing for the Alpine Club of Canada's mountaineering camp on Palliser Pass and the North Kananaskis Pass. They are: Mounts Evan-Thomas, Packenham, Hood, Brock, Blane, Burney, Jerram, and Wintour in the Opal Range and Tyrwhitt at Highwood Pass.

There were three Canadian army officers from World War I after whom mountains were also named. They are: Hart McHarg, W. E. Lawson and A. W. Northover.

R. W. Cautley, who was doing fieldwork for Wheeler, went over the North Kananaskis Pass on snowshoes on July 14th, 1916, which serves to remind us that the weather hasn't changed all that much. There are still summers when the pass is inaccessible to hikers until after the middle of July.

Endnotes
1. MacEwan, J. W. Grant and Foran, Maxwell, 1968, A short history of western Canada: Toronto, McGraw-Hill Ryerson Limited.
2. Spry, Irene M., 1963, Routes through the Rockies, Beaver Magazine Autumn, 02.6, Sp. 8, PAM.
3. Fraser, Esther, 1978, Wheeler: Banff, Summerthought, p. 111.
4. Smith, Donald, 1986, November 9, Majestic Monuments: Herald Magazine, p. 22-26.
5. Smith, Donald, 1986, November 9, Majestic Monuments: Herald Magazine, p. 22-26.

The Valley Changes

2

Logging

George M. Dawson and Louis B. Stewart's timber reports opened the way for the industrialists to enter the valley. Since most of early Calgary's buildings were of wood frame construction, the demand for lumber was high and most of this lumber came from the Kananaskis and Bow valleys. Several people were interested in the Kananaskis lumber; notably Kutusoff MacFee, an Ottawa lawyer, and James Walker, formerly of the mounted police and then manager of the Cochrane Ranche.

In the early 1880s, MacFee went to Eau Claire, Wisconsin, the logging capital of the midwestern United States, and interested I. K. Kerr, William Cameron and Dan Donnellan in the western Canadian lumber industry. MacFee proposed making an exploratory trip to the Kananaskis and Spray valleys to assess lumbering possibilities.

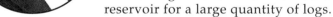

The men arrived in Calgary in 1883 and travelled by team and democrat to Morley, where they hired horses and guides for their investigative trip. They followed the Kananaskis River to the Kananaskis Lakes and while there named the lower lake Thorp, and the upper lake Ingram. Kerr's diary describes Thorp Lake as being "… an enlargement of the river, in some places three-quarters of a mile wide and four miles long." He felt this lake would be useful as a reservoir for a large quantity of logs.

Isaac Kendall Kerr.
Glenbow Alberta
Institute, NA-1432-1

From the two lakes the men crossed the height of land to the headwaters of the Spray River. This may have been the low pass at Mud Lake crossed by today's Smith-Dorrien/Spray Trail (road), as timber rights the company later acquired included this area. At the time of the Kerr party investigation the Spray Valley contained two lakes, commonly referred to as the Upper and Lower Spray Lakes, with the Spray River draining into the Bow River at Banff. One report calls one of the lakes Trout Lake.

From the Spray Lakes the Eau Claire men followed the Spray River to the Bow River and back to Morley via the Bow Valley. Their timber investigation proved favourable and in the fall of 1883, MacFee acquired the rights on 100 square miles of timber flanking the Bow, Kananaskis and Spray rivers.

Eau Claire lumber crew. Photo NA-1432-11 courtesy: Glenbow-Alberta Institute.

Eau Claire camp. Photo NA-1432-08 courtesy: Glenbow-Alberta Institute.

While the Eau Claire Company was still in the formative stages, before they actually commenced logging operations, James Walker established a mill at the hamlet of Kananaskis, three kilometres east of Exshaw, which was then a CPR divisional point, and proceeded with logging operations in the upper Kananaskis Valley. He operated from approximately 1883 to 1886. In 1884 alone his sawmill cut two million feet of logs and employed from 15 to 70 men, the number varying with the season.

Grant MacEwan and Max Foran in their book *A Short History of Western Canada* said:

> In this early period, logging was conducted by the most primitive and labourious methods. Cutting was done with hand axes and cross-cut saws; workers accepted humble living quarters and dietary fare was dominated by baked beans and fat pork. Heavy logs were dragged from the woods by multiple ox teams driven tandem. Waste left in the forest was shockingly high, however, new methods were introduced gradually: power-driven chain saws displaced hand tools, logging roads were built to areas considered inaccessible, and caterpillar tractors and heavy logging trucks took the place of oxen and bush horses.

In 1886 the Eau Claire and Bow River Lumber Company moved equipment for a mill to Calgary and two logging camps were established: one on the Kananaskis River and the other on the Bow River at Silver City (located about one kilometre east of the present Castle Junction on Highway #1A).

During the winter months three to five million feet of timber were cut. When the rivers were free of ice the logs were dumped in the Kananaskis River and floated downstream to the Bow River and then into Calgary to the mill (near the present-day Eau Claire Market). The log drives took about two months and required 30 to 40 men. The drives were 16 kilometres long and moved only three or four kilometres each day. The lumber consisted of spruce, jack pine and fir, and were cut into four- to five-metre lengths for the drive. The first lumber drives started in the spring of 1887 and continued until 1944.

During the first log drive six drivers drowned in Kananaskis Falls at the junction of the Kananaskis and Bow rivers. Theodore Strom, who worked for Eau Claire at the time, tells of this tragedy:

> The crew were crossing the river in a big boat above the falls, as they had done many times before, but this particular morning the current was a great deal stronger than they had figured on, as there had been a considerable amount of rain the night before. Before they reached the other side they lost control of the boat and were swept fast towards the falls. There were nine men in the boat and when they saw that they could not make it, they steered the boat right for the falls. The boat jumped the first falls and took in some water. It jumped the second falls and took in some water. When it went over the third falls it went under and six men were thrown out and killed against the rocks before they had any chance to save themselves. The three men who did not strike the rocks came out without being hurt at all. The bodies of five of the victims were found later during the summer in log jams, but the sixth was never recovered.

Eau Claire logging. Photo NA-1015-01 courtesy: Glenbow-Alberta Institute.

Eau Claire's main logging camp in the Kananaskis Valley was located at the site of the present Eau Claire Campground, on Highway #40, where a large number of buildings were in use at the time. A subsidiary camp was sited close to Evan-Thomas Creek near a log bridge, and consisted of a cookhouse, one bunkhouse, an office and a maintenance garage. Another camp, containing a cookhouse, bunkhouses, an office and a maintenance garage, was set up four or five kilometres along the south fork of Ribbon Creek in the late 1930s and early 1940s. The remains of two cabins can still be seen at this site, just beyond Dipper Canyon on the Ribbon Creek Trail. The Kananaskis Exploration and Development Company, during the time of the coal mine on Mount Allan, may have used some of these buildings, although they would have had to move them downstream. There may have been another camp across the creek from the present-day Ribbon Creek Hostel where a cement square in front of a hole over which a cabin obviously stood says: Moley's Manor 1900 Aug. In the early 1900s a wagon load of prostitutes was taken into the Kananaskis camps every other Saturday in an effort to retain the men.

In the early 1940s logging took place along Ribbon Creek and Evan-Thomas Creek. At this time logging trucks were taking the place of the traditional horse-drawn vehicles, because of the lack of skilled river drivers. Power saws were used for the first time as well. During the Second World War the prison-ers-of-war (discussed in Chapter 4) helped in these logging operations.

Logging frame that used to be along Baldy Pass Trail. Photo: Ruth Oltmann.

Old mill site on Baldy Pass trail. Photo: Ruth Oltmann.

The Eau Claire and Bow River Lumber Company was a well-known and esteemed logging company during the time of its operation. I. K. Kerr was president for many years. Peter A. Prince, after whom Prince's Island in Calgary is named, was manager of operations from 1886 until 1916. Prince had been brought from Eau Claire, Wisconsin to build the mill in Calgary. He retired on the same day as his son, John E. Prince (aged over 60), and died in Calgary in 1925 at 90 years of age. Charles E. Carr succeeded Peter Prince as manager of the mill and remained in that position until 1945 when the mill closed. His father had been an Eau Claire man as well. The Eau Claire Company had the first bank account with Calgary's main branch of the Bank of Montreal. Wm. Henry McLaws was the company lawyer from as early as 1905 and in 1928/29, when the company was reorganized, McLaws bought out Prince and Kerr just before the crash of 1929.

The main Eau Claire camp in the Kananaskis Valley was dismantled in 1948 by Joe Kovach, the chief ranger. In 1952 Kovach built a kitchen shelter for recreationists near the original logging camp. This is now the Opal picnic area. The site of the Calgary mill is now the trendy Eau Claire Market.

A number of other sawmills and logging camps operated in the valley over the years. In 1932-33 Claude Brewster had a sawmill at Upper Kananaskis Lake, where he logged timber prior to enlargement of the lake as a reservoir for water power. The Mannix company logged more timber here during the summer of 1942 and the winter of 1943 when Calgary Power made plans to raise the level of the reservoir. Starting in 1943, Claude Brewster again operated his sawmill for at least another four years. There appears to have been a Scott Sawmills at Upper Kananaskis Lake at some time. The Eau Claire company never logged around Upper Kananaskis Lake because of a canyon through which logs could not be driven owing to a log jam. The obstruction washed away in 1953.

In the 1950s Nelson Erickson and his three sons operated out of Canmore on Ribbon Creek cutting mine props, mostly from fire-killed trees, which he sold to Canmore Mines. A man named Webster may have worked in Ribbon Creek as well. Ken Olorenshaw operated a sawmill behind the present University of Calgary Kananaskis Field Stations, in the vicinity of Lusk Creek along Baldy Pass Trail. The north portion of Baldy Pass Trail was initially a logging road. Remains of the sawmill are still evident. Logging of green timber ceased after the fire of 1936, although burned timber was salvaged.

Forest Fires

Logging changed the look of the valley and so did forest fires. Early explorers and travellers frequently recorded seeing large burned areas of forest in the Kananaskis Valley. The location of the burned forests led James Hector to conclude some fires were caused by lightning. Slash left over after cutting on the Eau Claire and Bow River Lumber Company and James Walker berths was likely responsible for some of the fires. These early widespread forest fires affected stream flow rates on the eastern slopes and resulted in a decrease in the retentive capacity of the watersheds that was, in part, responsible for floods in Calgary in 1884 and 1897.

Pocaterra and Stoneys picking trail. Photo NA-695-20 courtesy: Glenbow-Alberta Institute.

Large fires have affected the valley's environment in the twentieth century. The first was in 1910, a drought year. This fire swept over approximately 2590 square kilometres of the eastern slopes, extending to the Chain Lakes area and south into Montana. At the time, George Pocaterra was prospecting for coal in the Evan-Thomas Creek valley. He kept two lookouts posted to warn of any danger. Later reports of mature timber standing in the Kananaskis Lakes region indicated this section of the valley was probably missed by the fire. There was a large fire at Kananaskis Lakes in 1920. Elizabeth Rummel said the peat bogs were still smouldering in 1922. Other major fires took place in what is now Peter Lougheed Provincial Park in 1712, 1765, 1803, 1858, 1890 and 1904. All of these fires would have been larger than 1000 acres. Throughout the valley today stands of trees remain that escaped fire damage. In the basin of Mount Allan there are fir trees 200 to 250 years old and spruce trees close to 300 years old.

The 1936 fire near Galatea Creek destroyed 18,000 acres and was often referred to as the Galatea Fire. Contrary to what has been said by old-timers, this fire was not within the boundaries of Peter Lougheed Provincial Park.

P. Campbell, December 19, 1936

The fire started in an area which was inaccessible and nothing could be done towards stopping it in the initial stage. Men were put to work widening the existing road between Boundary Cabin and Galatea Creek to act as a fire guard and to facilitate the movement of supplies and equipment closer to the fire. On account of the heavy pall of smoke drifting in from fires to the south, nothing could be seen of the progress of the fire until it climbed up to the top of Mount Galatea on August 4th.

Pumps were located every quarter of a mile from Rocky Creek down the Kananaskis River, along the river bank. Five pumps in all, with crews and hose. On the afternoon of August 8th a high wind sprang up from the southwest blowing down Galatea valley, but the draft seemed to be upward, carrying fire to the top of the mountains on the south side of Galatea Creek.

About 4:00 pm fire was carried from the top of the mountain across the Kananaskis Valley, a distance of one-and-a-half miles, and started up on the south side of the Kananaskis River across from the mouth of Galatea Creek. This was put out and up until 10:00 am on the 9th, no less than five separate fires were put out on the south side of the Kananaskis River, all blown from a distance of one-and-a-half miles.

About 12 noon on the 9th, several spot fires were noticed on the north side of Galatea Creek near the mouth. Having only three of my own private horses on the job, a pump and a small amount of hose was got across the Kananaskis River, but wind developed into a gale and the outfit had to be hastily withdrawn to the south side of the Kananaskis River, and all effort concentrated to keep the fire from crossing the river.

Men were strung along the riverbank with hand pumps, putting out dozens of spot fires.

By 1:00 pm the fire was a raging inferno in the old burn on the north side of the Kananaskis River, north from the mouth of Galatea Creek. It climbed up the side of Mount Bogart *(he may mean Mount Kidd)* and where it reached the top, live embers were carried across the Kananaskis Valley a distance of three-and-a-half miles, starting a fire two miles south of Boundary Cabin on the north side of the Evan-Thomas Creek, cutting off all the crew from Boundary Cabin. Several hasty trips were made with the truck and all but two men were got out. Equipment was hastily moved from Boundary Cabin by three trucks to Wasootch Camp.

By 6:00 pm the Kananaskis Valley was all on fire for a distance of six miles long by three miles wide. All the fire crew with the exception of two men turned up at the Wasootch Camp by 10:00 pm.

On August 10th a fire guard at Mile 10, Kananaskis Road, was fired with a favourable wind and fire stopped at that point.

Being greatly handicapped for lack of horses, very little work could be done on the north side of the river, but as the wind went down the fire did not spread. A crew was brought in from the Elk Pass Fire to work on the south end at Rocky Creek. Men cut fire guards and trenches were cut and the fire allowed to burn itself out against them. Fire is still burning in several places in the ground.

New methods of fire detection, modern equipment and a better transportation route into the valley presently enable forest fire control agencies to prevent extensive fires. Such complete control is not necessarily a good thing, as environmental management procedures now indicate forest fires are sometimes helpful. For example, in the Hidden Lake area between Mounts Sarrail and Lyautey, the forest is strewn with deadfall with 90 per cent of the standing timber either dead or diseased.

The most recent forest fire was in 1992 in the area of the Evan-Thomas bicycle trail, which runs from Kananaskis Village to Wedge Pond. Its cause was never determined.

Pigeon Lookout: Photo: Gillean Daffern.

ꝼire ꝸookouts

The fire management program consisted of having fire lookouts built on strategic points of land in order to detect any fires before they became unmanageable. A typical early era fire lookout was 12 square feet with a pyramid roof, anchored to the ground by four steel cables, one at each corner. There were windows on all sides and often a half glass door. The windows were shuttered in the winter and when opened were held up with iron rods. Inside there would be a map table with a map of the area, properly orientated. One side of the room would have a bed, one side a table with a Coleman cooking stove, and opposite the door there would be a long table fixed to the wall with cupboards beneath, a rack with tools and a backpack water bag with syringes to douse small fires. Meteorological instruments and a brass tube projecting through the roof for the anemometer, which was closed by a brass cap in the winter, would be part of the working tools. There were always plenty of blankets, an oil heater, pots and pans, boxes of magazines and a telephone. The weather report would have to be phoned into headquarters every morning at seven o'clock.

The chief task of the fire lookout person was, and still is, to watch for fires from dawn to dusk. After an electrical storm it is essential to scrutinize every inch of the district. The storms had to be tracked and their direction reported.

In the early days fire lookout personnel were seldom visited by people. I remember visiting Mary Roxburgh on the Pigeon Fire Lookout in the early seventies and being given tea and cookies, but I am seldom greeted at the lookouts today, unless it is remote by today's standards.

Lucille Roxburgh

Our daughter staffed the lookout tower that was on top of the peak across Barrier Lake for a summer. The mountain is actually called the EY Mountain. Nobody seems to know that. I saw it on one of our old maps as EY Mountain, which stands for Emily Yates. She used to own the Diamond Cross Ranch, which is now the YMCA. She was a rich New Yorker and lived there in the summertime for a few years. She had a little boy a bit younger than me. I used to ride my old buckskin pony over from Seebe and play with this little boy. Her brand was EY, so they called it the EY Mountain. When my daughter, Mary, was on the lookout, we called it Mary's Mountain.

There are three fire lookout stations located in the Kananaskis Valley. Kananaskis Lookout sits on a ridge overlooking the Kananaskis Lakes, and is reached via Whiskey Jack Trail and Lookout Trail; one is located on the northeast shoulder of Mount Kidd above Kananaskis Village; and a third overlooks Barrier Lake, and is reached via Prairie View Trail. The lookout on Mount Kidd was built in 1982, but has not been occupied since 1992, and unlike the other two has no designated trail to it. The others are occupied from May to October.

Today the fire lookouts are built and serviced by helicopter. This allows for a much higher position. The lookouts were supplied by the local ranger on horseback or by four-wheel drive truck. The Barrier Lake Lookout is typical of this. The original lookout tower, located at the first viewpoint on the present Prairie View Trail, was one of the guard towers from the prisoner-of-war camp. The lookout was called the Pigeon Fire Lookout, and was named after the camp guards, who were called stool pigeons by the prisoners. Recently the old guard tower was removed and taken down to sit beside the Colonel's Cabin, another historic site. It is set up for visitors with one level showing what the inside of a guard tower would be like and one level showing the inside of a fire lookout.

Rose Huston at Mt. Kidd Lookout, 1986. Photo: Param Sekhon.

Ingrid Von Darl

Jack Carter took me up to Kananaskis Lookout in 1987. You can drive up if it's a dry spring. You go from Highway #40. In those days there wasn't a bridge across Pocaterra Creek. I had to ford the creek and in the spring it was pretty full. It was touch and go getting through with a vehicle fully loaded with all the stuff I needed for the summer. I've been in Kananaskis for 10 years. They used to send me up to Keystone in the foothills for the spring hazard from the beginning of May until the first week of June or so. I'd then move out to Kananaskis and stay until the middle of September, although one year—I think it was 1990, I was there until the 3rd of October.

My primary duty is to make sure the area doesn't burn down. I'm there to watch for smoke, and catch fires when they are small. The primary cause of fires is lightning, so if there is a lightning storm it's very important to watch and if I see any smoke, to immediately report it. Then they send in the initial attack crews. If it isn't too big it's not necessary to call in the bombers or get a lot of people working on it. So far we haven't had any large fires in the Kananaskis Valley. We do get starts every year—last year I had three. One burned for six minutes fairly late at night. That particular night the wind was blowing at 60 and there was no rain. I had to wait six minutes for the rain. I got my scope on it but couldn't tell where it was because it was too dark to read the map. What I do is get the cross hairs on the flames. I know I've got the right degrees because the fire finder is set up and is accurate. If it had taken off I would have been phoning people all over the place. As it was I called my ranger after it went out and mentioned it. It's very important to have somebody check it out. If it's a dry time of the year and the hazard is high, it can start up again as soon as the sun hits it. So the next morning the helicopters check it out and I watch the area for a couple of days.

I have two radios—a simplex radio and a MDMRS. They have two different functions. Simplex is a system that only goes by line of sight, so if there is anything in the way like mountains it's sometimes difficult to get through. For example, I can't hear Barrier. The other system works via repeaters, so I key up one repeater, get through to a radio operator and then I am put through to the person I am calling. It's a much more complicated system to use than it used to be in the old days. We just had simple two-way radios when I first started—Century Two's, they were called. I seemed to be able to speak to just about everybody, so I'm not clear why they changed the system.

Now, if there is a smoke and the initial attack crew come along to fight it, and they are on the ground, I relay all the information about the smoke via radio. Headquarters talk to me and I pass the message along. I also relay messages between ground crews and aircraft.

I also take weather reports twice a day—at seven o'clock in the morning and again at one o'clock in the afternoon. I go to the Stevenson screen and take weather readings and temperatures. A Stevenson screen is a weather station. It has a wet bulb, a dry bulb and a maximum/minimum thermometer. I take all the readings and go back and do some calculations. I also measure rainfall. All this information gets passed on to headquarters. That's how they figure out the fire danger rating.

The day is full. I don't do a lot of sitting around. I prepare all my food and if it's really high hazard I can't be downstairs cooking in the afternoon for the

Kananaskis Lookout. Photo: Ingrid Von Darl.

evening meal, so a lot of the food gets prepared really early in the morning. If we are into really high hazard I like to be able to snack up in the cupola, so I bake cookies or a cake and make things that I can snack on. Popcorn is a great thing.

I have a generator, for electricity, so it's quite civilized. Most people think it must be awfully primitive. I have a fridge, stove and heater. I painted the cabin a couple of summers ago to brighten up the interior. Some days I can't see farther than my nose, it's so fogged in. Days like that I tend to spend inside the cabin and just turn on the computer. I write children's stories, poems and short stories. I've started to write about what it's been like for me as a lookout and what it is I enjoy about the job.

What I miss most are hot showers. They provide Lookouts with plenty of water and it rains fairly frequently in the Bow/Crow Forest so the water barrels are full most of the time, although the last two summers have been pretty dry (1995/96). Last summer I didn't have a drop in my rain barrel for over a month. That's when having my car is handy. Quite often Forestry is so busy I don't want to harass them for water every second week, so I just go down to Poca-terra Creek and bring up a few bottles and make do.

I take advantage of the low hazard and go for walks, following deer trails down through the forest, sitting quietly and seeing what comes by. I don't see as much wildlife as I'd like. I think it is because there are too many people around. Last year they shut the trails to the lookout, closing them off com-pletely to the public because of an agitated grizzly. I had the whole place to myself for almost a month. That was a first. It was interesting because all the animals started to come out of the forest into the clearing. They weren't just going through, either—they were hanging around. Moose grazed in the meadow, as well as elk and deer. A lynx came into the clearing after three or four days of rain and was just sunning herself. She was only about 50 or 60 yards from my cupola so I was able to study her through the binoculars. You feel really blessed when something like that happens, really honoured. I have a Steller's Jay that has come to me for a peanut every day for five years. He breeds down in the trees. There is a pair. I call them Lapis and Lazuli, like the stone. Every year they have offspring and in 1994 they had four, so I had six Steller's hopping around on my lawn all summer.

It's impossible to speak to everyone who comes up—my entire day would be given over to visitors if I did that. I get at least a hundred people every weekend and sometimes more. As soon as school is out I see a lot of families because it's a very easy trail for children. They mostly camp at Boulton Creek. I also get a lot of mountain bikers. It's a very popular trail with them. They can go the full circle up Whiskey Jack Trail and Lookout Trail, have a picnic at the top, then dip down to Elk Pass, turn right at the bottom and head back into Boulton Creek.

The number of hikers coming up on weekdays depends on the weather, although people sometimes come up in the most appalling weather. They are very cold by the time they get to the top and want to come in and dry off. I ask people, 'Why did you come up here?' Three gentlemen I was speaking to said, 'Well, you can always guarantee a view at a lookout.'

ℋydroelectric Schemes

*T*rees grow again and there is today no dramatic evidence of logging activities or forest fires, aside from the large numbers of lodgepole pine trees growing in the burned-over areas. The power development in the valley is a very different story as its effects and benefits are still present.

The story of power development begins in 1912, when the first Calgary Power Company people came to the Kananaskis Valley to assess the possibilities of hydroelectric development. This Canadian-owned company was formed in 1909 and reorganized in 1947 under the name Calgary Power Ltd. By 1911 Calgary Power had built the Horseshoe Falls power plant on the Bow River, 1.6 kilometres downstream from the Kananaskis and Bow rivers' confluence, where the village of Seebe came into existence as a housing complex for the company's employees. The Kananaskis Falls plant was completed in 1913, and was located right at the junction of the Bow and Kananaskis rivers on the Bow River.

Upper Kananaskis Lake

The following year, 1914, M. C. Hendry, of the Water Power Branch of the federal government, published a report of his assessment of the storage possibilities of the Kananaskis Lakes. Hendry felt the only place where water could be controlled was at the outlet of Upper Kananaskis Lake, but thought the engineering requirements would be too costly for the advantages obtained. He also thought: "…the beauty of the lake in its natural state and the extreme probability of its becoming a summer resort in the near future should not be lost sight of."

At this time a detailed survey of the Kananaskis Lakes vicinity was not carried out and the possibilities of storage were not considered further.

Work on Kananaskis River. Photo NA-33-530: R. M. Patterson.
Courtesy: Whyte Museum of the Canadian Rockies.

However, Hendry did see storage possibilities for the Kananaskis River, which he outlined in his 1914 report. This scheme consisted of building a canal, or flume, to convey water into Lake Chiniki, east of the river, on the Stoney Indian Reservation. It would involve building a dam on the Kananaskis River, and also building a 50 foot-high structure and a kilometre-long flume to raise the water over a low pass between Chiniki Lake and the Kananaskis River. There would also have to be a structure about 4,000 feet long to maintain the water required by the Kananaskis and Horseshoe Falls plants until it was re-turned to the Bow River. This scheme was never carried out.

Although the storage reservoir at Lake Minnewanka had been completed in 1912, there was still not enough water prior to 1927 for the power demands of Albertans. Development of the power in the Bow River and its tributaries was necessary to meet requirements for power in Calgary and Exshaw, where a cement plant was operating. The water flow through the Horseshoe plant was not, in 1911, as great as Calgary Power thought it would be. As engineering know-how in the electrical power field progressed, the Kananaskis River became a more practical power and water storage source, and in 1930 the possibility of using the Kanan-askis Valley for power development was explored further.

As early as 1909 P. M. Sauder had been doing preliminary measurements, and by the winter of 1932 the building of a hand-hewn spillway on Upper Kananaskis Lake was underway. This spillway was designed to raise the water level on the lake, thus increasing its storage capacity, and was followed 10 years later by a

Building Interlakes power plant, June 1955. Photo: J. D. Francis. Courtesy: TransAlta Utilities.

Upper Kananaskis Lake, 1937. Photo NA-33-497: R. M. Patterson.

Kananaskis Lakes, 1937. Photo NA-33-561: R. M. Patterson.
Both photos courtesy: Whyte Museum of the Canadian Rockies.

Partly completed Interlakes powerhouse, June 1955. Courtesy: TransAlta Utilities.

higher dam, which further increased the lake's storage capacity. The dam built in 1932 was a 30-foot log structure, with the flow controlled by pulling out two logs every two or three weeks in the spring and again in the fall.

During the summer of 1932, Calgary Power sent a crew of men into the valley to do survey work around the Kananaskis Lakes. These men created their own colourful saga.

Jack S. Charlesworth
Jack S. Charlesworth was a young lad employed at this time, and remembered it as a thrilling experience. Jobs were scarce and he was pleased, not only to get a job, but to get one with adventure. There were no roads into the Kananaskis Valley, so the mode of travel was by horse along a hand-cut trail that was kept open by the local ranger.

Charlesworth went into the valley for his first summer's work as a member of a four-man survey crew. It was high water time, and after completing eight hours of hard work on the trail, they were forced to turn back and spend a week in Seebe waiting for the water to subside. While thus delayed they lived at the Brewster's Lodge (Kananaskis Guest Ranch) and worked at pushing floating debris down the spillways of the Kananaskis and Horseshoe dams. When a week had passed, about 11 riders and 18 packhorses set off from Seebe for the Kananaskis Lakes. En route they stayed overnight at Boundary Cabin, the ranger stopover near Ribbon Creek, rolling out their bedrolls in the roofless cabin. (The present site of the Kananaskis Emergency Services Centre. The cabin still exists, but now has a roof.) Through the night all was not peaceful; one of the men woke up to find a bear walking on top of the walls of the roofless cabin!

The survey crew consisted of 10 men and a cook. When it was discovered the cook's culinary skills were limited to frying eggs, bacon and bannock, he was fired and replaced by a little wizened man who fed the crew royally. The camp at the Kananaskis Lakes was relocated two or three times, first at Pocaterra Creek and later on the shore of Upper Kananaskis Lake. This particular crew was at the Kananaskis Lakes to do topographical survey work, mostly around Lower Kananaskis Lake, to calculate the volume of the storage area. Although Charlesworth, who was hired as one of three axemen, had never used an axe before, he soon became adept. William (Bill) Wolley-Dod, a tall, lanky Englishman, was the boss of the outfit and extremely well liked. Wolley-Dod's name was soon to become synonymous with Calgary Power in the Kananaskis Valley.

As in John Palliser's time, the country was difficult to travel through. Deadfall and new growth in burned-over areas created a real tangle underfoot. However, the valley was an unending source of interest to the men, and Charlesworth, as had many before him, saw the nude woman that Jack Fuller had carved on a living tree by the ranger's cabin, located on the shore of Lower Kananaskis Lake.

Charlesworth enjoyed his summer and was back working for the power company in 1933. He was sent to the Kananaskis Lakes to help complete and clean up the survey work. At this time a beautiful peeled log cabin was built for Dr. Geoffrey Gaherty, president of Calgary Power until his death in 1954, on a spectacular point of land jutting out into Upper Kananaskis Lake. Here Dr. Gaherty spent his honeymoon with his new wife and 30 engineers! Charlesworth's father, Lionel, was one of the engineers. (The chimney and part of the foundation for the cabin, and its outhouse, can still be seen at the end of the peninsula directly across from the White Spruce parking lot. The chimney can also be seen by hiking Upper Lake Trail from Upper Lake picnic site along the west side of the lake.) Dr. Gaherty and T. F. Hogg, also of Calgary Power, were the two foremost power people in Canada at the time.

When the survey crew was at the Kananaskis Lakes in 1933, a sizable forest fire broke out near the ranger station on Lower Kananaskis Lake. Two hundred men were brought from Calgary to fight the fire, and the survey crew was also enlisted. The fire had been started by a fisherman's cigarette, and had spread in a V from the outhouse door! Since it was difficult to feed so many men with fresh meat, because of the lack of refrigeration, the ranger had permission to hunt wild game. He supplied the fire fighters with fresh moose and deer. The valley was a game preserve at the time, but an exception was made owing to the unusual circumstances.

During this year the initial storage development of 35,000 acre feet was completed on Upper Kananaskis Lake.

Charlesworth was hired again in 1936 and was sent once more to the Kananaskis Lakes. This was the year Jimmy Symington was sent out from Montreal by his father, who was an official of the power company. Symington created a crisis when he accidentally cut his foot while swiping at a tree with Charlesworth's razor-sharp axe. He was seriously injured and had to be carried back to the camp by his teammates, Jack and Gordon. After waiting about a week in camp for the foot to heal, Bill Wolley-Dod decided it would be best to send the fellow out to civilization. Infection had set in and the wound was not responding to first-aid treatment. Clarence and Jenny Sage, a young couple who had come from Calgary for a fishing holiday at the lakes, were asked to cut their stay short and, along with their guide, accompany Symington and Charlesworth on the two-day horse trip out of the valley.

The Sages had come into the valley via Sheep River and Rickert's Pass; leaving their car at the Bighorn Ranger Station. (The station still exists, but is now a field station. It can be seen on Highway #546 west of Turner Valley.) They had only spent three days at the Kananaskis Lakes and were loathe to leave, but kindly put their personal desires aside and accompanied the two young men. It was not a pleasant trip, as Symington was delirious from the infection and had to be tied to his horse. They camped overnight at Burns Mine on the Sheep River, but it was an anxious time for Jenny Sage, who was extremely worried about Symington. Eventually they reached their car and Symington was taken to hospital where he recovered, none the worse for his ordeal.

Charlesworth, who had left the Sages and Symington when they reached the Sages' car, had to turn around the following day and ride back to the Kananaskis Lakes. To make matters worse, the ranger at the Bighorn Station told him the saddles on the two Calgary Power horses were his and he promptly retrieved them, giving Charlesworth an English polo saddle that belonged to Wolley-Dod. Charlesworth's trip back to the Kananaskis Lakes was done in one day, but not without incident. Since the horses had their tails clipped and he had no saddle horn on the polo saddle, he had to lead the one while riding the other, with his arm stretched out behind him. He might have escaped with only a sore arm if it hadn't been for the polo saddle. When one horse wanted to trot the other one didn't, and every time the horse he was riding wanted to trot he would slide off the back end in an effort to hang on to the other horse! This memorable trip began at 5:00 am and did not end until 6:00 pm. In spite of a very sore rear end, Charlesworth still recalled the times as being good days.

The power development work in 1936 consisted of cutting a channel directly through the centre of the riverbed, almost to the top of the falls that were between the two lakes, so that by pulling out stop logs at the appropriate time of year, more water could be released from Upper Kananaskis Lake. The channel was close to 20 feet across and the men put a six-inch timber across it as a bridge, which they used every day during the course of their work. The first time Charlesworth saw this log bridge, he watched open-mouthed as Wolley-Dod picked up a transit, threw it across his shoulder and sauntered across. Charlesworth sat down and inched his way across in abject terror. Before long he also was sauntering across as nonchalantly as the rest of the crew.

Fishing parties, made up of Calgary Power friends, often came into the Kananaskis Lakes, and the young fellows in the crew were asked to show them around. On such occasions the fellows would spend a day hauling the old flat-bottomed scow, which had been built years before, from Lower Kananaskis

Lake to Upper Kananaskis Lake, in order for the men to fish the upper lake. Calgary city commissioner, Van Newhall, the general manager of Calgary Power, Bert Howard, and the head of the Boy Scouts Association of Chicago, Al Nichols, were all recipients of the fellows' mountain hospitality. Even Dr. John Allan, who was head of the Geology Department of the University of Alberta and geological consultant to Calgary Power, enjoyed this hospitality.

Among the many other events that took place during the survey and dam work was the forest fire of 1936, commonly referred to as the Phillips Fire, which completely surrounded the camp for 10 days. (This fire was not the same one that took place near Galatea Creek, which was called the Galatea Fire.) There was also the odd moose snorting and sniffing, making the men apprehensive while they worked.

As time progressed, Calgary Power had a greater demand for electricity, and the Upper Kananaskis Lake storage was increased in 1942 to 100,000 acre feet.

Art Longair

When I got out of high school in 1943, I worked for Calgary Power for a little bit before I went into the air force. Those were the days when we had a Chev truck, before the power wagon, and it was either a one-and-a-half or two ton truck. Ted Schulte, Ernie Thompson and myself drove into the Kananaskis during the winter. At that time there was no power house. They had a big culvert they shut up in the summertime to let the lake fill up and then opened it up in the winter. It flowed out all winter just like a creek.

They were interested in knowing what level the water came out, because if the water becomes super cool you get frazzle ice that blocks everything up. We went in with a truck to some cabins left over from building the dam. We stayed in those old log cabins—the kind with low walls. They were located on Upper Kananaskis Lake, just about where the Upper Lake day-use area is now. We had to walk across the dam.

We had a thermometer that measured the temperature of the water every 10 feet. You would let it down and it would take the water in and turn it over and it would seal. You'd bring it up and you would know the temperature of the water all the way down. That was my first chance to go in there. As I remember there were still parts of the road that were corduroy, going across the creeks.

I was in the air force reserve for a while and after I came back I worked for Calgary Power again. At that time I remember going into the Kananaskis Valley in, probably, March of 1944. There used to be a small cabin at Pocaterra, right by the creek, on the west side of the road. All the cabins in those days had sleeping bags and food hung from the ceiling on wire so mice wouldn't get in them.

The big culvert was about eight feet in diameter, and had been flowing all winter. It had a butterfly valve you could shut down and then another plate that bolted on the front to close it, so they could let the lake fill up in the summertime. We were going in to do this and got to Pocaterra with a power wagon and couldn't go any farther. We both had snowshoes, it was spring, and the snow was wet and there was a guy in there with a caterpillar tractor, a bulldozer. It was also Hockey Night in Canada. We decided to carry in the big C battery. Since this fellow was going to come in and clear the road we left our food and decided to take this battery in, as it was a load by itself, so we could listen to the hockey games. The snowshoes got wet and I remember I pulled a leg muscle and Ernie kept saying, 'It's just around the corner.' I think he said that for about 10 corners! We finally got into the cabin, and there was food, but it was all frozen. Frozen beans are mush.

We stayed and kept going back and forth closing this valve. We had all the bolts to put on. We were probably in there four or five days. The fellow never got in with the cat. The reason he didn't was because the trail was one vehicle width through the trees. He was afraid to get in with the cat because there was nowhere to push the snow, and as there was no side to push it to, he was afraid of getting high centred. We ate frozen food the whole time. We went back out on our snowshoes.

That was my first experience at Upper Kananaskis Lake. I was working, at that time, in the Production Department. Ted Schulte and Ernie Thompson did most of the survey exploratory work for the company.

Barrier Lake

Shortly after, in 1945, Calgary Power moved north to the Barrier site with construction of a dam and power plant along the Kananaskis River. Barrier Lake was created by flooding 673 acres of land just off the Forestry Trunk Road.

Throughout that summer prisoners-of-war, confined in the valley at that time, were hired for timber clearing in preparation for Barrier Lake. The pay was not high—50 cents for a full day, paid by the government of Canada, plus $3.00 a day, paid by Calgary Power. However, the men preferred to work rather than sit around camp, and they were good workers. They were all crosshanded swingers, a seemingly awkward way to hold an axe, but the result was the trees were cut closer to the ground. Consequently, Barrier Lake had less stumpage than the Kananaskis Lakes. The trees were all cut, piled and burned by the time the men were repatriated at the end of the war. The timber was burned because it was not merchantable.

The Barrier plant, with a capacity of 12,900 kilowatts and a head of approximately 155 feet, began operations July 18, 1947, using water that had been stored at the Kananaskis Lakes, and with a reservoir storage of 20,000 acre feet. Today, Barrier Lake is a popular fishing, boating and windsurfing lake with two day-use facilities; one called Barrier Dam and one called Barrier Lake. The section of the river below the dam is a mecca for kayakers, canoeists and white water rafters.

Art Longair

After I came back from the war in 1945 I started working for them again and at that time they were building Barrier Dam. My brother and I both worked there. I worked on building the diversion tunnel, because if you're going to build a dam, you have to divert the water around. I also worked on figuring out the volume of water that had to be held back by the dam. You don't just build the dam and fill it with water; when it gets halfway built you start to fill it up, but you don't want it to flow over the top either, so you have to know how much water it will hold.

Actually, building the tunnel was kind of interesting. It surprised me that they started at both ends. I thought you'd just start at one end and go right through.

Our job was surveying the tunnel. Of course, it doesn't take very long because all we did was go out and get a centre line and an elevation and they'd have to drill and muck the rock out.

Barrier Lake site before the dam and lake, 1941. Photos: J. C. Jackson.
Courtesy: Canadian Forestry Service.

That was the time the German officers from the camp cut all the trees. I thought they'd all have German accents, but they didn't. Ninety per cent of them had English accents, as they'd been educated out of the country and were all officers. That was a total surprise to me. We talked to them and had tea with them. They got a lot of axes to start with and they got onto it. I think they worked half a day each, different shifts.

That was the time we rode our horses up. My brother and I had a couple of saddle horses and came out through Jumpingpound from Calgary. We had our horses kind of half broken. He rode his all the way out and the next week I was going to bring my horse out. I didn't know anything about the route, so I got lost. I went back and stayed at the ranger station in Jumpingpound. There was a hostel behind it, so the ranger let me stay there and he looked after my horse. At that time there was no road through there, it was a trail. They logged on the Jumpingpound side, and actually logged on the Kananaskis side too. There was a little wee logging camp called Lusk Creek. In between there was just a trail. We came through *(the Sibbald area)* with our horses and we had an old corral. That was a miraculous thing, seeing that meadow *(Sibbald Flats)* way out in the middle of nowhere. It was never cleared—it was a natural meadow. We had built a little corral and the truckers who ran dump trucks would go into Calgary to Love's Feed and pick up a half dozen bales of hay and bring them out for us on the weekend.

It took me two days to ride out, but it took my brother just one day. We started right from Bowness and went up through Springbank, through Jumpingpound and straight through Lusk Creek. We rode back in the fall, but kept the horses there all summer. At that time Bowness was a little farm where we kept the horses. We totally enjoyed it.

One time a wild stallion broke into the corral. We had the corral divided in half so the horses wouldn't eat each other's feed. The stallion broke in and stole one of the mares. Calgary Power gave us four days off to look for these horses. We found them eventually and they were lined up just where the edge of the dam is across from the internment camp. Our horse was on the end and all the wild horses wouldn't move because they'd never seen bare ground before. They were afraid to walk across the bare ground. Our horse had a halter on so we were able to get her with some oats. The wild horses didn't even know what oats were. When we got our horse she had a shoe off—she was like a half-wild horse. You could pick up her front feet, but you couldn't pick up her back feet. When we got her shod in Calgary they used to put a twitch on her nose and then she'd sit on the blacksmith while he put her shoes on her back feet. We took her down to Brewsters, and Bud Brewster threw her down and she had shoes on before she knew what was happening!

When we were looking for her we went down to Soapy Smith's *(Rafter Six Ranch)* and met an artist who was sketching. I said, 'Do you sell those in Calgary?' He said, 'If I sold those in Calgary I'd starve to death.' He was from New York. *(Belmore Browne, who owned a cabin right beside Rafter Six Ranch.)* There is some kind of plaque there in his memory. Gillean Daffern discovered it and it was written up in the Calgary Herald about four or five years ago. It's around Rafter Six Ranch someplace, but it's not a public thing.

We were instrument men, as was Pete Roxburgh. When the dam was finished, my brother and I wanted to be farmers, so we took a degree in agriculture, whereas Pete went on and became an engineer and then worked for Calgary Power.

Peter Roxburgh

I started in the fall of 1945 after I finished high school. One of my first jobs was the Barrier Dam construction project. I worked there for two years while I decided a little more education would be better and saved up my money and went to university. During those two years I went through just about every phase of construction activity there was on the project. You name it, I did it.

Initially I was part of a survey crew. I started in October. Winter was coming on and most of the earth-moving activity slowed down. Clearing of the reservoir began that winter and it was done by the prisoners-of-war from the nearby internment camp.

When the prisoners went out in the morning from the camp, there could be anywhere from 70 to 100 at a time, and they never went with a cook. They had one home guard soldier who went with them, unarmed. He carried his lunch and a first-aid kit and that was it. These were all officers who were on parole every day, and they had to give their word to return. The enlisted men worked in the internment camp, and there were a few around who were mostly batmen for the officers. They did all the menial jobs; cleaned up the garbage, did the dishes, washed the kitchen, probably did the cooking. I was never in the camp at the time as it was closed to civilians. The prisoners would stream out in the morning, when there was snow on the ground, and begin cutting the trees into short lengths and piling them up for burning. When there was enough snow on the ground, and forest fire danger was low, they would burn them. In those days they would have, in addition to the axes and saws they carried every day, a little can of kerosene to light the piles. There was the delicious smell of burning wood all that winter, which I always enjoyed.

The survey activity I was involved with was defining the clearing line around the reservoir. We worked with two or three survey crews. Art Longair was on a different crew than I was as a rule, but Art's younger brother, Ernie, and I worked together for half the time I was there. One crew took one side of the river valley and just carried levels to obtain a level line around the reservoir, and we marked it. The clearing crew would cut the trees until they came to the line. That's the edge of the treeline now. I can't remember for sure whether they finished all the clearing in one winter or if there was some left over for the second winter.

In the summertime when the earth-moving activity started up I worked again and did many things. During the winter when we weren't surveying we were working with other engineers doing concrete tests and designing concrete mixes. These were young engineers, fresh out of university, and they were practising their skills designing concrete mixes. I was just a kid out of high school and didn't know what the heck we were doing. We did the labourious work of taking a bag of cement and a bunch of sand and gravel, pouring water in it and mixing up cement and pouring, which would then be cured and broken in a testing machine. We just did the bull work. These guys would sit there with their slide rules and change the water content, the cement content and the sand content, and design these things. It was like a witches' brew as far as I was concerned. I found out more a few years later when I went through the same process in university.

We did compaction tests on the soils this dam would be made out of, and again, I really didn't understand what we were doing at the time—it was just hard physical labour mixing this stuff. In the summer when the contractor was back at work moving dirt I worked on the survey crew that did the layout and staked where the

Barrier Dam construction. Photos: Art Longair.

dirt, structures and excavations would go. That winter they finished pouring the concrete for the powerhouse and late in the winter the installation of the turbine parts began. I worked with the turbine rector as one of his helpers for most of the erection of the hydraulic turbine in the powerhouse.

At about the same time another gang of men were building the generator and it was set off on one side of the floor. It was assembled from a lot of small parts—a very labour-intensive activity. I helped install the conduit in the floor of the power-house where all the wires were eventually run and did testing on the concrete when it was being poured—supervising to make sure the right amount of materials were put into the concrete. I had the dirtiest job in the project—at the end of the concrete pour. The cement was always supplied in bags. To make sure the cement quantity was correct, for the quality of the concrete, the contractor had to empty the bags and put them in a big hopper and at the end of the pour it was my job to go and count them. There would be several hundred empty paper bags full of cement dust stored in this, plus the ones that the wind had blown into the trees all over the project! I had to go and find them and physically retrieve them, and then burn them after I counted them. Every time you touched them the residual dust was terrible. There was no such thing as a mask. It would get in your eyes and your nose and your ears. It was awful. The bathing facilities were pretty primitive. It really was a filthy job. I was elected to do it, but I hated it.

Through the course of the two years I saw everything from the ground up, literally. The plant went on line before I left to go to university in the fall of 1947. It was the first automated plant in the Calgary Power system, and it was one of the few in North America at that time. It was impressive to know that there was a man in the Horseshoe powerhouse who pushed a button and started the Barrier plant. Subsequently, the remote control centre was removed and relocated to Seebe at the Kananaskis plant. It was a very simple control panel with a few switches.

The bears were a fact of life around the camp. We saw them frequently. I had some close encounters myself and I remember one in particular. I went to the outhouse one evening when it was pitch dark and I didn't take a flashlight. I left the door open as usual and was sitting there communing with nature. The little corral was 100 feet away from the outhouse, and I could hear Art and Ernie's horses crashing around, so I figured there was a bear around some-where. The next thing I realized there was a shadow on the path coming right toward the door of the outhouse and the shadow was a black bear! He stuck his head in through the door, right between my knees. I was paralyzed. I didn't breathe. He was sort of snuffling, but he couldn't smell me for the outhouse. He kind of half turned around and started away and I went 'Ssssnt,' and he just exploded and went straight up! There was a tree beside the door and the door was six feet high and he was in the tree above the door! Then I thought, 'Man, that was a stupid thing to do. Now what do I do?' I knew I couldn't outrun him, so I just sat there and didn't say another word. He snuffled and snorted and backed down the tree and got on the ground and grumbled and walked away. I left and went back to the camp and I never, ever went out again without a flashlight!

Powerline

During the period between 1948 and 1953 Calgary Power had a crew of men clear-ing the right-of-way for the high-tension powerline between Ribbon Creek and the Kananaskis Lakes. The line on the British Columbia side of Elk Pass was owned by

Mount Baldy and Barrier Lake. Photo: Ruth Oltmann.

Kanelk Transmission Company Limited, a wholly owned subsidiary of Calgary Power, and was completed in 1951.

The crew clearing the section from Ribbon Creek to the Kananaskis Lakes was housed at Ribbon Creek on the south side of the creek from the coal mining village. They worked their way south from Ribbon Creek in the spring, and as soon as the snow was gone at the Kananaskis Lakes they moved their camp to a marshy plain near the present Elkwood Campground on Lower Kananaskis Lake. From here they worked north in clearing operations.

George Bearns, who was in charge of the crew of men, was newly married when living at Ribbon Creek. Chris, his wife, was a hardy woman with an enthusiastic and adventurous spirit, who had come to Canada from Scotland because she loved snow and mountains. She had met George on a bus trip between Butte, Montana, and Calgary, Alberta. During the course of their courtship, which was mainly by correspondence, she laughingly told him she would marry him if he got a job in the mountains where there was lots of snow. George promised her snow and lived up to his promise. Chris proved invaluable to him, as she spent the summers cooking for the power company crew and during the winter of 1952/53 taught school at the mining village of Ribbon Creek. Chris was equal to the challenge of teaching 26 children in a one room school all winter, and the day after school closed, beginning her summer job as cook for 30 men. She managed magnificently, although she said years later, "I was daft ever to do it."

During the course of the Bearns' sojourn at their Kananaskis Lakes camp they met Old Man Phillips who had a cabin over the pass at Elk Lakes in British Columbia. Phillips had been taking hunting parties down the Kananaskis Valley into the Elk Lakes for many years and was well known. Bearns, a man with a heart of gold, took supplies over the pass to Phillips once a week. (It is possible the Phillips Fire of 1936, on the British Columbia side of the Divide, was named after this man.) The Bearns became good friends with Phillips and understood his grief, even though they worked for the company, when Calgary Power built the powerline over Elk Pass into British Columbia, passing close to his cabin and changing forever the wilderness aspect of the location.

Lower Kananaskis Lake

Clearing for the reservoir on Lower Kananaskis Lake began in 1954. This time the clearing was done by machine. By 1955 the work was completed and the Pocaterra plant had been built. The plant has a capacity of 14,900 kilowatts and a head of 207 feet with usable storage of 50,000 acre feet. By 1955, the Interlakes plant was completed on Upper Kananaskis Lake, with a capacity of 5,000 kilowatts, a head of 127 feet and a usable storage area of 100,000 acre feet. The three plants: Interlakes, Pocaterra and Barrier were remotely controlled from Seebe for many years, but are now controlled in Calgary.

Thus, Calgary Power met the power demands of the public, in particular the growing city of Calgary. This absolved the federal government from being involved, which saved the taxpayer money. (The federal government commissioned M. C. Hendry to do the survey in 1912.) Calgary Power changed its name to TransAlta Utilities on May 3, 1979.

Mining and Quarrying

Exploration for coal began early in the history of the Kananaskis Valley. The earliest records of the geology of the area were made by Dr. James Hector, a member of Captain John Palliser's 1857-1860 expedition. Palliser's map of the Kananaskis Valley was one of the earliest to be compiled. George M. Dawson, the Dominion surveyor, further investigated the geology of the Ribbon Creek area in the years 1881-84. Richard G. McConnell, formerly an assistant to Dawson, also did geological work in the Rocky Mountains, and his division of the rock succession into lithologic units is still in use today. Donald Bogart Dowling made the first detailed geological surveys of the Ribbon Creek area in 1903 and 1904, and in subsequent years provided further knowledge of the structure, stratigraphy and economic possibilities of the coal seams of the Cascade coal basin. It was Dowling who published the first large-scale maps of the area. Dowling's work in 1903/04 probably contributed to the influx at that time of a number of people to Ribbon Creek who were prospecting for coal. Mount Bogart (3144 m), located between Mount Kidd and Mount Allan, is named after Dowling.

The first detailed information regarding the Ribbon Creek area was recorded by Dowling in 1909, who reported the three measured sections along Ribbon Creek and on Mount Allan. He discovered, "The coal seams in the Ribbon Creek area belong to the Kootenay formation, which is considered to be Lower Cretaceous in age. The coals rank from low volatile bituminous to semi-anthracite, and are, therefore, of high quality. The seams vary in thickness from a fraction of an inch to 34-1/2 feet. Though the seams are distributed throughout the 3,400 feet of the formation, those of commercial importance, that is, those three feet or more thick, appear to be restricted to the lower 1,200 feet." Later, prior to World War I, Lionel Charlesworth, who owned mining property on Ribbon Creek, ran a preliminary survey for a railroad into the property. He

Mackay coal claim in Evan-Thomas Creek. Photo NA-695-28 courtesy: Glenbow-Alberta Institute.

J. Ashworth near Pocaterra's coal claim in Evan-Thomas Creek.
Photo NA-695-27 courtesy: Glenbow-Alberta Institute.

lost out on this venture because of a lack of development money and the out-break of World War I.

Subsequent to the beginning of prospecting at Ribbon Creek, George Pocaterra prospected for coal for Mackay and Dippie Coal Syndicate in the area now known as Pocaterra Creek, and in 1910 and 1916 in the Evan-Thomas Creek valley. A report on this latter coal field by Calgary engineer John Haddin predicted it contained at least 125,000,000 tons of recoverable coal. He estimated the cost of strip mining would not exceed $2 per ton, but railway transportation was "… of first and last importance." The coal deposit was located on the east side of the Opal Range and was eight miles long. At one time there was talk of running a railroad into the coal claim over Elk Pass. (The Canadian Pacific Railway and the Great Northern Railway had surveyed from Michel in the Crowsnest Pass.) There was also talk of a rail line from Ozada (near Highway #1), up the Kananaskis Valley and up Evan-Thomas Creek. It was thought this railroad could be built for $250,000. The branch railroad never materialized and the markets declined, so interest in mining the coal dissolved.

The Cloudburst Coal Company Limited acquired a lease on the coal in the Evan-Thomas Creek valley in October 1949. Construction of a pilot road up the valley was undertaken for 7.5 miles to a cabin that had been built on what was called Camp Creek. A camp was constructed with a bunkhouse and cookhouse for eight to 10 men. The boggy area between Evan-Thomas Creek and Rocky Creek was known as "Moose Wallow." Gillean Daffern, in her book *Kananaskis Country Trail Guide*, calls it Cloudburst Pass. The coal quality was classed as medium volatile bituminous, but was certainly not proven in 1951. Joe Kovach, the district ranger, mentions in his work diaries that during his tenure (1940-1953) he checked on the Cloudburst Coal Company's work at their site.

During the 1960s Minorex Ltd. did some diamond drilling in the Evan-Thomas Valley, cores of which were still around in 1974. In 1973, CanPac Minerals Ltd., a subsidiary of CPR, published a leaflet showing they were the leasees of approximately 15,700 acres, but they did not carry out any drilling at that time.

Eventually, coal exploration expanded to include Elk Pass, and revealed one seam 13 feet thick. George and Chris Bearns heard the rumblings of a coal fire underground on Elk Pass when George was working for Calgary Power at the Kananaskis Lakes.

Martin Nordegg

One of the most interesting characters connected with coal mining in the Kananaskis Valley was Martin Nordegg. Although Nordegg's name is associated with the town of Nordegg, west of the city of Red Deer, and the coal fields there, few people realize he was the person who started the development of coal on Mount Allan.

During the summer of 1907, Nordegg, accompanied by D. B. Dowling of the Geological Survey of Canada, made an exploratory trip into the Kananaskis Valley. Forty years passed from this date until actual mining took place, and while Nordegg was no longer associated with the coal industry, it was his company that mined for coal.

Nordegg's adventures regarding the Kananaskis coal field are colourful and thought provoking. He arrived in Canada from Charlottenburg, Germany, on May 1, 1906, as the emissary of the German Development Company, which was formed for the purpose of developing Canada's natural resources. At this time the government of Canada was anxiously soliciting investors in the development of its natural resources.

Before coming west, Nordegg had unsuccessfully explored for precious metals in northern Ontario, particularly around the town of Cobalt where silver had been found. Supplying steam coal for the transcontinental railway through the Yellowhead Pass seemed to him a practical, economic venture. He was, therefore, anxious to find coal somewhere in the eastern slopes of the Rockies between Canmore and the Yellowhead Pass. Making a calculated guess as to where the coal would be, Nordegg began his exploration in 1907. Starting from Morley by horse, with D. B. Dowling and Tom Lusk as head packer, he entered the Kananaskis Valley, staked a claim on Mount Allan and left several workers to dig a tunnel to assess the coal.

After his explorations were completed, Nordegg returned to Germany with his report on the coal fields in Canada, and a large lump of coal to show to his financial backers. His financiers requested him to show the coal sample to Professor Pontonié, who was the German authority on coal. When Nordegg told Professor Pontonié the coal had come from the Canadian Rocky Mountains, the professor, whose book on the origin of coal said coal did not come from Cretaceous rock, accused Nordegg of swindling him. Though Nordegg told him of the 2,000 tons of coal per day coming out of the Crowsnest Pass and Canmore mines, Pontonié refused to believe him. Since the reputation of Canada and its coal was at stake with this most noted German coal authority, the Canadian Mining Institute invited the professor to Canada to see for himself the natural resources of Canada from the Atlantic to the Pacific.

Nordegg chose to show Pontonié the coal on Mount Allan as it was nearest to the railway. It was a memorable trip. The professor had never ridden a horse and he encountered difficulties during the ride from Morley to Ribbon Creek. When they arrived and entered the tunnel on Mount Allan, Pontonié asked a miner to pry a chunk of coal loose for him. After examining it he meekly uttered: "There is coal in the Cretaceous. I must rewrite my book." His glowing report on the Canadian Rockies coal fields solidified Canada's reputation in the coal industry abroad, but it did not immediately result in Nordegg successfully securing financing for the coal extraction.

By 1909 all was not going well in the coal development field for Martin Nordegg. He had returned to Canada from a trip abroad only to find:

"A party from Edmonton had also applied for the lease of a coal field (*on Mount Allan*) and claimed that theirs covered the outcrops while ours covered the hills; in other words, that they had the entry to our seams. That was very serious, because it would have necessitated our sinking deep shafts to reach the coal, and every ton hoisted would have been too expensive to compete... with Canmore." Upon investigation it appeared one of the parties to this "hold-up" was a high official in the government at Edmonton. He would have "received his knowledge from reports made to his department. The eventual outcome of the dispute came only two years afterwards, when the minister in charge decided the section containing the entry to the seam would remain the property of the Crown, and both parties would be permitted to drive their tunnels from there into the coal." Eventually the Edmonton party crept out of the situation entirely.

While obtaining financing for his coal enterprises, Nordegg entered into a business arrangement with Messrs. MacKenzie and Mann, who owned the Canadian Northern Railway. Nordegg hoped to sell his coal to this railway, and in order to do so he had to do some hard bargaining. The outcome of his negotiations "… was that two companies were to be formed, one in the north, comprising our northern fields and those of MacKenzie and Mann, and one in the south for our Kananaskis field." Nordegg had incorporated the Kananaskis field under the name Rocky Mountain Collieries Ltd., with MacKenzie as president and himself as vice-president.

In the spring of 1910, after making a trip to the Kananaskis field to ascertain that the exploration and official surveying were progressing well, Nordegg was requested to return to Berlin to continue the financial negotiations. It was felt development of the Kananaskis field would require $2,000,000 for the mine and $600,000 for the railway spur. The big question at the time was: Which field to open first, the South Brazeau or the Kananaskis? The directors of the development company felt a negotiator should be consulted.

Nordegg said, "The question arose, 'Who was the most clever negotiator in the capitals of Europe?' One of the directors said he had a cousin in Brussels who was the ideal man for the job. He was a banker and very well connected with the great financing houses of Europe. His name was Eugene de Wassermann, the brother of the famous professor who discovered the 'Wassermann test.'" When Nordegg went to see this man he found: "… his luxurious apartment, filled with beautiful art treasures, paintings, and a library famous more for its antique bindings than for its contents, which had been described to me as being mainly pornographic, the cousin received me most cordially. Whenever I related the economic prospects of our enterprise he seemed bored and yawned, and wanted only to know how much money was involved. The property itself did not seem to interest him. When I told him that the money needed for the railway depended on the decision which field to open first he said that was easy to decide. The farthest field was the best. In fact, if we had a coal field still farther away than the South Brazeau, he would prefer it for financing. I tried to argue this point with him, saying that if we opened the Kananaskis field, we would only save a couple of years in the construction of the railway, but we would save money in the transportation of coal and find immediately a ready market."

"You do not understand the matter. It is easier and more profitable for me to find several millions than a few hundred thousand. I am not a piker and if you people do not agree with me, you can go elsewhere," Wassermann stated. Thus, in this bachelor's apartment in Brussels, it was decided which field, 12,000 kilometres away in the Rocky Mountains of Canada, should be opened. "In the future, actual facts proved that the cousin was right and I wrong. But that could not be foreseen at the time."

Why Nordegg later felt Wassermann was right is obscure, but it could have been the South Brazeau contained more coal than the Kananaskis field.

These financial negotiations in Europe left Nordegg morally disgusted and he reveals his true character in the statement: "The financial discussions showed the greed of all and I felt that I did not belong there, in fact that I did not belong in Europe any more. Even the luxury and comfort, with all its artificiality, had no attraction for me. I belonged to Canada. The air there was not so contaminated."

Subsequently, Nordegg spent many years developing the Brazeau coal field, where the town of Nordegg was built and named after him. But because of his German nationality, during the First World War Nordegg was deprived of his interest in the company. At the end of his memoirs he could still say, "… often I longed for the Rocky Mountains, and travelled again over the trails and to the town which still bears my name."

Mount Allan Coal Mine

All of the seams at Ribbon Creek had been prospected by the time geologist M. B. B. Crockford visited the area in 1947. His work revealed a one-metre coal seam on Mount Kidd that was over the 2154-metre elevation level, and three measured sections that contained 23 seams along Ribbon Creek and on Mount Allan. He determined that 16 of these were workable and estimated they contained a total of 27 metres of coal. Crockford stated that Brazeau Collieries, Nordegg's company that operated the coal field at the town of Nordegg, had considered opening an operation in the Ribbon Creek area in 1924, but carried no development beyond the prospect stage.

Dynamite shed, c. 1975
Photo: Ruth Oltmann,

Also in 1947, a subsidiary of Brazeau Collieries, Kananaskis Exploration and Development Company, undertook a core drilling program on their Mount Allan holdings. This program was followed by the opening of a strip mine, which was followed in 1948 by an underground mine. Eventually the Belgian and German interests in Brazeau Collieries lost out to the British firm of Lazard Brothers & Co. Ltd., who, as at April 15, 1952, owned nearly the whole of the capital.

In the beginning the mine operation on Mount Allan used horses that were kept between the mine and the miners' village. The Coal Mine cross-country ski and hiking trail has a small cabin and other old bits of buildings on it. This could have been the location of the horse camp. (A boardwalk in front of what had been three cabins, and an outhouse was still evident in the 1970s.)

It was not long before the operation of the Mount Allan mine was fully mechanized, with coal-cutting machines, duckbill loaders, shaker conveyors and belt conveyors. Electrical power was furnished by Calgary Power. Approximately 100,000 tons of coal were developed underground and the estimate of coal reserves ran into many millions of tons. The original purpose in

Ribbon Creek mine. Photo: Otto Johnson. Courtesy: Vereda McAffer.

Painting of Ribbon Creek mine by Mr. Earle.
Photo given to Ruth Oltmann by Donald Barnes.

developing this property, according to Kananaskis Exploration and Development Company records, was to displace United States anthracite coal in the Ontario market. The coal was also used to make briquettes. This took place at the tipple, located on Morley Flats (sometimes called Ozada Flats) at Ozada, a CPR station on the Stoney Indian Reservation directly north of the present Highways #1 and #40 inter change. The tipple had a capacity of 75 tons an hour. There were two briquetting units with a rated capacity of 24 tons per hour. At Ozada the mine company provided cottages, bunk houses and a dining room, with the accommodation housing 25 to 50 men.

Three things happened that ultimately caused the suspension of operations of the mine in February 1952. One, on April 1, 1951, the freight rate to the central Ontario market was increased; two, the policy of conserving United States dollars changed considerably; and three, briquettes proved difficult to sell.

Coal mining on Mount Allan ceased in February 1952 and coal development in the Kananaskis Valley never extended beyond this mine. When the province of Alberta was establishing Kananaskis Provincial Park (now Peter Lougheed Provincial Park) and Kananaskis Country, they issued a coal policy on June 15, 1976, that stated, "The Kananaskis Valley will have no exploration or commercial development within it." Exploration for other minerals continued, however.

Gypsum and Rundle Stone

George Pocaterra staked out, but did not record, a gypsum deposit in 1920 on what appears to be Mount Invincible. He said it was "a tremendous body. The whole side of a great big mountain." He followed the deposit for over 1 1/2 miles, and said it ran over "one thousand feet from the woods," above treeline. He felt the "quantity was certainly incalculable" and the quality was "93 per cent pure gypsum."[1] Pocaterra was interested in getting financial backing to mine the gypsum. He also tried to sell his knowledge of this deposit for $5,000. Nothing further happened.

Much later, the Geological Survey of Canada published a report in 1964 about gypsum on a north ridge of Mount Invincible, above Lower Kananaskis Lake, and early in 1965 Canadian Pacific Oil and Gas filed a permit. The following year, W. R. Smith acquired a 21-year lease for 70 hectares, which he subsequently assigned to H. R. Morris, who assigned it to Alberta Gypsum. Alberta Gypsum commenced to build a road into the gypsum deposit via a small valley on the south side of the ridge from Smith-Dorrien Creek. The road came within three-quarters of the way to the deposit when the builders could go no farther. Another road was then built on the north slope of the ridge.

There is some speculation as to the amount of gypsum in the mountain. Although the first carload of gypsum taken out was classed as impure, Smith declared the gypsum was high-grade. He believed the first carload had rubble in it. During early August of 1970, Alberta Gypsum's lease was cancelled because the company failed to make a cash deposit to cover land restoration costs. The bridge across the Smith-Dorrien Creek was removed and used for firewood and the road was reseeded. It was further reclaimed in the late 1980s. The site is now within Peter Lougheed Provincial Park and the road has become a popular ski touring trail and is renowned for its wonderful snow conditions.

A small Rundle rock quarry operated on the north side of Ribbon Creek at the beginning of the present Ribbon Creek trail. Elmer Smith operated this quarry for a number of years in the 1960s, periodically living on the site. The quarry changed ownership several times and was last owned by Spud McCormac of Calgary, before the formation of Kananaskis Country. He was extracting rock from the quarry as late as the mid-1970s.

Ribbon Crick

*W*hen the Kananaskis Exploration and Development Company began mining coal on Mount Allan in 1947, a small settlement sprang up at the bottom of the mountain. The people who came to live in Ribbon Creek village were attracted to the beauty around them and learned to enjoy it in their own way.

Plans for a townsite were under consideration during Crockford's visit in 1947, but the settlement was never incorporated as a town and could only be classed as a village or hamlet. Although the village was listed as the Locality of Kovach in the Gazetteer of Canada, after district ranger Joe Kovach, most of the inhabitants referred to the village as "camp" or "Ribbon Crick."

Bunkhouses providing accommodation for 100 to 150 men, a cookhouse and a mine office occupied a section in the general area of the present Ribbon Creek parking lot. The mine office stood in front of the spring where the residents collected most of their water. The pipe for the spring was still there in the 1970s until trail construction eliminated it. It came out of the ground right behind the present information kiosk. The cookhouse was a large log building with a full basement. Scotty and Nellie Patterson were the cooks, Isabel Bradford the pastry cook and John Johanson the bull cook. Several buildings were made of logs, and may have been brought down Ribbon Creek from the Eau Claire and Bow River Lumber Company campsite. Approximately 15 homes lined both sides of the road just east of the mine office group of buildings, most of them tar paper shacks. A few good homes were built later.

The school was located on the north side of the road, in the most westerly clearing of the present hostel grounds. The truck camp, together with some homes and trailers of the truckers, was situated to the north of the present Kovach Pond site. The concrete floor of the garage can still be seen if you poke around in the brush. The garage could hold as many as two or three coal trucks for repairs. Norman Holt held the contract for hauling the coal to Ozada where the briquette plant and railway siding were located. Calgary Power had a bunkhouse and one or two other buildings across Ribbon Creek from the mine buildings for personnel, who were clearing the right-of-way for the high-tension powerline between Ribbon Creek and the Kananaskis Lakes. The Calgary Power crew including George Bearns and his wife, Chris, lived in small cabins on the site and ate at the mine cookhouse until the mine closed, at which time they brought in their own cook.

Until the schoolhouse was built in 1950, the children went to school in Seebe, 32 kilometres away. One day a week they remained after school for Sunday School. With the help of the mine manager's daughter the children took their schooling by correspondence after the school was built. In September 1951, Chris Bearns was hired as the school teacher by the school inspector in Calgary who became the trustee for the school. The school had hardwood floors and a piano that 26 children from grades one to eight were able to enjoy.

In Grade Seven the students studied a bit of geology and, with the help of Mrs. Bearns, found agates and jasper among the handfuls of raspberries along Ribbon Creek. Mrs. Bearns acquired topographical maps to help the students identify the mountains and learn more of their environment. Long before outdoor education became a school subject these children were going on hikes along Marmot Creek to see the seven falls and other natural features.

Verda (Johnson) McAffer

My dad was the mine carpenter for Kananaskis Exploration and Development Company, and he was the foreman when they first built the tipple. My parents' names were Erma and Otto Johnson. I was about eight years old when he started working in Ozada, I think it was 1947, and Mom and I were in Calgary for a while. Then we moved to Ozada and lived in half of a house, which meant we lived in two rooms. After that we went up to Ribbon Creek and lived in the Ritz Hotel—one of those black tar paper houses! I think it had one room, but it was quite long. We lived there for a while and then went back to Ozada and lived in a

Ribbon Creek Village, 1950. Photo: Joanne Goodwin.

whole house, with four rooms. In the meantime my dad decided he was going to build our own house and he did that at Ozada.

All summer, when he was building it, we lived in a tent that was put on wooden walls. They made a movie on Ozada Flats and left some props there, so some of the guys hauled the big floor (about 15x15 feet) to us, and Dad built walls and put a big, white, canvas tent on top. Mom did most of the cooking outside on a little stove while Dad built the house.

The company leased one square mile and it was fenced all around, the rest was the Indian reserve. It took in part of the hill and the backside of the hill where the local Indians lived, and we had our houses and the tipple over by the railroad tracks, almost to where the railroad station was. The railroad station was just a building with a phone in it that you could use to call, I believe Canmore, when you wanted a train. There was a flag on a stick that you had to wave when the train was coming by; the train would stop and away you would go. The station was east of the tipple.

The houses were south of the tipple behind the hill—on the other side of the hill from what is presently Highway #1. There were about three houses and then a couple farther down. You can still see the foundation of the house that I lived in. There is a new split level house at the very end of the hill now. Last time I was out there, the pump that used to be by the cookhouse was still there, sitting on an angle, but it still works. The water is delicious, clear and clean. There was no indoor plumbing, just outhouses. We had wood stove heating and a slop pail under the sink. Even in 1948 it was fairly primitive.

When we first moved, I was the only school-age child for a while, and there was no school and no way to get to the Seebe school. When more families moved in, we started going to school by car to Seebe. Marilyn Fleming's father drove the car, and there must have been half a dozen of us that would squeeze into it. The road, which had two tracks and a wood cattle guard, would go across the flats between the Ozada hill and the overpass. When I was first learning to drive, I think I was 11 or 12, my mother would hold her breath while I was driving through the little cattle guard, as she was sure I'd hit the side.

Occasionally we'd walk home along the railroad tracks right to Ozada. There are a couple of really nice sloughs in there. The wind from Exshaw blows so hard that it would blow all the snow off and we'd skate on them. Sometimes the ice would be covered with the dust emissions from the plant. There were spells when we wouldn't go to school for three or four days because of the snowdrifts. They'd finally get some trucks out to clear it so a car could go through. It was exciting.

We used to go over to the Bow River for walks and fishing a lot. The natives didn't mind us. We lived in the centre of their property and were friends with the people who lived there. My dad was friendly with the Indian children and they had horses, so we rode them. There is a great Saskatoon patch on the way to the river. Going east of Ozada we used to drive down a little trail and up the backside of another hill and on the top there was an artesian well with salt water, which ran all the time.

My brother, Vider, worked at the tipple for a while. We called him Johnny most of the time; for Johnson. There was a huge slack pile. I remember wearing gum boots and running around that when I was eight years old.

We had skis that were straight with a strap you put over your foot, but no ski boots. There was a water tower on the top of the hill, with a swath cut in the trees that we would go down with a toboggan, piece of cardboard or our skis.

I used to go around to the bunkhouses and collect all the beer bottles the guys had thrown out. I saved them until I had a huge stack, then my dad got a truck to come and take them away and get some money for them. I got my bicycle with the money—for $52.50, which is why I called it my 'beer bottle bicycle.' I can remember trying to learn to ride it and just about breaking my neck.

After the prisoner-of-war camp had closed we used to go to movies there. They had a projector and screen and we'd drive down in my dad's old car, for a night out on the town. One night we were driving home and the moon was out—it was a beautiful night—we were just by the hill at Ozada. All of a sudden a wheel fell off the car and went rolling into the ditch and the car hit the ground. No one was hurt. My brother was driving and my mother must have been in the front and my father said, '!!!!!! did the gas tank blow up?' It was so funny.

My dad was the carpenter in the mine at Ribbon Creek, too. The house my dad built in Ozada was hauled up to Ribbon Creek. They put it on skids and skidded it up, floating it across the Kananaskis River. They pulled it in and plunked it down. That was exciting.

Unlike Muscles, whose wife had to haul their water, my dad carried our water. He was an old Swede who was born in Sweden and came to Canada when he was pretty young, and he was very inventive. He made a yoke to fit over his shoulders with a big hook on it and a pail hooked into each hook. Behind our house he built a box about two feet by two feet with four sides and a top, not a bottom, which he stuck into the rocks in the creek. The water was so cold you couldn't ask for a better fridge.

You had to drink canned milk mixed with water, and I didn't like it very much, so I have had coffee since I was eight years old. I expect there was lots of canned milk in it, but at least it was better than canned milk mixed with water. Subsequently, I have had coffee all my life.

Ribbon Crick Schoolhouse. Photo NA-2468-13, courtesy: Glenbow-Alberta Institute.

When I first started school at Ribbon Creek, the daughter of the mine manager, Isobel Shanks, looked after the students, and later Mrs. Chris Bearns was my teacher. She was a real character. I think there were eight grades in that school.

I remember Scotty and Nellie Patterson. Nellie was killed when her car went off the road by the Barrier Dam and she broke her neck and back. All her children went to the Ribbon Creek School. The littlest girl was very young, about four, but Chris Bearns let her go to school because she had nobody at home to look after her as the dad was busy cooking and the boys were all going to school. Mrs. Bearns just loved to play the piano, and she pounded it really loud!

Lil and Harold Falt had a cafe, with a counter, stools and a kitchen in the back. They made lunches for the guys—the drivers or the miners. They had a good business, but it burned to the ground. I don't know what caused it, but I know they left there after that and I think we saw them in Edmonton later. They were good friends of my parents. Their son, Lawrence, and I used to do a lot of hiking.

We called Mount Bogart, Stormy Mountain (*Ribbon Peak is often mistaken for Mount Bogart*). If there was going to be bad weather it would come in behind Mount Allan and cross over Mount Bogart and obliterate it. Mount Allan was called Windy Mountain. We laughed when we heard they were putting the ski hill there and had trouble keeping snow on the runs. No wonder, its name is Windy Mountain!

There is a spot up on the mountain, and it was probably because of the forest fire, where there were trees with great big gnarls on them. They had been burnt. It was the eeriest place. I wonder if they are up there somewhere now?

The women got together to go hiking. I remember hiking with Eileen Langille and a couple of younger girls and a couple of ladies. Thunder Mountain had a creek—where O'Shaughnessy Falls is today—it sort of ran down there and we'd stop where there was a tin cup hanging on a branch for a drink.

We'd hike up the canyon from there. We called the mountain Thunder Mountain because the creek made such a noise coming down that canyon.

There used to be a dark wood trapper's cabin on the east side of the Kananaskis River from the village. One of the fellows had some horses for some reason, so we decided we would go horseback riding in the winter to this cabin. There were only four of us and two horses, so we had two people on each horse going through the deep snow. We finally got up there and were nearly frozen, so we had to light a fire and get warm in the cabin. My mother was so upset by the time we got home because it took us forever. They were ready to send out a search party.

The truck drivers were amazing. Barrier Hill was so steep. It went right up over the top—no rock cut like today. It was hard for the trucks to get up, let alone cars. Going up in the wintertime with the road sheer ice, stepping out and trying to push and falling because the road was so icy, was scary. The road was close to the steep rock face. There were grizzly bears in that rock at one time.

There were a lot of young men—they seemed old to me because I was pretty young—who drove the trucks. I can remember they would sing for hours. Norma Holt and I would camp out in this little tent trailer thing; it was the back of an ambulance with no wheels—like the military ambulances that were trucks. We would listen to this one fellow sing and play his guitar in the bunkhouse. They were mournful songs.

I was thinking today of a song that I heard when I was up there. I can't remember it all, although it's really funny.

'The old truck ain't had no horn since the day it was born,
but I never seem to worry any time,
I just load it up with coal before I let her roll
from the Kananaskis Exploration Mine.
I just started down the hill
but I forgot to make my will
And there's a thrill awaiting for me down the line
If there's anyone around they should give me lots of ground
For here comes old faithful number nine.'

There are many verses, but I can't think of them. Toward the end…

'I just headed down the bank and I hopes they all sank
For there was Kelly's shack around the bend
There was Kelly's underwear just a flying through the air
On the grill guard of old faithful number nine.'

Kelly and Lucy Gallagher lived right where the road came down from the mine. The road turned sharply to go through the village and their shack was right there.

One of the most interesting aspects of the village was its pioneering spirit. Although the time was the 1950s, many characteristics of the early 1900s prevailed. For instance, in western Canada men wrote to eastern Canada looking for wives, telling of their big ranches and substantial herds of cattle. Many of these early pioneer women came to live in what they thought was a large ranch house, only to find it was a small log cabin with no running water. John Johanson, a good-hearted Dane, answered an advertisement in a newspaper written by a lady in Calgary interested in getting married. The letter, which was composed mainly by the miners, was very impressive. It said, among other things, that Johanson was the mine manager. Johanson, who was the bull cook alias camp flunky, went to Calgary, accompanied by the Micheners, to meet the lady, get married and bring her back to Ribbon Creek to his two-room shack with its one bed, one table and two chairs. Mama, as she was to become known, was a half-Scot from Ontario. The letdown must have been a heartbreak, but Mama was a true pioneer and did not allow this rude awakening to dampen her spirits for long.

The miners, no doubt motivated by a guilty conscience, contributed some money to purchase furniture and Mama distributed the linens, blankets, cutlery and dishes that she had brought with her around the little shack and made a home for John and herself. She and Chris Bearns, who was living just across the creek, established a friendship that lasted for many years. On the day of the coronation of Queen Elizabeth II the two women hoisted a Union Jack and sang "God Save the Queen." The men thought they were "daft," but they "enjoyed their daftness."

In the beginning, the village did not have a store. Some of the people went to Canmore or Banff for their groceries, while others used the services of Ken Lyster, who owned the Seebe General Store. (North of Highway #1 off Highway #1X.) Lyster would drive into Ribbon Creek on Tuesdays and pick up the grocery orders from various residents and the cookhouse; and deliver the orders on Fridays. He started this service in 1950 and continued until sometime in 1952 when the families left the village. One year when the creek flooded across the Ribbon Creek road (the creek has since been diverted) he had to put planks across the road and walk into the village carrying the groceries. In time, Harry and Lil Falt opened a small coffee shop and store, but not long before the mine closed it burned down. The store had a stock of gun shells so the fire was a noisy affair!

Other aspects of village life were quite primitive. Water came either from the creek, which was not polluted by the mining activity, or from the spring behind the mine office. It had to be hauled and heated before washing could be started. Not everyone was as fortunate as Eileen Langille, who had a wagon, with wheels in the summer and runners in the winter, to carry her water pails. Isabel Bradford's daughter, Joanne (Goodwin), a young girl at the time, recalled getting up one morning to go for water to do the family wash: she was frightened by an encounter with a moose, dropped her buckets and ran to the nearest house. Grappling with the problems of wildlife in the village was just one of the adjustments the villagers made, the other was living without electric washing machines and doing the family laundry with a scrub board. A few people may have had electric machines, but most did not.

Sometimes the problem was living with the vagaries of the weather, such as the time a big snowstorm made the road impassable. Some of the men walked over the Canmore Trail (now called Skogan Pass Trail) to Canmore to get more supplies. This trail had been used for many years by people going to Ribbon Creek from Canmore, and had the telephone line strung along it to the ranger's Boundary Cabin. (Site of the present Kananaskis Emergency Services Centre.)

In spite of the primitive conditions, even for that age, the villagers were innovative and used their skills to entertain themselves. Singing and playing the guitar, sharing coffee from house to house, drinking, card games and fishing were some of the things they did to amuse themselves. The drinking that went on led to an interesting bet between the Calgary Power fellows across the creek and the miners, as to how many hairs the Calgary Power fellows could pull out of bears' rear ends! We don't know who won the bet.

Eileen Langille
The men did a lot of fishing—they would get in the car and take their booze with them and go down the road and throw in their line and hope the fish wouldn't get on and interrupt their little party. Some of them ended up in the water!

Hiking and mountain climbing were also popular pastimes. Gordon Langille, his wife, Eileen, and several others, felt the call of Mount McDougall and Mount Allan and managed to make it to the summits.

Ribbon Creek had its share of interesting people. Gordon Langille, a tall, lanky fellow who worked first in the mine and then in the mine office, was the scapegoat of the miners. He was known by many people as Muscles or Mr. Muscles; his wife, Eileen, was called Mrs. Muscles and the children were Little Muscles. This term was so popular among the people that one day Langille received a letter addressed to Mr. Muscles of Ribbon Creek.

Eileen Langille had a neighbour who was the friendly type and who

…would get up early in the morning, I mean early—about four o'clock in the morning—and go right through her house and have everything spotless by about eight o'clock in the morning. And she had a wooden floor that she scrubbed with a scrubbing brush. She would throw open the window in her house and holler around to everybody to come over for coffee. She had an old grey blanket that she laid down on the wooden floor as her rug, and it looked great.

During the years the coal mine operated on Mount Allan, people were not aware of the damage a small open-pit mine could do to the environment. Therefore, it was much easier for them to accept the existence of the mine and still appreciate the beauty of the area the mining operation did not touch. Although Eileen Langille often thought the trucks running down the mine road and rounding the corner by her cabin might come right through the wall, she did not make a derogatory remark about the coal mine in relation to the environment. The mine was their living, why would they complain?

When the mine closed in February 1952, the miners moved on to other jobs in either Canmore or Drumheller. The women stayed in the village until the end of June when the school term was completed, whereupon they joined their husbands. The people dispersed in different directions, while the love of Ribbon Creek remained in many hearts.

Until 1962, most of the buildings from the village were still standing. The final demolition took place in 1969. At that time some of the chimney blocks and lumber were used in the building of a research cabin on Marmot Creek by the University of Alberta, and the Ribbon Creek Hostel people were allowed to salvage what they wanted.

Endnotes
1. *J. A. Haddin Papers 1910-1961, Letter to Haddin from George W. Pocaterra, September 20, 1920: Glenbow-Alberta Institute Archives, Calgary.*

Researching the Valley

3

The Kananaskis Forest Experiment Station

The Kananaskis Forest Experiment Station was the first research facility in the valley. It was located where the Barrier Lake Station of the University of Calgary Kananaskis Field Stations is today, on the east side of Highway #40 by Barrier Lake.

It came into being on November 15, 1934, when negotiations were completed for the return to the federal government of 162.12 square kilometres of the Kananaskis Valley for a forest experimental station. The site, which straddles the Kananaskis River for 28 kilometres, was chosen after a survey was completed by the Alberta staff of the Dominion Forest Service (now the Canadian Forestry Service), to determine the most representative area of the Rocky Mountain's eastern slopes.

The purpose of the station was to provide an outdoor laboratory for research on forest ecology, tree growth, soils, insects and diseases, watershed and forest fires. Research began in 1936 and continued for more than four decades. Almost immediately upon its establishment the station became the site of an unemployed relief camp under the federal Department of National Defence. This was the era known as the Dirty Thirties. The men in the relief camp helped set up the research station. This camp came to an end in June 1936.

A road construction program was given high priority and about 32 kilometres of road was built from Seebe to the station headquarters, located where Canoe Meadows picnic site is today. Sections of this road can still be seen, as well as the remains of the log bridge built over the Kananaskis River. (The best vantage point to view the old bridge is from the river via canoe, kayak or raft.)

An administration office and superintendent's cottage were constructed of logs across the road from the station headquarters (opposite Canoe Meadows picnic site), and telephone facilities were installed from Seebe by bringing a line on trees up the valley. One of the first buildings constructed (now called the Colonel's Cabin) is located at the Kananaskis Field Station. The fireplaces in both the Colonel's Cabin and the superintendent's cottage were built of Rundle stone and are of particularly fine workmanship. The Colonel's Cabin was used first as the relief camp superintendent's office, in 1936, then became a guest house, and was later used as the commandant's office for the prisoner-of-war camp, from whence it got its name. Today the Colonel's Cabin is an interpretive centre, offering displays and information on the prisoner-of-war camp.

In the autumn of 1936 H. A. Parker was appointed research forester. He initially established a number of permanent sample plots and transect plots in various stands of trees. Studies at that time included nursery work, planting of exotic species, experimental thinning, measurements of tree volumes and identification of soils. A climatological station was established at the site of the headquarters in August 1939. That summer, H. W. Beall initiated forest fire hazard studies at the station and in adjacent national parks. During the fire season the forest fire hazard was calculated daily.

The station's research activities was interrupted on September 29, 1939 when it became part of the Department of National Defence. An internment and prisoner-of-war camp was opened on the site and remained in existence until January 28, 1946 (see Chapter 4).

By 1948, when the station had returned to its former forestry studies, there were four couples and two single men living at the station at the northeast end of Barrier Lake. These people worked for the Forest Biology division of the Department of Agriculture. Each apartment had a potbellied stove for heat and there was also a potbellied stove to warm the big room in the middle. Later a furnace was installed in the basement that burned coal from the Ribbon Creek mine. The station, at this time, was maintained by staff from the Canadian Department of Resources and Development and included a cook, assistant cook, a camp foreman and a mechanic. Ed Rogers, whose job it was to take the mail deposited in the cookhouse into Seebe and bring back the incoming mail, would also pick up incidental groceries at the Seebe store, deliver passengers to the bus at the highway, the present Highway #1A, and bring incoming people back to the station. It was a busy and happy life for the residents of the small community. The men were occupied with their research work while, "every Friday a panel truck took the girls and one or two men to Banff for grocery shopping, and once a month or so they went to Calgary for an overnight trip to shop and visit headquarters for orders."[1]

As in most isolated communities, the residents made their own fun. In the summer hiking and climbing mountains, and observing plant and animal life were popular activities. W. C. McGuffin tells of seeing bears mating at the dump and watching lynx with their young at the beaver ponds near Lusk Creek. In the winter the residents' recreational activities included skiing, tobogganing and skating. A few curled at Seebe, where there was a one-sheet curling rink. On New Year's Eve 1948, the few people who were left at the station celebrated the new year by going skating at 2:30 am. In the summer the skating rink was converted into a volleyball court.

Desmond J. Crossley

The Canadian Forestry Service research organization in Alberta came about in 1930 as a result of the natural resources being transferred from federal responsibility to the provinces. Until that time the forests had been administered from Ottawa, and all the staff involved in both administration and field work were on the federal payroll. Following the transfer, the superfluous staff accepted employment with the Alberta Forest Service. However, a nucleus remained with the federal government in its Alberta office until a decision could be made about what the future role of the federal government would be in Alberta. For some time it had been toying with the idea of moving into research. The transfer of resources raised the question of the need for such a program in Alberta. If the need could be justified, should a research station be established, and where? Harry Holman was in charge of the remnant staff in the Alberta District Office, and he, of course, was questioned on these subjects. Apparently it was his opinion a need for a research program was evident. As an aside, I don't think—from what I subsequently learned—there was any crying demand for it from anybody in Alberta, but it was a national decision that this field of forestry should be embraced by the federal government, and plans proceeded to that end, which included the establishment of a research station.

The next question, therefore, was its location. The chief forester in Ottawa, at that time, was a man named Finlayson. He used to come out once a year to visit the districts: one at Riding Mountain in Manitoba, and one in Alberta. This was a result of the 1930 change of authority. This is all early history before I arrived in 1945. This information was all garnered from Holman and other people, and from reading reports in the office library.

As I said, Finlayson came out every year, but he was never satisfied with the proposed research station locations Holman suggested. By chance they were both ardent fishermen and Harry arranged to introduce Finlayson to a new fishing stream each time he visited the Alberta district. This time Holman decided to take him to the Kananaskis River in the mountains west of Calgary. Apparently the fall colours were in all their splendour and the fishing was exceptionally good. Harry took the opportunity to introduce the idea that the Kananaskis Valley would make a fine location for the proposed research centre and it was instantly approved! Obviously, no thought was given to site suitability, its very high elevation, its prime use as a source of water for prairie irrigation, the lack of interest as an industrial source of timber, and so on.

The Alberta Forest Service, upon request, reserved the necessary acreage and a great deal of money was spent developing the station to accommodate the necessary research facilities. Of course, it was never intended that research be confined to this location, although in the early years most of it was. It was convenient to the Calgary office and was a delightful place to spend the field season with your family, but it eventually became obvious a location in the heart of the forest utilization areas in the province would have been much more practical.

The public knew little about what was done at the Kananaskis research station and probably cared less. This got to me after a while and we decided we should have something to attract their attention and arouse their curiosity. As one approach, a stand of young lodgepole pine was selected, bordering the trunk road that passed through the Experiment Station. This dense, fire-origin 15 year-old stand was thinned out to a more suitable density. We then proceeded to remove the buds from all but the terminal leader, so each tree would develop without branches at the lower levels, and this should result in tree boles free of any knots. The idea was to continue annual debudding until each tree reached a height of 16 to 18 feet. At this point, debudding was discontinued and the tree allowed to resume its natural lateral branch growth beyond that level. Since this was mainly initiated as an eye-catcher, we placed signs on the edge of the road to attract the public and to explain the scientific purpose of the study, as well as its history of establishment and the results to that point in time. It attracted the most attention of

Administration building built between 1934-36, 1975. Photo: Ruth Oltmann.

"Colonel's Cabin," 1975. Photo: Ruth Oltmann.

any project we had ever established on that station, but many were still at a loss as to its purpose. Actually, the study yielded the knowledge that debudding in lodgepole resulted in adventitious budding on the main stem and, therefore, was unsuccessful in providing knot-free boles, so the project was discontinued. It required too much maintenance. We had to keep going back year after year to pick the buds off the boles so they didn't start putting branches on again.

Lynne (Crossley) Bowen
We were there for five summers: the summers of 1946-1950. My father was a senior research officer of the Dominion Forestry Experimental Station.

I have only a child's memory of the work my father did. He had forestry students with him every summer and at that time they would have been from the University of British Columbia as there was no forestry school in Alberta. He conducted various experiments, thinning lodgepole pine and observing how it regenerates after a fire. It takes the heat of the fire to open the cones, so the stands are very thick. He was working on ways of thinning them efficiently. I remember a lot of seed plots. We would go back up into the bush and all of a sudden we would come across a plot. He would have my mother down on her hands and knees counting how much regeneration had occurred. Why his students weren't doing this I don't know!

Looking back, it was absolutely idyllic, although at the time I was taken away from my friends for the summer and I always resented that a little bit, but we settled in. I can remember going barefoot all summer. The first couple of weeks it was hard to walk and then our feet toughened up and we went everywhere barefoot. My mother would turn us loose in the morning and we'd be gone. My brother, when we first went up there, was just a little tiny guy. He was only two years old and I was six.

The very best part of playing there were the old guard towers. One of them was down in the camp where the entomologists' cabin was, and I think that cabin is still there. They were big, long buildings. All the buildings were from the Canadian side of the prisoner-of-war camp—the guard's side. They had gotten rid of all the prisoner's side, which was sort of on the foot of Baldy Mountain. The other guard tower that we played in was up in an open field where the German camp had been. It was located as you faced Barrier (*Mount Baldy*) on the left. All the barbed wire had been removed and it was like a super fort. It was in really good shape because it had just been abandoned the year before. It had a downstairs, an upstairs and a balcony. There were frequently several kids playing on that balcony. Where the mess hall had been for the prisoners was just a foundation and there were still a lot of pots and pans around. I scavenged some of those for my mother. We found an old stove and pushed it end over end all the way to the guard tower. We wrestled it into the lower building and had a stove in our fort. That was wonderful.

The first year we were at Kananaskis we lived in a cabin. It must have been a bunkhouse for the guards because it was a long, narrow building. It was divided up into rooms. I don't have a clear memory of the inside of that house. I do remember one night a thunderstorm was happening and we were making fudge to keep our minds off the thunder and lightning. The next year we lived in what had been the hospital. It was two bunkhouses joined, with a connecting hallway that made it H shaped. It was across the road from the cookhouse, down farther, away from Barrier Mountain *(Mount Baldy)*. Each side was divided into two rooms: a kitchen and living room and two bedrooms.

The third, fourth and fifth year we lived in what we called the Lusk Creek Cabin, which overlooked the Kananaskis River, situated right where the kayaker's parking lot is now *(Widowmaker Day Use)*. It had been the commandant's cabin. It was about a mile from the camp and had a kitchen, a living room with a potbellied stove and two tiny bedrooms. My brother and I had a bunk bed, and it was just big enough for a bunk bed and a bit of floor to jump out on. There was a little outhouse down behind. My brother stored frogs in there one year and I hated going to that outhouse. I would open the door and all the frogs would jump out! The house was facing the river and on the other side right above where the Widowmaker rock sticks out there was a smaller cabin that someone else from the camp lived in. Behind that was a spring with a crib down in the ground, and that was wonderful water.

We had a wood stove, Coleman lamps, and it was usually cold enough even in the summer that Dad would get up and make a fire in the morning, and we would get up when the house was warm. The floor of the living room was painted in big flagstones: red, green and white with black borders. It was painted by the prisoners-of-war for the camp commandant. On a rainy day my brother and I would amuse ourselves by saying, 'Okay, today we will only step on the red ones, tomorrow the green ones.' We had a washing machine that was made out of wood and had a hand crank to make the agitator go and another hand crank for the wringer. By the end of the summer the wood had shrunk so that it wouldn't hold water very well, so Dad would lower it down the bank on a rope and leave it in the river all winter to make it swell up.

One of the expeditions was to Pigeon fire lookout *(located on what is now Prairie View Trail.)* We went in army surplus 4x4s. They must have come from the British army because they had right-hand drive. They would load up people sitting on the two benches in the back and drive up on Sunday; during the week you weren't supposed to use the road. I'm not too sure why because forest fires don't necessarily happen during the week, do they? We would have a picnic up at the top. I think Bob Waldron was the lookout guy, but as I think about it I wonder if he wasn't the cook. I remember there was a little Willy's jeep as well, the little ones that you see in war movies in which the general is being driven. The man we called the weatherman drove that. He would go up to what, I believe, was the headquarters and check the weather-reading equipment. The equipment looked like honey hives in the front yard, but they were weather instruments. He also had instruments to read down at the camp. When we lived at the Lusk Creek Cabin my brother and I would walk the switchback road up to the main road and then we would walk along there knowing the weatherman would be coming along. He'd pick us up and drive us down to the camp and we would play there all day. My father would bring us back home.

I am not absolutely sure how we met Belmore and George Browne. They were a family of artists who lived on the other side of what we called Pigeon Mountain, in the plains where the Rafter Six Ranch is. The father and his wife and the son and his wife had separate cabins close together, which are still there. They and my parents hit it off fairly well, so we visited them a lot. In order to get there we had to open and close 12 gates, like ranching gates, so my brother and I took turns getting out of the car, opening the gate, standing on it

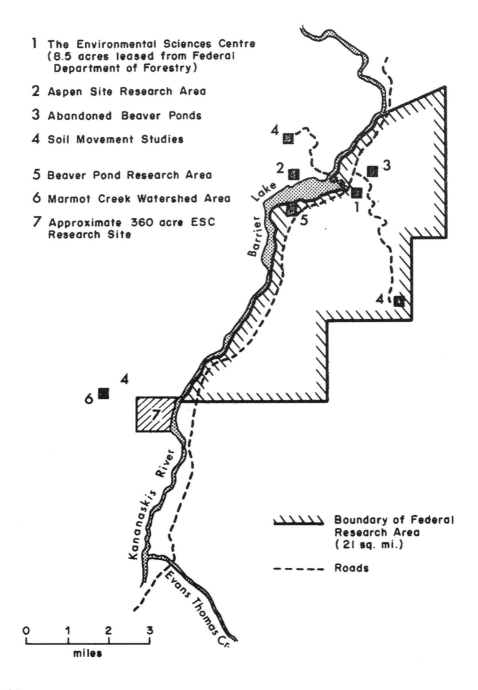

1 The Environmental Sciences Centre
   (8.5 acres leased from Federal
   Department of Forestry)

2 Aspen Site Research Area

3 Abandoned Beaver Ponds

4 Soil Movement Studies

5 Beaver Pond Research Area

6 Marmot Creek Watershed Area

7 Approximate 360 acre ESC
   Research Site

Barrier Lake

Kananaskis River

Evans Thomas Cr.

⟍⟍⟍⟍ Boundary of Federal
        Research Area
        (21 sq. mi.)

- - - - - Roads

0   1   2   3
    miles

while it swung open for the car to go through, then we'd push it back and get in the car and go on to the next gate. It was quite a labourious process.

Belmore Browne would have been in his late fifties or early sixties. He was a well-established big game artist at the time. George's specialty was game birds. The Brownes were Americans. They spent half the year at what they called Seebe, and half the year in Connecticut, which is where their markets were—where the people with the money to buy the pictures were. They were outdoors men, both the father and the son. Both of them were missing an eye. It was just a freak—some kind of an accident. Belmore was a wonderful storyteller and I can remember sitting in front of this huge fireplace with three sofas making a square around the fireplace and him telling us stories. He and his wife had been coming out there for a long time, because their children spent their summers there—George and Evelyn.

Dr. L. A. (Bud) Smithers

I was working as a forester from '52 to '59. I didn't spend all my time at the station. I was basically trying to apply mathematics and mathematical analysis to the age of trees, so I had a lot of these experiments at Kananaskis, but I had established others all through Alberta. I was a research scientist and when Des left—he had been the senior scientific officer—they asked me to take on that job. This meant overseeing other people's experiments as well.

We spent summers there until '56. We'd go up in early May and stay until October. We had the Lusk Creek cabin. It was a gorgeous spot with fish in the river. What more could you wish for? There used to be a lot of cutthroat trout. I used to keep a fly rod set up against the cottage and every morning I would go down and pick up a couple of trout for breakfast. We used to keep a couple of milk bottles at the back door. We had a little ice box—there were no refrigerators around in those days, just ice boxes. While I was down fishing Verna let out a yip, so I came up to see what was going on. Well, in the bottom of each of these milk bottles was a small deer mouse! They were still alive, so I shook them out and away they went. We had pack rats who used to come out and get any silverware if you'd left it out. They would grab it and haul it off and pack it away in the rafters.

The province had a very interesting system of managing those watersheds. The main Kananaskis River was open every year, but all the tributaries coming in on one side of the river would be closed one year and the next year the tributaries coming in on the other side would be closed to fishing. It wasn't outstanding fishing, but it was pleasant. Cutthroat liked the small silver doctor fly. They seemed to work every time. We didn't kill a lot of fish; there was a lot of catch and release going on.

As I mentioned, they were looking for somebody to take over a bunch of experiments that had been established back about 1937 by Harry Parker. Harry was one of the original staff members who had established these experiments and he was retiring. He had put it in plots and made the measurements, but the material had never been written up, so they asked me to go while he was still around and available to pass on his information. I set to work to analyze this huge mess of information that had been collected from 1937 right through until 1952. None of it had ever been analyzed or reviewed or checked.

About three years afterwards a position opened up at the new pulp mill at Hinton and Des took that job as chief forester for the North Western Pulp and

Power company. So he was gone from the station, but there were a lot of his old experiments there. He did a lot of work on direct seeding of lodgepole pine, on seed supplies, seed distribution and so on. I imagine a lot of his experiments are still there and probably being remeasured regularly. A large portion of it had burned over in 1937. It's kind of interesting, almost the same conditions we have occurring in the west now had occurred just prior to 1937, in British Columbia and Alberta. There had been a major infestation of mountain pine beetle and then there was the drought cycle. The agriculturists believe there is a 30-year cycle of drought. There's an 11-year cycle caused by sun spots and then when you get the third multiple of that, roughly 33 years, you get a very deep drought often followed by forest fires—if there's abundant fuel. That was the condition that prevailed at that time. The fire started in B.C., all up through the Kootenays, and it came right through the Rocky Mountains, although it didn't hit the park too much, and it came over the Highwood summit—all along that country. The '37 burn is what is shown in Des's experimental records. A lot of it was young seedlings that were established immediately after the fire—the cones open and you get a seed supply.

We had some interesting people there. There was a character named Hugh Cameron. Hugh worked for the meteorological service and the forestry service had an agreement with them to assign people to study weather patterns in relation to fire behaviour. Hugh was at Kananaskis for two or three summers. He got terribly interested in trees and forestry and Des Crossley was trying to figure out what was going on. Lodgepole pine cones tend to remain closed until you have a fire and then open and, of course, the seed is viable and you get new regeneration. Hugh got interested in this and he and Crossley worked diligently. They were taking the resin that was bonding the tips of the scales of the cones and collecting it, extracting it and determining the melting point. It turned out the melting point of that resin was only achieved at 145°F. It could

Lusk Creek Cabin. Left to right: Agnes Browne (Mrs. Belmore), Tibby Browne (Mrs. George), Caroline Scott (Mrs. David), Isabel Crossley (Mrs. Desmond). Photo: Lynne Bowen.

only be achieved by getting that kind of temperature during fire conditions. This was the basis from which Des worked with his whole practice around Hinton, but it started at Kananaskis.

J. L. McLenahan would have been there from about 1926 until 1944. He was at Kananaskis earlier than the establishment of the forestry station. He surveyed all that area by going in with pack trains. We called him Shiner. He was one of six McLenahan boys from Fredericton, New Brunswick.

Shiner had gone in there with a pack string to assess the area for an experiment station. I think it would have been 1926 or '27, thereabouts. He was riding a saddle horse and had a pack string of four or five horses loaded with equipment behind him, and he had the rawhide lead from the pack string around his thumb. He stumbled right onto a grizzly. The saddle horse went one way and the pack string went the other way and it took his thumb off like that! It was just a rawhide lace, so he had an amputation right then and there. Kananaskis was a long way in at that time. He was by himself and I guess he had a pretty rough time of it. He bandaged it up and kept on working and did his job.

There's another wonderful story about McLenahan. Apparently there was a huge scree slope on the fire lookout peak across the valley from the research station, and McLenahan kept seeing this grizzly up on the slope wandering around and digging. He decided he wanted a grizzly bear rug for the cabin, so he would sit and watch with the glasses to see this bear. One day he saw the bear and started across the valley, with a horse pack, and decided to put out bait. I don't know whether it was a cow's head, a steer's head or a dead horse's head, but they put this head up on the scree slope as bait and then wired it up to the rocks. He looked across the valley, saw the bear bouncing around where they'd put the bait, so decided it was time to go and get the bear! He rode across and climbed up the scree slope. The bait had been put back amongst the rocks, about 50 yards from the top of the scree slope on a bit of a flat depression, which he thought would be a nice shot with a .30-30. When he got up the scree slope and looked over the top of it with rifle at the ready, he was looking at the bear about 10 feet from him! The bear had hauled this carcass over to the edge of the scree slope. The people who were watching this from down below said they never saw anybody go backwards down a scree slope faster in all their life! He had a bear skin rug in the cabin, but whether it was that bear I don't know.

George Tunstall is another name that crops up. George was working out of Winnipeg and I think he was in charge of the whole western region. I can remember making a trip with George when they appointed an Eastern Rockies Forest Conservation Board. George was its first chairman and he came out and wanted to travel down this new Highwood road, when the road was first built. So we went up through the Kananaskis, up the gravel road and we got up to the Highwood summit and started down and got to about the Highwood River, where the road crossed it on an old log bridge and he said, 'Stop the car.' We stopped and got out and he headed down the river a piece and first thing I knew he came back and had four bottles of beer.

'Where did you get those?'

'Oh,' he said, 'I brought these in here by pack train, back in the early forties. If you know the right places to look, the whole distance down the height of land from here to the Crowsnest Pass there's beer stashed.' And there was. We drove all the way down to the Crowsnest Pass and every time we crossed a river we had to stop for one of his caches of beer! He was a wonderful, amazing character.

I guess I had four students that summer. We were doing a series of studies out at Wasootch wash. There were a number of Harry Parker's old sample plots there and then I established 50 or 60 additional plots in the Wasootch area. I was trying to determine the relative growth rate of lodgepole pine on different site quality conditions. It seemed to grade off from a very impoverished soil, close to Wasootch, and then as you went back away from it there was an alluvial fan and the soils got richer and deeper. We covered the area with sample plots.

The students were doing stem analysis. Those little metal things on the trees would be some of Harry's original plots of 74 to 80, a thinning experiment on 60 year-old lodgepole pine, thinned to varying densities, then they remeasured it periodically and I rethinned it. It was thinned originally in '37, then I thinned it again about '54. We were trying to study how much you could increase the growth and improve the quality of the trees by cutting them and improving the space.

(Jack Quaite) had a logging operation (in Quaite Valley) for the purposes of experimentation. We were trying to develop better methods of regenerating over-matured Engelmann spruce, white spruce and alpine fir in that valley. We tried to play with the spruce as most of the natural regeneration is alpine fir, and we wanted to improve the spruce. So it was being logged experimentally to try and achieve that.

A lot of the original logging in the Kananaskis was done by the Eau Claire Lumber Company. Bob Cummins, who had been the foreman for the logging operations, came to work for McLenahan as foreman of the experiment station, probably after the '36/37 fire. I think Eau Claire pretty well pulled out of that area about that time. Bob was quite a character, an old logger. He'd been all through that country. An amusing tale about Bob was when we were having a lot of bear trouble around the cookery at the station headquarters where the officer prison camp had been. Our garbage box was a large wooden box with a lift-type lid and it would accommodate about four of these big galvanized cans. The cook put all the wastes out there and the bears were forever getting into this thing and carrying it off and then bashing the cans around and raising hell. Bob got pretty peeved at the bears and would have none of this nonsense. 'That's enough of these bears,' so he proceeded to get hold of Jimmy Naylor, who was the mechanic at the garage, and got him to wire up a heavy copper wire from the main line coming into the cookery to the galvanized lining of this box. Then they proceeded to sit in the cookhouse—there were three or four of us sitting and watching the window, with the switch in the off position. The bear got into the box and started rattling around the cans. At this point, Cummins threw the switch and the whole operation came alive. The roars that came out of this bear were something to behold. I guess his feet must have been burned because he took off away from the cookhouse—the cookhouse was quite close to the old road that ran alongside the lake—heading for the lake. I guess he wanted to get his feet cooled off. As luck would have it, an American tourist was coming down the road in his car and the bear was so stupefied by the partial electrocution that he ran right into the side of the guy's car and put a huge dint in the side. The bear bounced off the car and ran down to the lake. The guy drove into the camp and he was just shaking. He was telling us how he had been attacked by this bear. All the bear was trying to do was get his feet in the lake and cool off!

Just after the war things were not all sweetness and light in the Canadian Forestry Service. For at least four years we ate Hong Kong butter and applesauce. There had been a whole shipload of canned butter and applesauce that was on the high seas, heading for Hong Kong before it fell. This stuff was all shipped back, and was owned by the Canadian government, Department of National Defence. They didn't know what to do with it, so they simply distributed it to all the government establishments all over the country. We were eating this stuff for at least four years!

I guess the eventual Olympic ski site was on that west slope at the base of Wind and Storm Mountain. Mount Allan was originally known as Storm Mountain. Wind Mountain was right next and above the mine and directly next to Mount Kidd *(the south ridge of Mount Allan)*. The next peak over was the one we called Storm Mountain *(Mount Allan)* and then Mount Lorette. We skied in that valley *(the basin of Mount Allan)*. I think Pat Duffy was skiing in there with me in 1954. We'd ski up there in late May, early June, on the snowfields on the top. It was a lovely spot. I said at the time, 'This is a perfect slope for a future ski development.'

We drove into the Kananaskis Valley when we were driving out to Vancouver from back east. That would have been about 1978. We drove just as far as Wedge Mountain and the road was paved that far at that time. That was the last time we were there. I remember looking back at that spot across from Wedge Mountain and saying, 'Wouldn't that make a marvellous golf course!'

Dr. Patrick Duffy

I worked at the Kananaskis Forest Experiment Station in the summers of 1953 and 1954 and then I returned to work for what is now known as the Canadian Forestry Service in June 1957. I was associated with the station until September of 1959 when I went back to university for a while, and then later in 1961 to 1968 when I had to do some work at the station. After that my visits were sporadic, but I kept an interest in the place because of my love for the valley and the people who were associated with it over the years.

In the sixties the forestry work I was doing dealt with using aerial photographs and some soil survey work, digging soil pits and understanding how soils are formed after glaciation, and mapping soil types and correlating the soil types with tree growth and vegetation, so you could say, 'This area is a class one area for growing lodgepole pine, and over here you have a class two, and this poor soil over here may be a class five.' We would work out of Kananaskis, up the foothills into this spruce-aspen type of north-central Alberta. About 1965 or '66 the idea of computer mapping became very important, so with Professor Lou Hamil, from the University of Calgary Geography Department, and a grad student, whose name I think was Ray England, we undertook to map the Kananaskis Forest Experiment Station area soils for forestry purposes, and we did all this on a computer. I think it was the first time it had been done in that valley.

North of the station there were extensive stands of immature lodgepole pine, about eight or nine centimetres in diameter. We had to prune these trees up about 20 feet, so when the trees were harvested they would have no knots on the wood. Therefore we had piles of slash we had to dispose of, and in those days permission was given to burn the stuff, so we had to burn it in the rain. And it does rain a lot at the station, particularly in June. We would drag these great mounds of slash through the bush and, of course, we were university students not given to boredom. At one point we were so desperate for something to do we used to take heavy army blankets from the camp and get the fire going and stand around in a circle, talking about everything we could think of, or have one of the guys read the Bible to us. It was half serious. Every now and then our boss, Larry Skov, would come along and there would be a big scramble to ditch everything and to be seen to be throwing branches on this gigantic fire. That is a recollection of a hilarious side play of an otherwise boring activity.

On February 5, 1952, 47 square kilometres of the Kananaskis Forest Experiment Station were returned to the province of Alberta, which simultaneously set aside an additional 4.53 square kilometres of provincial land. On February 4, 1961, the station's area was again reduced to 61.79 square kilometres when all the lands lying west of the Kananaskis River were returned to the province.

One of the largest projects was the Marmot Creek project on Mount Allan. This project began in 1962 when the Marmot Creek basin on Mount Allan was set aside as an experimental watershed. The objective of the project was to increase water production while maintaining water quality and improving the timing of flow. As time went on the research activities in this basin broadened until they included geohydrology, groundwater instrumentation, water quality studies, meteorological, precipitation and evapotranspiration research, research into the hydrologic properties of the forest floor, geology and geomorphology.

Marmot Creek basin was legally closed to public vehicular traffic and to hunting on August 13, 1971, for the protection of the research equipment from vandalism. In the summer of 1974, 100 acres of Engelmann spruce-alpine fir forest was logged for the purposes of this research. The area represented 30 per cent of the forest on Cabin Creek, but only two per cent of the Marmot Creek basin. Instrumentation was returned to the logged areas and further data was taken under the new conditions. At that time there was talk of a major recreational facility being built in the basin. This recreational facility would have a large element of experimentation, such as experimental ski runs, and experimental housing that would include housing for a wide range of socioeconomic classes.

Dr. Robert H. Swanson

The Marmot watershed became our primary focus of research, at least in the subalpine. The research program didn't get started until around 1964 when a chap named Dr. Walt W. Jeffrey was with the Canadian Forestry Service. He was charged with doing watershed management work to learn how to manage the eastern slopes for water yield.

I was there from 1968 to 1986.

When I came up to Barrier for the job, the guys took me up to show me Marmot. It was kind of funny because we started walking up the slope and about halfway up I asked, 'Aren't you feeling well?' as I was puffing less than they were. It turned out they had forgotten I had been working at Fraser in Colorado and the place where we lived was 9,500 feet and it went up to 11,800 feet and more. The elevation in Kananaskis wasn't bothering me a bit.

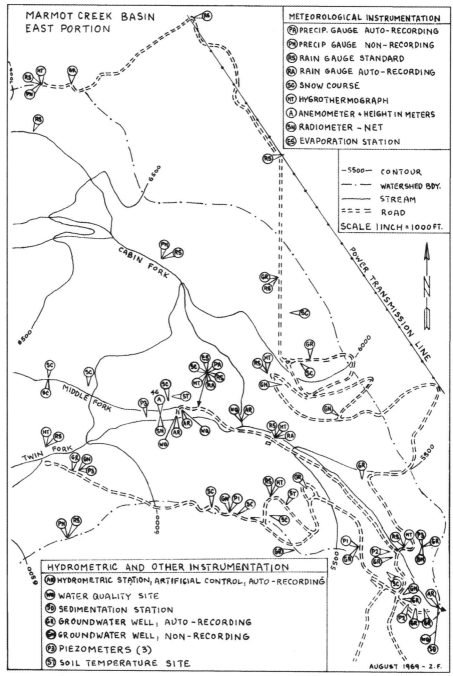

MARMOT CREEK BASIN
EAST PORTION

METEOROLOGICAL INSTRUMENTATION
(PA) PRECIP. GAUGE AUTO-RECORDING
(PN) PRECIP GAUGE NON-RECORDING
(RS) RAIN GAUGE STANDARD
(RA) RAIN GAUGE AUTO-RECORDING
(SC) SNOW COURSE
(HT) HYGROTHERMOGRAPH
(A) ANEMOMETER + HEIGHT IN METERS
(SN) RADIOMETER - NET
(ES) EVAPORATION STATION

—5500— CONTOUR
—··— WATERSHED BDY.
——— STREAM
=== ROAD
SCALE 1 INCH = 1000 FT.

HYDROMETRIC AND OTHER INSTRUMENTATION
(AR) HYDROMETRIC STATION, ARTIFICIAL CONTROL, AUTO-RECORDING
(WQ) WATER QUALITY SITE
(SD) SEDIMENTATION STATION
(GR) GROUNDWATER WELL, AUTO-RECORDING
(GN) GROUNDWATER WELL, NON-RECORDING
(P3) PIEZOMETERS (3)
(ST) SOIL TEMPERATURE SITE

AUGUST 1969 - Z.F.

Map: Kananaskis Forest Experiment Station. Drawn by Denny Fisera.

Sacramento gauge used for precipitation measurements. Photo: Denny Fisera.

The objective was pretty well set up and all the research sites chosen. They really didn't need all the experimental watersheds they had. They had three, and at that time they had five scientists and five technicians. Even if we had put everyone on one watershed we couldn't have done an adequate job. They were supposed to have 10 scientists and 20 technicians, which they promised me when I came. When they had a reduction in force in 1969 I got cut back to four scientists, plus myself, and five technicians. Our focal point then became Marmot because that was the most advanced of all the experimental watersheds set up. Marmot Basin was on Mount Allan. Marmot was just the basin and Marmot Creek flowed from the basin. It was a bit confusing for me because I kept hearing about skiing at Marmot and I thought they meant skiing down there. I said, 'There are no lifts there. I cross-country ski there when I work.'

What they wanted to do was cut three areas. One was to be used as a control, which would be what we'd measure the other two against. One was to be clear-cut and one was to be cut with something else in mind—some purposeful thing for water. Middle Creek was to be left as control. I felt we knew enough about clear-cut practises to not have to do that, so we took Cabin Creek, the one that was least useful as far as a basin was concerned, and put the commercial cutting on that. That went on from 1973-75. The other one we reserved for something that would be more exotic.

Out of this research came the fact that by cutting one tree height diameter clearing (essentially cutting holes in the forest), more snow accumulated, but it also melted slower. It looked like you could probably get a delay of about two weeks in the runoff if we put in that kind of cutting. So Cabin Creek in Marmot was cut that way. Our modelling experiments and everything else told us it would probably take about 25 years to evaluate. We had something like four years before Nakiska came along.

Some of that logging was done with horses. We used them in the circular cuts as well as regular skidders, too. We wanted to use horses, but Brewster's horses would only work five hours a day. I was told this was the horses' union. They only worked these hours and they weren't going to work very hard. It was getting so costly, it just wasn't worthwhile.

We hand-felled everything and the contract paid for that. Spray Lakes Sawmills hauled out what they could with their rubber tired skidders. You can see where they have gone quite aways up on the side of the hill. The top part of the basin was cut and everything was knocked down so it was flat on the ground as much as possible. We had crews for two years doing this—laying things down flat so it would rot faster.

Denny Fisera was the layout man. When it came time to lay out a cut it required knowing where you were and making sure things didn't overlap all over the place with a bunch of tree height diameter circles. He was put in charge of that because he knew most of the basin. He kept real good records. In fact, we had every clearing numbered and he knew exactly where it was and kept track of when we had cut it and who had done it, so we knew who to pay. It was the kind of work he loved to do.

The bottom part of the basin was logged by Spray Lakes Sawmills. By the time the commercial cut was completed we had done a computer model that had evolved out of our own and U.S. research. It was an easy way to predict what the water yield change was going to be. We used the commercial cut as a test of the model to see how well it worked. Our predictions were for about seven millimetres of annual yield change and it actually came out to be about 17 millimetres. Much of the development of that model came about as a result of our efforts, and it is being used all over Canada and in much of the U.S. There was no direct benefit in managing those slopes for water because by the time the results were in, the Alberta Forest Service had decided that was not its mandate. They did look at stream protection a little bit. They would not allow so much cutting so they could protect the integrity of stream soils. To some degree the research is still being used for that, but it is not for the purpose it was originally intended.

I hired the first women students we had ever had in the Canadian Forestry Service. They worked with chain saws in the watershed. They did the bucking up of the lengths of logs to make them lay down on the ground. Denny was the supervisor of this all-girl crew. Some of them were good, although their upper body strength took a bit of time to develop.

We also had crews from the STEP program the province ran, and there were some weird ones. We did a spring snow survey every year to measure the snow at something like 2,000 points on the watershed, so we knew the extent of it over the whole Marmot Basin. We would bring down all the technicians I could find from our outfit up in Edmonton, divide them up into 10 crews of two men each and just blanket the thing in two days. I got assigned one guy from the STEP program who couldn't run the snow tube—he was too stupid for that, so I had him writing down the data. We would go along and I'd call out the data, the depth and density of the snow. I stopped one place to ask him, 'What was the last reading I gave you?'

'I don't know.'

'What do you mean you don't know? Look in your note book.'

'Well, I didn't write it down.'

'Why didn't you write it down?'

'Well, my pencil broke.'

'When did your pencil break?'

'Oh, probably a couple of hours ago.'

I was so mad! I had to go back and redo the whole thing.

Denny had wanted a pistol to protect himself from bears. We applied to the RCMP and, of course, it came back to the director. The director said, 'I'd rather take my chance with a bear than with Denny with a gun.' He didn't get a permit for a pistol, but he could have carried a shotgun. I've never seen a bear in Marmot, although I've seen very fresh bear scat. One time we were putting up a weather station and when we came down in the mid or late afternoon there were a couple of hunters along Cabin Creek spotting with a spotting scope. They said, 'Did you know there was a bear just up above you guys?'

'No, we didn't see him.'

If you don't bother them, they won't bother you, I guess. I have seen moose up on the top of Marmot in the larch.

Once we were up inspecting the layout of the road for the small cuttings. We had backed off the side of the road and were sitting talking when a lynx came out, walked around the car, peed on one of the wheels and walked off down the road. We were part of his territory at that point. We ran into another lynx when we were fishing at the ponds below O'Shaughnessy Falls. He was fishing, I guess, and he wasn't about to leave. He just stared and glared. We went around the corner to fish and left him there. Pretty animals. I've never heard of any attacking anyone.

We did the snow surveys in March. One time, when we had moved to Calgary, we came out to do the snow survey and they still had the cook out at Kananaskis. We wanted to get out early in the morning while there was still crust on the snow as it was beginning to get rotten, so we got the cook up at four to prepare breakfast and we got out there and the darn chinooks—it was about 14 degrees Celsius and there was no crust, no nothing! After that we forgot about getting up early and did like everybody else. Then the next year it was so crusted up you could walk without snowshoes! You had to be careful to get off the hill before noon. Other years it would be totally powder. It was a tricky thing to get the right time, which is fairly close to maximum pack before it starts melting too much.

We were more interested in snow distribution than we were in maximum. We wanted to get the snow survey done before it had been modified by melt. It did not change much from year to year, which was the nice part about it. Quantity changed a lot, but not distribution. We got to a point where we could predict what it was going to be in any given point from another point with about 95 per cent confidence.

I occasionally helped Denny Fisera with his Marmot Basin readings. Sometimes at the beginning of the season he would stop at Ribbon Creek Hostel and ask if I was going skiing. If so, would I go up and pack the switchback trail? He would pull me behind the skidoo and then at the switchbacks I would go ahead and pack the trail with my skis so he could get the skidoo up for that first time of the year.

The first time I went up in the basin Denny had gone up the day before. It had snowed about a foot overnight and it was still snowing heavily. I broke trail all the way, on top of his covered skidoo track. I could see he had gone onto the ridge that morning (eventually I named it Fisera Ridge). I knew he was in the hut when I arrived, as I could see the smoke coming out of the chimney and his skidoo outside. I skied over, but realized if I knocked on the door I'd really scare him, so I yodelled instead. He came leaping out of the cabin in great surprise and was amazed to see me.

Denny's research cabin,
1984. Mt. Allan cirque.
Photo: Ruth Oltmann.

Twin 1 Meteorological
Station. Photo: Denny Fisera.

97

At that time Denny didn't really know me and the kinds of things I did, but eventually he got so he could tell when a ski track was mine, over someone else's. He said mine were more even and straight, they didn't go off to the sides. Consequently, I never worried because I figured if he was around and I ran into problems he'd find me.

The establishment of the Canadian Forestry Service research laboratory in Edmonton in 1969-1970 reduced the importance of the Kananaskis Forest Experiment Station in the Kananaskis Valley. There wasn't much research in the last two years; mostly tree measurement and monitoring of cutover blocks. The Forest Management Trail was built as a recreation trail and is now called the Barrier Lake Forestry Trail.

The administration office and superintendent's cottage were used well into the 1980s and then sold. The houses were loaded onto flatbeds and taken south along Highway #40 and were last seen for sale in Aldersyde, south of Calgary. I remember standing in the Barrier Lake Information Centre and seeing the houses go by on the flatbeds. It was like seeing history driving away.

Denny and Yvonne Fisera had lived in the superintendent's cottage with their two sons, Peter and John, for 20 years while Denny was the research technician on the Marmot Basin watershed research project on Mount Allan. They moved to Edmonton when the station closed.

In 1979 the federal government transferred the research station site to the provincial government and it was operated under the Alberta Forest Service, mainly for the use of Boy Scouts and Girl Guides involved in outdoor activities.

In 1993 the province transferred the facilities to the University of Calgary.

The University of Calgary, Kananaskis Field Stations

The Barrier Lake Station of the University of Calgary's Kananaskis Field Stations (formerly the Environmental Sciences Centre [Kananaskis] and the Kananaskis Centre for Environmental Research) was the second research centre established in the Kananaskis Valley.

When the university was still the Calgary Campus of the University of Alberta in 1962, it undertook to establish a coordinated program of field work. Dr. P. K. Anderson, of the Biology Department of the Calgary Campus, started looking for a site for a field station. He had hoped to be able to acquire some of the old buildings left after the mining village at Ribbon Creek closed down, but this was not feasible.

Meanwhile, the university was given a half section of land downstream from what is now Troll Falls, not far from the Kananaskis River. In the summer of 1963 Calgary Power donated a power pole and transformer for the site and two portable buildings from the Calgary Campus of the university were hauled to the site and installed on either side of Marmot Creek. Dr. Anderson and three students (Raymond Sloan, Clive Eliott and George Holeton) built a log bridge across the creek and installed the buildings. The students then commenced work: collecting birds, frogs, amphibians and small mammals in the Marmot Creek basin. They worked from the Kananaskis River level up to the top of Mount Allan, setting traps at 500-foot intervals. One of their problems was bighorn sheep stealing peanut butter from the mouse traps!

Dr. Anderson felt that at the time the Kananaskis Valley was relatively unspoiled. Civilization was pulling out of the valley rather than coming in. The village at Ribbon Creek was deserted and, except for Calgary Power and the Kananaskis Forest Experiment Station, there was little activity in the valley.

Shortly after the research work commenced at Marmot Creek, the Canadian Forestry Service offered the university the use of the prisoner-of-war camp site adjoining its Kananaskis Forest Experiment Station. There were several things favouring acceptance: sewer and water systems were already installed and the road was snowplowed in winter. Subsequently, in the spring of 1964, $100,000 was allocated by the University of Alberta to erect buildings. Cedar log buildings were initially considered, but for various reasons these plans were not used and frame construction was adopted. By the summer of 1965 the first stage of the laboratory block was completed. Atco trailers were used for accommodation, and the first courses, in geology and field natural history, were offered. On April 1, 1966, Dr. J. B. Cragg, chairman of the Biology Department on the Calgary Campus, was appointed director of the field station. Under Dr. Cragg's guidance the field station was named the Environmental Sciences Centre and its aims were established.

The Environmental Sciences Centre had a broad program covering natural resources studies. At one end of the scale students would learn about the fundamental properties of the natural environment, and the interrelations between organisms and that environment. At the other end, they would learn about the economic and social implications of natural resource problems in relation to man.

The facilities were extended in 1966/67. A lodge was built that housed a kitchen, cook's apartment, men's and women's dormitories, and a fireside lounge. In 1968 the laboratory was extended and an environmental sciences library was built. Both a Kananaskis Committee and a Kananaskis Building Committee were formed to manage the affairs of the Environmental Sciences Centre under the chairmanship of Dr. Anderson. Further construction commenced in 1970 to erect five duplex housing units that provided accommodation for staff members and visiting researchers.

While the University of Alberta supplied financing for the buildings, equipment expenses, salaries and travel expenses were paid out of a National Research Council Negotiated Development Grant extended over a period of three years, from April 1, 1968 to March 31, 1971. Under its financing the following research programs were developed: studies on decomposer systems, environmental chemistry and physiology, large mammal studies, production studies on Rocky Mountain ecosystems, aquatic biology, studies related to land management, and geomorphological investigations.

When the University of Calgary was independently established on April 1, 1966, the Environmental Sciences Centre became a separate academic unit of the University of Calgary.

Dr. Gordon W. Hodgson became full-time director on January 1, 1973, and worked to raise the profile of the Environmental Sciences Centre throughout the scientific community. Under his direction the centre's mandate was to promote teaching and research in the natural environment through the encouragement and conduct of interdisciplinary studies. A strong core staff of interdisciplinary scientists with primary interests in environmental research was augmented by visiting scientists. As a result, a substantial number of funded programs were undertaken dealing with resource inventory, water quality, air quality and the quality of life; involving, to a large degree, recreation and tourism. The centre recognized the conflicts in land use in the mountain environment. There were conflicts, for example, between forestry and hydro companies, between hunters and conservationists, and between recreationists and mining companies. Accordingly, the University of Calgary established research projects that transcended pure science and moved toward social and economic issues.

The name of the centre changed several times. On July 4, 1978, it was changed to the Kananaskis Centre for Environmental Research, and then in 1993 it was again changed to the University of Calgary, Kananaskis Field Stations. The word "Stations" was plural because it included the A. B. Miller station in the Sheep River valley.

I first became involved in the centre in 1972 when I moved to the Ribbon Creek Hostel. The centre had the nearest telephone (16 kilometres away), and by using their pay phone I became friends with some of the people working there. In 1973, when I realized I couldn't live on a hostel houseparent's honorarium, which was about $85 a month, I asked the director's assistant, Linda Jones, for a part-time job. I fully expected to be scrubbing floors, but found myself organizing their technical library, and about a year later working on the Man and the Biosphere, Kananaskis Pilot Study, project as the human history historian. Eventually the director continued funding me to put the material into a book, called *The Valley of Rumours ... the Kananaskis*.

Dr. Gordon W. Hodgson

I was the director of the Kananaskis Centre for Environmental Research for 10 years. I started in 1973.

We were unsuccessful in getting funding from Man and the Biosphere, but in our attempt we found our footing in the mountains. The pilot study that we did do, as I recall, was looking at the resources in the Kananaskis Valley and starting to think in terms of making an inventory of those resources. For example: this is what we have in terms of water, this is what we have in terms of vegetation, visual beauty and all of that good stuff, this is where we are in relation to a major urban centre like Calgary and Vancouver, and given all of those things, then we hope to build on the cataloguing of the resources and reasonable expectations of what the valley might evolve into in coming years. The university gave me $30,000, as director of the centre, to fund the start of the program and it was that $30,000 that produced the report The Mountain Environment and Urban Society, Kananaskis Pilot Study.

As I look back on it, one of the most interesting things we did in the whole centre was something totally off beat. We thought we would do an analysis of what might happen to the Kananaskis Valley in the future. This was with Janet Marsh. We put together a short story that projected that the Kananaskis Valley could become the Disneyland of the Rocky Mountains. We aren't very far off that right now, with golf courses, hotels and swimming pools, and everything else all over the place. We attracted enough attention with the paper Janet wrote that it became a curriculum item in one or more of the local colleges. We were perhaps more knowledgeable than we thought.

Right at the end of my 10-year tenure the Olympics came crashing in on us. I had seen this coming as inevitable, and I had tried to encourage my masters to take full advantage of that. The university wasn't in the slightest interested: that we could have had the entire Kananaskis Centre totally redesigned and rebuilt at that time had we had the will to do so. The money was flowing so freely, there was the possibility that we could have diverted a couple of million dollars of the whole Olympic money to rebuilding the entire centre into something that would be in tune with the times and would allow us, after the Olympics had finished, to have a very strong base from which to continue full-scale environmental work.

Dennis Jaques, Ginny Jaques

We came to Kananaskis in June 1974. I had come the year before to look the place over and decided to go to San Francisco to work instead. A year later a good buddy called me and said, 'We need you up here. We are doing work on a project, Man and the Biosphere, where we are getting a group of scientists together in all disciplines, including Ruth Oltmann, doing the history of the valley.'

When I arrived I was doing forest ecology studies in the Kananaskis Valley and region, along with geologists and plant physiologists. We were all putting together studies of the current state of all the knowledge of scientific work in the east slopes of Alberta. The work went on for a year or so, and we published a report on the Kananaskis Valley called The Mountain Environment and Urban Society, Kananaskis Pilot Study. Also, I was called there to prepare for a conference in October, an international remote sensing conference. I presented a paper with Dr. Allan Legge on remote sensing work I'd done that summer in the Kananaskis Valley, Mount Allan and the Evan-Thomas Creek area in particular, where I did a lot of field work. Ruth Oltmann led me up Old Baldy in June that year and introduced me to the trails in the area.

At the remote sensing conference in 1974 I met Dr. Bill Wishart, who was the research wildlife biologist with Alberta Fish and Wildlife at the time. He liked what my talk was about and said, 'We need some work done on some wildlife populations, could you help us?' That was the start of wildlife studies.

For the next four or five years I was doing studies on grasslands, alpine ecosystems and fire-burned areas, and fire ecology of the east slopes, all the way from Waterton Lakes National Park north to the Smoky River and almost every river in between—looking at the quality of range in the Rocky Mountains. That kind of work hadn't been done on range ecology in Alberta since about 1920.

The Kananaskis Valley in '74, of course, was a little more isolated than now. The road was real rocky and we lost a few mufflers, as did everybody on the rocky old Morley Flats. In those days the kids had to go to school in Seebe, a one-room school house. We finally got a little bus that would come and drive them back and forth.

There was a great kindergarten at Exshaw in the old church, and a pre-school. One other interesting thing about life there in the seventies was when a bunch of us got together at Seebe to form a baseball club, and Calgary Power at the time, TransAlta Utilities now, loaned the guys at Seebe a bunch of heavy equipment, and we built our own baseball diamond. It is now a real nice base-ball diamond right in Seebe. We had tournaments every year in July and Sep-tember on the long weekends. That was a lot of fun.

Ginny: I remember how we started to worry about the water at Kananaskis, because over the seven or eight years we were there, we began to realize that all of the children conceived in Kananaskis were girls! Every time somebody got preg-nant we kept waiting for a boy and the boys never came, and after a while we got to wondering if there was something in the water that kept the boys away!

It was Marcia's baby shower—I think it was for Mandy—and I had made a cake for the shower and was trying to cool it so I could ice it. It was the afternoon and the kids were all down for a nap and it was in August, so it was really hot. The cake was cooling in the kitchen and the front door was open, the screen door was shut. I heard a noise and thought it was the kids not going to sleep, so I yelled at the kids. I think I was lying on the couch in the living room. The noise kept going on, so I got up to see about it, took one look down the hall, and there was this black bear trying to open the door to get to the cake. I ran down the hall to slam the door in his face, but of course, as soon as he saw me he turned around and ran off. Every year in early August, right about that same time, we'd have a black bear hanging around the duplex units.

Dennis: That reminds me, too, of one episode that was interesting. We had a young family come from South Africa, Chris and Gail Whiteley. I am a jogger, so after work at the lab I would often take off on the back roads and run up to the old sawmill at the pass on Barrier Mountain *(now called Baldy Mountain)* and down Lusk Creek, or something like that. When Chris arrived, he was pretty overweight—30 or 40 pounds—with a big paunch on him (he loved beer and made his own), he decided to go jogging. So I took off with him in pursuit.

My normal routine was to go up the water supply route—the old flume that was built by the prisoners-of-war, which was still pretty much intact—and run up the hill behind that little pond and then up the hill to the road *(Baldy Pass Trail)*. Well, the hill was steep, so if you're not in shape it would be kind of a rough go. Poor Chris was half dead after our trip up there.

Shortly after that Chris took off on his own and got into jogging, and became a long-distance marathon runner. The next time I went out with him, about a month-and-a-half later, I couldn't keep up with him. He'd lost all the weight. After he started jogging he took it seriously. For me it was recreation, relaxing after work, for him it was dead serious. He initiated a spring Kananaskis Fun Run—10 miles (16 kilometres)—starting at Ribbon Creek and running to the research centre for the finish line. Sure enough on the first race Chris won, I was second, then all the others came trooping in—mothers walking with their carriages and people cycling.

Ginny: I think the reason Chris got into jogging was because he figured the best bear protection when you are out is to take someone who can't run as fast as you can. He probably figured he'd better run faster than Dennis!

In the wintertime the people at the research centre started a cross-country ski race. They skied on the trails up behind the research centre.

Dennis: I think it was in 1975 that a young man came to work with us—Ed Van Zinderenbakker, he was also from South Africa. His father was a famous

U of C, Kananaskis
Field Stations, lodge
and duplex units.
November 28, 1970.

Lodge at Kananaskis
Field Stations.

103

pollenologist down in South Africa. I took Ed on a hike up Mount Allan. This was in spring—late May or early June—and we were up on the top of the first peak, before you go down and back up to the actual peak. We sat there catching our breath and looked down the valley. I've never seen anything like it, before or since, but we had had a cold winter and then it warmed up very quickly, so the pine pollen all matured simultaneously and big winds were whipping up from the south—from the Kananaskis Lakes, Evan-Thomas Creek and up toward Barrier Lake. There were huge clouds of pine pollen thousands of feet above our heads. I got a beautiful picture of this mass of huge clouds of pine pollen. It was so unique I sent a picture to his father in South Africa.

I was doing studies on winter range for bighorn sheep, which eventually led to helping them design the winter Olympics downhill ski run *(Nakiska at Mount Allan)*. They had originally positioned it in the wrong area and I was able to convince them to move the ski runs to avoid wildlife paths and escape terrain.

Leading up to those studies, I was up working on the wintering habitat of the bighorn sheep. I was sitting on the saddle east of the main peak of Mount Allan, looking down into Twin Creek. This is an area where we were doing a lot of studies with Dr. Telang, Eric Peak and Dr. Doug Golding on hydrology and the effects of logging in Marmot Basin. I knew the area well. I was looking into the clear-cut areas and all of a sudden a lynx came out of the forest on Twin Creek. He was padding through the deep, deep snow—this must have been in December of '77 or '78—and in just a few seconds had come all the way up above treeline, right to the saddle in front of me, and padded along like he was snowshoeing or snowskiing through the snow. He padded right on top, just amazing. Then he zoomed down the north fork side through the snow and in a few minutes he was gone up the north fork. He traversed miles in just a few minutes!

Dr. Robert Mutch, Dr. Cynthia Mutch

I started working in the valley about 1974/75 on a master's degree, a M.Sc. degree in biology. I worked there, initially, just in the summers—up in the Marmot Basin. It was a really remarkable wilderness experience being in Marmot Basin in those days, because early on the only people I would ever see would be Denny Fisera when we crossed each other's path, and maybe *Ruthie* on the way out when I stopped in at the hostel for tea. I suppose one of the depressing things, in a way, was to discover that one of my research sites is now underneath the Men's Downhill run for the Olympics. In the days when I worked there I would never have thought that would happen.

Basically what I was doing was studying the invertebrates that live in the streams. I was looking at the role of the invertebrates, insect larvae, in the energy transfer within the stream. For example, how quickly they processed the organic matter that fell into the stream from the trees around it. I was looking at what the energy sources were, to know whether it was from the surrounding trees or bushes, or whether it was from the in-stream mosses and algae. Also, how much of that energy got washed downstream and how much of it was processed in-stream by all the wonderful bugs. It was very esoteric work, but really enjoyable. Especially having to ski up there in mid-winter, and sometimes digging through five and six feet of snow to get to this tiny alpine stream and finding that beneath that there was life going on. That was an eye-opener to me. We discovered one new genus within the streams of the basin. It was a philoscasca.

John Corbin and Jeff Jaques sampling bighorn habitat, 1975. Photo: Dennis Jaques.

One of the most memorable things, because it was frightening, was the time that John Corbin, Janet Marsh and Colin James got hung up in the Bow River in an aluminum canoe. It got jammed under a log jam and they had to get out onto this little island. Janet went right under the log jam and came out the other end. We worried a lot about them being lost. I remember being out, driving up and down the side of the Bow River looking for them. The helicopter found them. They had a fire going because John's lighter worked. They got badly bitten by mosquitoes.

That was the winter Mike Mappin and Judy Buchanan persuaded me to enter the Kananaskis cross-country ski race. February 1980 that would be. It was 49 kilometres that year.

Cynthia: They all discussed it the night before and they persuaded you to enter. In bed in the morning Bob said, 'Oh, I don't think I'm going to do this.' Then there was a knock on the door and it was Mike and Judy and Bob said, 'I'm coming.' He got ready in about five minutes.

Bob: And I finished it and got done well under the five hours. That was the time limit. You couldn't get any slower than that, or you were not allowed to finish. That was a fun winter. Mike and Judy and I did a lot. I introduced them to backcountry skiing and then they got into racing and, of course, they never looked back since then. I can remember quite often taking off after supper with big Dennis Jaques and doing the loop up the hill, Barrier Mountain Trail, and hooking up with the Old Mill Road *(Baldy Pass Trail)*.

I remember staying at that forester's hut on the Old Mill Road, the hidden one. We had a wonderful rested night in there. We got a fire going in the old stove and had our warmish sleeping bag, which wasn't overly warm, and we were sleeping in the bunks. It was funny because there was no caulking between the logs. You could see light and the wind blowing in through the logs. With a fire going it got too warm. We almost set fire to the cabin. We always meant to go back and check on that cabin, but never have. It was a nice place to stay. It was very cold. It was about -30°C with the windchill. There was good snow, although the last bit of the trail was very steep.

Dr. Peter Wallis

We came in 1978 and arrived the 6th of June. Our children were born there and spent at least part of their life there, except John, who didn't show up until we were in Exshaw. We lived at the field station for six years, from '78 until '84, then we moved to Exshaw because the apartments at the field station were pretty small and we were tired of living there.

I think you had to be a bit on the different side, at the very least, to spend any amount of time out there and be prepared to live in fairly isolated circumstances. It was still a dirt road, and all of the development that is currently there—the Kananaskis Country development—wasn't there at that time. It was semi-protected because it was a forest reserve. The population pressure was much, much less than it is now. We lived pretty much beyond everybody's notice. It was great, because you didn't have people telling you what you could or couldn't do. It was very good for doing research. Nobody really cared if you cut a hole in the forest floor to see what roots were there. Nowadays you have to have six permits. Nobody wanted to build a golf course on top of your research site, either. It was a very different world.

When I first took up residence, I was mostly interested in things that went on in ground water coal mine sites. We did a lot of work at Canmore—the old coal mine site there—and we also expanded the work later to other mine sites in Alberta, particularly Forestburg and Wabamun, and some on Mount Allan. The projects in the coal mine sites occupied me for three years.

I remember two people who were studying katydids, because the first summer I was there as a student in 1976 those guys were there, too. They were up half the night looking for these insects. I still remember waking up one morning listening to their conversation. The walls were about half-an-inch thick. As I remember his father had come up to help him that summer. The first thing I heard the son say to the father was, 'Did you get a female last night?' He said, 'Yup, I got two.' I thought, 'What a greedy old guy!' You have to realize there weren't a whole lot of eligible young ladies in this field station at that time. I eventually realized what they were talking about.

The strongest in-house research projects we had were based on Dennis Jaques and his botany group, who did lots of work all over the province, but particularly in that area, looking at reclamation problems. *(Related to wildlife habitat and coal extraction.)* They worked in conjunction with some of the mammalogists on the main campus, because they were always interested in things that bears and other animals eat. Peter Van Eck was part of that group. He was actually there because of his photogrammetry skills—interpretation of aerial photographs. Then there was our group, which worked in the microbiology and water quality section. We worked initially in the local area, working at the Marmot Basin site, which is now the site of the Nakiska ski hill. It is also where we met *Ruthie*, who was houseparent at the hostel.

I remember the night I drove into the swamp and had to go and get some help at the hostel. We were fishing, back before the gates were all locked, and I took a shortcut, but it wasn't a shortcut—only in distance. This was about eleven o'clock at night. We got down to the hostel and discovered it didn't have a telephone, and *Ruthie* had to drive me up to the field station in her own vehicle. (I paid her back for that by installing a radio in her car.) I felt pretty stupid—pitching my old Volvo in the mud and having to get somebody else's 4x4 to winch it out the next day!

I guess no account of the field station would be complete without saying something about the Olympics in 1988. We lobbied long and hard to have the field station used as a facility for the volunteers, because we wanted to be involved like everybody else. The university was heavily involved anyway and we wound up housing volunteers who worked at Nakiska. We didn't have athletes, only the people who were grooming the hills and looking after the facilities—maximum about 120 people.

We took over the management of the Forestry Station as well, because we couldn't possibly accommodate all those people in our place, even though we'd outfitted the labs as dormitories. We hired lots of cooks and groundspeople—it was quite an operation.

We cleared an enormous amount of money at the end. It was never intended to make money, we were doing it on a volunteer basis, but the way the Olympic organization worked was they insisted on contracts and they were very, very picky. In the end they didn't come up with the number of people they had contracted for, and they tried in a halfhearted way to get out of the contract, but they didn't try very hard. By that time it was obvious the Olympics were going to make money. You have to remember everybody expected them to lose money, and the doomsayers said it was going to break Calgary and it wouldn't be paid off until into the next millennium. It was such a big success and in spite of all the problems it was well managed. So we ended up with a hundred thousand bucks at the end.

We spent thirty thousand bucks upgrading the dormitory facility. Then we used another thirty thousand bucks to launch a program for kids. It was designed to bring them out and let them be part of the university field station operation as a science camp. That still runs—the Young Scientists' program. It was extremely successful.

The research from the staff members gradually wound down as the eighties wore on, and as the budgets got tighter. Not only was the university money drying up, but all of the grant and contract money was just not there anymore.

In the end they kept the field station and dropped the Kananaskis Centre on campus in all but name. In 1990 they let the eight professionals go, and most of the support staff. The field station now operates purely as a facility. There is no in-house science that I know of, but they still operate for graduate students and professors. They still have lots of courses. Mike Mappin was there and running the Young Scientists' program, so he and Judy Buchanan-Mappin stayed on.

Marcia Wallis, Dr. Peter Wallis, Dr. Robert Mutch

Bob: The sauna was really Peter Van Eck's idea. I helped to build it. It was *Ruthie's* wood stove.

Peter: The problem I had, as station manager, was that this was an illegal building because we didn't have a building permit, among other things. Not that it would have mattered much—the guys had gone off and erected this thing. It was a decent little sauna hidden away in the trees. The problem was there was no way of getting power to it, other than running a long extension cord, which is what we did. The extension cord went over the road and no one thought anything of it. Then the university maintenance officials were out one day and they saw this extension cord running off into the woods, so they followed the cord and discovered the sauna. Boy, they just went ballistic when they saw that! We had erected a building, on our lease, and without permission! To make a long story short, the order was to 'tear it down forthwith.'

We were saved by Barb Zailo, Frank Tester's wife, because she worked for the Kananaskis Country office. When we looked into it very carefully and took a look at the site, we discovered the sauna had actually been erected about six feet off the university lease, so it wasn't even on our land. We thought, 'Ahah.' We got Barb to mention it to the chief administrator of Kananaskis Country, Bob Reynolds, who said, 'So?'

Barb wrote up a letter that gave us official permission to have this sauna. I don't know how she got him to sign it, but she did! Barb gave it to me and I went to the university and said, 'Hey, I have permission.' In the end there wasn't a single thing they could do, except they refused to give us permission to plug in our extension cord.

Pollen cloud, biggest one I've ever seen, 1977. Photo: Dennis Jaques.

In the end it became part of the research establishment, because when people became tired of the sauna it was turned into the wood rat emporium. One of *(Dr.)* Jack Miller's people was working on wood rats and he wanted to keep these things somewhere. They stunk so badly we couldn't have them in the building, so we banished him to the sauna and it became the wood rat emporium. So it had its use.

Marcia: Do you remember the summer of the bed bugs?

Peter: That would have been Rick Samuto. Rick was one of Jack Miller's students initially, and his interest was birds, particularly the swallows that loved to nest around the lab. We had hundreds of them, but they were getting a little bit out of hand because there were nests everywhere. They were very attractive, but toward the end of the summer the nests began to dry out because they were made out of clay. They would fall off the building and often they would have little baby birds still alive inside them. The baby birds would be strung all over the lawn and the cats and other animals would get them. It was a bit distressing.

Nobody really worried that much about the birds until we had the invasion of the bed bugs. Initially the itchy bites didn't attract much attention because there were so many biting things, but somebody finally produced some of these bugs. I didn't know what they were, so I took a look in the medical entomology book that I had stuck on the shelf. These things were bed bugs! To make a long story short, we discovered the bed bugs had, in fact, been carried by the birds and they were infesting the building because the birds were all up in the eaves.

The obvious thing to do was to get rid of the birds, but it was an environmental research institute and we couldn't get rid of birds! I remember at one point we tried to control them by organic means. We dragged every single mattress, mattress cover, blanket, pillow, pillow slip, you name it, all out onto the lawn and we autoclaved the whole works. We had a big autoclave for the lab and we actually sterilized this stuff. In fact, we probably reduced all the pillow slips to doilies by the time we got finished. It didn't do the slightest bit of good because that was not where they were coming from.

In the end we had to hire an exterminator. The compromise was they would spray this insecticide inside the building and outside all around the eaves. The stuff was guaranteed not to bother birds and if a single bird died, I guess I would have been hung, but we had to do something. It was an enormous amount of money, and I remember being very disappointed because the guy just showed up with a pressurized container and sprayed all around the baseboards in the lodge. I could have done this! They were right though, it worked. We figured after that we could do this ourselves and that is what we did from then on every year.

We suspected the birds. When the nests started falling off in late August I made a point of examining some of them. We'd see this thing go splat on the pavement, and if you looked very closely, half the nest would get up and walk away. It was really disgusting. I don't know how the birds tolerated it.

Marcia: I happened to be in Ginny's duplex one spring, and I guess because that corner had a nice exposure and there were bearberries there, the bears came. There was a young one that kept coming back, and I would go out to do laundry and wouldn't be able to get back in the house.

I phoned Fish and Wildlife and got them to bring a live trap out. Pete had left a shotgun over the door for any problems. One day I wanted to go shop-

Dr. Peter Wallis, 1995.
Photo: Ruth Oltmann.

ping in Canmore and wanted to get the kids out to the car, but that bear was sitting right beside the car. I got the gun out and shot twice in the air and scared it off. When I came back there was the bear, sitting where I park! I honked the horn and got the bear out of the way and got the kids inside and was unloading the groceries when the bear came back. I got the gun out and shot it into the air again.

At this point I think most of the young people were concerned I was dangerous, so they said if the bear was going to be a problem I should call them and they would come and throw rocks at it. The next time it was a problem they came up and threw rocks and chased it back in the bush. They were convinced this was going to be more effective and the bear would not come back, especially if it was hit with a rock. It was true that it didn't seem to be too disturbed by the sound of the gun. I made myself really unpopular. The bear came back, but it did move for them.

Peter: The bear story has some background to it, because in the original days of the field station there was a dump that everybody used, and all the bears frequented it. The bears were never a problem then because they always went to the dump. When the dumps were closed, which was at the beginning of the Kananaskis Country era, the bears had nowhere to go, so they would just mosey around and became more curious and aggressive.

Dr. Lionel Jackson

I came to the Kananaskis Centre for Environmental Research in late May of 1974 as a graduate student of the University of Calgary, working on my Ph.D. in geology.

The work consisted of making a surficial geology map of the Kananaskis Lakes map area and investigating the ice age history of the region by looking at the succession of ice age deposits. There are a number of rock glaciers high in the mountains in the source area of the Kananaskis River. There are also glacial

110

moraines and we discovered, up in the Lawson Lake area, several layers of volcanic ash. The oldest one fell in the area when Crater Lake in Oregon was created in a cataclysmic eruption about 7,000 years ago. The younger one, I believe, came from Mount St. Helens. We know that by doing chemical analysis and optical tests on the ash. There are also big piles of debris at the east end of Lawson lake. These were probably landslide deposits that fell on the ice during the recession of the ice in the last ice age, and were dumped off the end of the glacier in big heaps—very similar to the moraines at Moraine Lake. If you dig into those big boulders there are pockets of fine material where you'll find the ash layers.

We also found probably the oldest tree in the entire Kananaskis watershed. We called it Methuselah Larch. We took a core and figured the tree is at least 500 years old. In fact, I still have the core kicking around in my office. It is right at Lawson Lake, near the ridge. Part of it has rotted away and part is still living. I think there were 450 rings in that and we cored nowhere near the whole tree. It is probably a couple of hundred years older than that. I was trying to date the moraines to see whether the moraines were relatively young. If there was a deposit of the recent advance of the glacier, then we could get a minimum age from the age of the tree.

We had an experience in the Lawson Lake area we still can't explain. We were wondering whether we had our camp visited by the Sasquatch himself. It was when Gerry Osborne was with me. It was my first trip in there. I was in one tent sharing with the assistant and Gerry was in another one. We did our work and it was getting dark and, of course, it was the middle of summer. The evenings were very long, so we ended up turning in and then it started to rain. Just as we were drifting off to sleep—this was close to midnight—we could hear footfalls. It was not a four-legged animal at all. It got louder and closer and you could almost feel yourself bouncing in your sleeping bag. These footfalls went all around our tents. I heard this and figured it was really strange, but thought it had to be Gerry getting up to answer nature's call or something like that. There was nobody else there, nobody in our valley at all. We were all by ourselves. We had come in by helicopter and were right near the trail. If you came from the Upper Kananaskis River up the trail, you would have had to go right by our tent. We never saw anybody go through at all. There was no flashlight, it was pitch dark—a moonless night—and there were these tremendous heavy footfalls. After pacing all around our tents, we could hear the footsteps going off.

Next morning we were up and cooking breakfast when Gerry said, 'Which one of you guys got up to take a pee last night?' Well, we started looking around for tracks. We couldn't see anything as it's all mossy. There was no snorting. It was something walking on two legs—really heavy—boom, boom, all around the tent. I can't explain that one.

Cross-country skiing was my main passion when I lived there. Occasionally, I guess maybe it was Tuesdays if the snow was good, Ruth and I would ski up to the top of Skogan Pass and back. I think we did that a few times. We'd often stop by the youth hostel and have a cup of tea with Ruth and her cats, Ribbon and Creekie.

I also remember that when we would have a cold, snowless autumn, we would get enough ice on Barrier Lake that we could get out and ice skate in February. Another place we'd ice skate was down at Wedge Pond. There'd be good skating on that as it was relatively shallow.

Somebody I helped get going on his master's degree, Len McDonald (now a professor at McMaster University), seized an opportunity when they drained

Wedge Pond and excavated it. This was when they took the fill out for the golf course. That lake had an incredible paleoclimatic record contained in it. They drained it and he sampled the sediments that had accumulated a millimetre a year or better, over almost 10,000 years. He was able to take the pollen contained in those sediments and analyzed it so he could see how the vegetation had changed in the valley over 9,000 or 10,000 years.

I can tell you a story about when my dog blew away in a chinook! The chinook winds could really howl there. I remember one Halloween when I don't think anybody slept for three nights it was so windy. Just as you come into the lab building you go through a little anteroom, and then into her office (my wife Carol used to be the director's secretary). Our dog, Brandy, used to be chained to a cinder block outside. She was a small dog and weighed about 10 or 12 pounds. We'd have her chained so she wouldn't wander off, because often times she would go over to Forestry where the Colonel's Cabin was. In the summertime there would be people who acted as interpreters and they would always have dog biscuits, so she would go over for a handout. We didn't want her to wander off because of coyotes and other nasties that might have gotten her. One day it was blowing particularly hard and she was outside and I could see she was suffering. I can't remember if I picked her up and took her up to the house, or if I moved the cinder block and her around to the other side of the building where she was out of the wind. All of a sudden there was a tremendous gust of wind that really shook the place. Carol went out to check on the dog, but the dog and the cinder block were gone. Carol came running in saying, 'The dog has blown away!'

The ultimate story is one that is personally embarrassing to me: the saga of the bushy-tailed wood rat from the lab. They say there are no rats in Alberta, but it's not true. There is a resident species, the bushy-tailed wood rat. People call them pack rats. This animal looks just like a rat except it has a bushy tail like a squirrel. One of these rats found its way into the lab and it caused all sorts of havoc. It got into Dennis Jaques' herbarium and started eating his specimens, and it loved to relieve itself on top of calculators so the keys were totally welded together. I didn't realize how large this creature was. I started setting live traps around and thought somebody was playing tricks because I'd set these traps and they'd be shoved all around. Finally I just had enough and I came out and said, 'Who's the idiot who's been kicking the traps in my office?' It turned out it was this bushy-tailed wood rat! It was so big it wouldn't fit into any of these live traps. Finally we got a really big trap and we caught the thing, took it outside and let it go, and it was back in the lab in 25 minutes!

There was one girl who worked at the centre, Karen Larson, who said, 'Maybe we can donate it to the Calgary Zoo.' She phoned up the zoo and asked them if they needed one of these. They said, 'Oh yeah, bring it in.' She was excited about this, so she took it and drove all around Calgary and showed all her friends this animal she was donating to the Calgary Zoo. When she finally got down to the zoo, I don't know who she talked to originally, but the head zookeeper said, 'Oh no, we already have one of those. We can't put two together, they'll fight.' So they wouldn't take it. She ended up stopping the car somewhere in the Stoney Reserve and letting it go, a safe distance from the Kananaskis Centre. That was the end of the bushy-tailed wood rat. We never saw it come back. The rat made a monkey out of me, I'm afraid.

Dr. Allan Legge

My mother and father and I used to go down to the Kananaskis in the fifties to fish in the beaver dams. That's where I learned to fly fish, because it was always fairly open. I can't remember which beaver dam it was, but one of them had a hot spring in it. I was on a raft on one of the dams, fishing with a fly rod, and given the raft was not too thick, when floating around, you would hit these warm spots. You could really tell. I've actually gone back to look for it, but never found it. The fishing was always pretty good. Rather than deplete the population, we'd just fish with barbless hooks.

Basically I was hired to do research in the area of alpine ecology and arrived at the centre in April 1972. When Dr. Gordon Hodgson was made the director of the centre in January of 1973, the emphasis of the centre shifted from basic field research on plants and animals to contract grant research that had more applied overtones than basic overtones.

The first contract I got was with the Canadian Forestry Service to do a characterization of the vegetation in the Kananaskis Valley using satellite imagery and aerial photography. The net result of that was a remote-sensing test corridor was set up to develop a vegetation map and means of classifying vegetation using satellite and aerial photography for the valley. We were some of the first to use that imagery in western Canada.

In a lot of the locations I would use my telescope to characterize the vegetation types and when I was uncertain I would hike into the area to determine exactly what was present. Occasionally when using the telescope I would find people climbing, could see them sitting on top of mountains and stuff like that, which was interesting, but right across the valley was the forest lookout. This one particular summer there was a woman working there and I really didn't think too much about it, until I was siting my telescope in to make sure I had all the optics with me, because I was going out in the field. I didn't realize this woman liked to sunbathe nude on top of the tower! My telescope was a major attraction when people discovered it could site in on some of the local colour!

The next contract came from a consulting firm in Calgary that asked if anybody in the university would be prepared to look at the effect of sulphur dioxide from sour gas plants on trees. Although I had never looked at pollution as a stress, my background was fairly extensive in stress physiology, so I thought, 'Well, why not?'

In order to do this we had to grow our seedlings. During that time we developed a facility in the basement of the lab building to do the exposure experiments. We were using cuvettes, which were small, controlled environment chambers that housed the seedlings to expose them to varying environmental conditions.

In 1973 we started lab experiments and, basically, what we found was the vegetation was sensitive to the SO_2 exposures we were doing in the lab. Being a field-oriented person, I was always a little nervous we might not be getting the whole picture by simply doing laboratory experiments. In 1974, while our work on the exposures in the laboratory continued, I was able to look at the response of trees under field conditions near a sour gas processing plant northwest of Edmonton in the Whitecourt district. We did, in fact, see the trees had been affected by the sulphur emissions. There were noticeable affects on the physiological level as well as at the physical level in a few locations. This gas plant was one of the oldest in the area. It had been in operation since '58/59. It became a classic study of how to look at mature trees in the field exposed to air pollution.

Air pollution concerns, when we first started in 1972/73, were rather minor. People were just beginning to recognize that it was an issue to be addressed, so during the seventies we were approached by industry and government to look at other pollutants besides SO_2. In the early eighties we started looking at the effect of nitrogen oxides (NO_2 and NO). Again, we were looking at the effect on the trees, primarily as it related to compressor stations in Alberta.

In the early 1980s there was a recognition that acid rain might be a problem and it could be affecting the environment. The major source of acid gas emissions was the oil and gas industry, because a lot of the natural gas that is present in Alberta contains hydrogen sulphide. The project officially started the first of February 1985.

How does this relate to the Kananaskis Valley? One of the major air quality locations chosen for air entering the province was Fortress Mountain. Since we had the electronics shop developed for the cuvettes, we just used it, to not only modify, but also build electronic equipment for use in the station at Fortress, as well as several other locations in Alberta. This Fortress air quality station was referred to as our background air quality station for the province, because we were essentially looking at air entering the province from British Columbia. We could then compare that with the air we measured north of Calgary at several locations and determine how much hydrogen sulphide was being contributed by sources within the province.

When the project first started, there were about 55 people involved in it around North America. The final funding for the project, in terms of the contract, was 5.3 million dollars. It was at the time, and I believe still to this day, the largest contract in the history of the University of Calgary. It was all operated out of the Kananaskis Centre for Environmental Research in both the Kananaskis Valley as well as in Calgary at the facilities there. It lasted 42 months and we finished officially the end of September 1988. We published the results as a report and as a book. It represents the best air quality study for Alberta that has ever been done. People from all over the world, to this day, ask about the study.

Primarily I worked on the effect of air pollution on trees, but there was one study that we were requested to do in the middle seventies, '75/76, which was very interesting. That was to look at the potential for algae, primarily a combination of fresh water, as well as salt water algae, as a source of hydrocarbons. In the early seventies there was what was called the "energy crisis," and the price of oil and gas, particularly oil, just skyrocketed. People were looking for potential alternative sources. The idea was to see if we could actually get algae, in culture, to produce hydrocarbons in sufficient quantities to be able to make it economically feasible. We ran the program for two years, through 1976, and primarily the conclusion was, yes it could be done, but at the time the price of oil was beginning to drop and the economics were on the edge.

When I became acting director and moved into town, I was still known for constantly fixing things. On my birthday, on the 11th of August, 1979, I got a call saying one of the growth chambers had broken down and there was nobody around to fix it and would I mind coming out? I drove into the station and noticed there weren't many cars around. That fitted with what I was told. I decided I would check in the lodge first before I went down to the lab, to see what specific growth chamber it was and how long it had been down.

I walked into the lodge and hadn't walked but a few feet when I was showered with styrofoam chips from the balcony. It turned out to be a surprise birthday party for me. People were laughing and talking and there were a few funny gifts, then

Dr. Michael H. Benn, chemistry lab, 1971. Photo: University of Calgary, Kananaskis Field Stations.

they said, 'We have all gotten together to give you one big gift.' There was a huge box sitting in the middle of the room, and I was thinking, 'What can this be?' I didn't have a clue as to what these people had dreamed up.

Anyway, I began to undo the top of the box when out popped *Ruthie* in a wedding dress! No sooner had she popped out when two close friends sidled up to me with a shotgun. The idea was they were going to have a shotgun wedding. Peter Van Eck was the preacher, he had his collar turned up. It was Cindy Savage's wedding dress. So, *Ruthie* and I had a shotgun marriage in the lodge as part of my surprise birthday party!

Today, the Barrier Lake Station operates year-round, and has two lodges with dorms and kitchen/dining facilities, 10 duplex units and a laboratory building. In 1993 the provincial government transferred the forestry facilities on the site to the University of Calgary, thus doubling its size.

Throughout the year it offers university credit courses, school programs and non-formal adult education programs. Generally, 10 to 14 courses are offered each summer.

In the area of school programs, the field station provides the unique opportunity to link scientific research and outdoor science education programs for upper elementary, junior high and senior high students and teachers.

In the area of non-formal adult education opportunities, programs are offered through a number of agencies. For example, the University of Calgary's outdoor program centre has initiated an Elderhostel program with a focus on combining outdoor recreation with natural and human history education of the valley.

Wolf, Bear and Moose Research

*I*n Peter Lougheed Provincial Park and in designated Recreation Areas where hunting is not allowed, the Land Management unit of Kananaskis Country is responsible for protecting the vegetation, historic and archaeological sites of significance, and wildlife.

Steve Donelon

I am the Land Management Coordinator for Kananaskis Country, Natural Resources Service. We have a responsibility to maintain wildlife and to make good planning decisions. To do this we have to understand what the requirements are for these creatures. We usually don't provide direct funding, but we provide logistical support and housing for people working on the studies in Peter Lougheed Park. For example, the bear people are out today with the BATUS (British Army Training Unit Suffield) helicopter guys who come out twice a year and help us do telemetry.

Wolf Study

The wolf study started in 1989 in Peter Lougheed Provincial Park in a cooperative effort between ourselves, Parks Canada and Dr. Paul Paquet, who was contracted by Banff Park to do the study. We had wolves who were recolonizing in Peter Lougheed Provincial Park both from Montana, we believe, and from Banff Park. We think we had the original alpha male, the lead male of the pack—a black wolf from Banff called Midnight, who was with a couple of wolves that came from Montana. The spring of 1989 was the first year we believe they denned in Peter Lougheed Provincial Park, somewhere around Black Prince. In the spring of 1990 they denned again along the Kananaskis River in the north part of the park. That year we believe there were seven adults in the pack and six pups that spring.

It was the spring of 1990 when we began collaring wolves to study the movement of the pack in relation to other packs in the central Rockies. We collared two wolves in the spring of 1990 with funding supplied by both Banff Park and the World Wildlife Fund. One of those was Pluie, and the other was, we believe, the alpha male of the pack called Peter after Peter Lougheed because he was found in Peter Lougheed Park, not because of Peter the wolf. We monitored Pluie for about nine months by satellite. Between June and about January she travelled from Peter Lougheed Park right down into Montana and into Idaho and back again at least three times, perhaps as many as four times. She is the one who really opened everyone's eyes as to how far some of the wolves were actually travelling from the pack. On one of those trips she went over as far as Flathead Lake in Idaho and on another occasion she went as far east as Browning in Montana and back again. The first time she went down we know she went to Eureka, Montana in a matter of four days. As the crow flies it is about 300 kilometres. They go over Elk Pass in Peter Lougheed Park and straight down the Elk Valley to Highway #3. A French exchange student, Christian Landry, working on the project had the privilege of naming Pluie, which means rain in French.

Peter was with that pack right through the summer and the following year until late in the spring, at which time he began to do a fair bit of travelling himself. He was known at different times to be in Kootenay Park, out in the Elbow, Bragg Creek and in Banff Park. Our pack often moved up the Spray Valley past Spray Lakes into the Spray Valley toward Banff, where they would meet up with what is called the Spray Pack. We think that was where some of the roots of the pack originated with Midnight. Unfortunately, Midnight was shot in the Elk Valley, B.C. in 1990. We know that because we got the collar back from the hunter who shot him.

In 1991 we captured two more wolves. We capture them in a leg hold trap specially designed not to hurt the wolf, but to hold them in place. We put out lots of those traps and we usually scent them with wolf urine, which is the most common way. The trapper will spend the winter tracking wolves in different locations, collecting urine from the snow. He melts it down and ends up with a bucketful of the stuff by the spring.

In 1992 we caught another wolf called Opal, who was a female from the Highwood pack. During that period (1992 to 1993) we had a fairly stable pack that formed in the Highwood south of Peter Lougheed Park. So we had a pack in the park and another pack in the Highwood. The pack in the Highwood also contained wolves that had moved north from Montana. We know that because of work with Diane Boyd, a research biologist who has done lots of collaring of wolves and following wolves in the Flathead Valley area of northern Montana and southern B.C. Several of her wolves came up here and had collars on them. She would lose them and would regularly phone us and say, 'I can't find these particular wolves, will you listen for them when you're doing your telemetry runs?' We would end up picking them up and finding them. We had one called Montana, who came north and settled in the Highwood area for some time. The Highwood pack has been really decimated in the last three to four years. In 1992-93 they started to go downhill from hunting and from ranchers who were shooting. There was some predation happening to livestock south and east of the Highwood, out along Highway #22.

We trapped again in the summer of 1995, and we have another wolf that we captured this spring in the park (1996) called Nakoda. The pack is fairly active. We know we had two sets of pups in the last two years.

Unfortunately, we had a road kill wolf a short time ago near Rocky Creek, which was undoubtedly from our pack in the park. They don't just stay in the park, they often utilize areas around Kananaskis Village and the golf course in the winter. They are there because of the elk and the moose. There are lots of sheep around Rocky Creek and they were on a moose kill, I believe, when this one got hit by a car.

Grizzly Bear Study

The two primary researchers are Mike Gibeau, a bear biologist, and John Kansas, a vegetation ecologist doing the mapping and the vegetation side of the work. They are overseen by (Dr.) Steve Herrero who is involved with the study as well.

The study started in the spring of 1994. In that first year across the study area we trapped 22 or 23 bears. The study area is most of the northern portion of Kananaskis Country and much of Banff Park—essentially defined by the Bow River watershed. Because grizzly bears don't pay attention to boundaries, we are getting information from a much larger area. For example, many of our bears come into Peter Lougheed Park in mid-August for the berry season and then as the berries disappear in early September, they move down to the Highwood. The season is a little longer there because it's warmer and at a lower elevation. They've done that every year so far. They feed on Shepherdia (Shepherdia canadensis, Buffalo Berry), their favourite food in terms of the berry crop. In August they will be in the Peter Lougheed Park facility area, from the office down to the Upper Kananaskis Lake, along that corridor on the east side of Lower Kananaskis Lake.

One of the things we are looking at in Peter Lougheed Park is a regular seasonal closure of the bike trail between Canyon and Boulton for the bear's sake. It's always a problem as soon as the berries come into season. Elkwood Campground is built right smack in the middle of what is probably the best piece of grizzly bear seasonal habitat anywhere in the Rockies. It is just loaded with Shepherdia (buffalo berry) so we have consistently had bear sightings there. There is always the potential that some day someone's going to get hurt because of that. If we knew in 1978 what we know now we would probably have put the campground somewhere else.

In that first year in Peter Lougheed Park, we trapped seven bears as our contribution to the study. We used Fish and Wildlife officers, ranger staff and one contracted biologist, Chuck (Charles) Mamo, who was hired as the team leader. He's worked on bears for many years, and was part of the original study done in Kananaskis Country back in the early 1980s down in the Highwood. We even captured one bear that still had a collar on from that study. The idea of recapturing is to replace lost collars. Sometimes the bears will drop a collar or it will malfunction or they'll rip it off. In the case of a couple of them, they actually pulled them off.

The most common way we capture them is with leg snares. We use a quarter inch aircraft cable and attach it to a fairly large tree, usually 10 inches in diameter, minimum. A big spring hooks onto one side of the cable. There is a little pad in the middle of the circle that releases the spring when the bear steps on it. They build what is called a cubby, something with bait in the back of it. Usually they put what is called step logs there, so the bear has to step over the log to get at the bait. By stepping over the log it forces their foot right into the exact spot we want them to place it. The spring comes up and pulls the cable tight. The bear gets real mad and will rip the tree apart and dig up the ground until we come along and dart them. We use a drug called Telezol, which is very safe for bears. When they are immobilized we measure for the length, size of their paw and their girth. We take a fecal sample, blood samples and a tooth sample for aging, then we weigh them. We use a big tripod with a spring and pulley system and have a set of shackles that go on the four legs to hold them up under the tripod. The average weight on the low scale is 125 pounds for a small bear. If they are a real big male, maybe 600 pounds, but not much over that. I would say your average adult male grizzly bear in this part of the country is 300 - 350 pounds and the average adult female 200 - 225 pounds. They are not the 1000 pound marauders people make them out to be.

We're now involved with DNA analysis, so we know the lineages of the bears. For the bears we catch we know how they relate to one another if it shows up in the DNA—and many of those have shown up. The broader picture for using DNA is looking at lineages between populations. We can get an idea of how much movement there has been or is between populations by the lineages of the females.

We had a plane crash in the summer of 1994, the first year of the study, up on Highwood Pass. It was before the road was open in the spring. Nobody got hurt. They did a hard landing on the highway near Rock Glacier. The biologist, John Pazowski, and the pilot were following bear #24, which was a subadult female we had captured a couple of weeks earlier near the fire lookout in Peter Lougheed Park. They skidded into the ditch and decided they shouldn't sit in the plane in case there was a fuel leak. They got out of the plane and as they stood outside and looked down the highway, they saw #24 slowly making her way up the ditch to where they were. They crawled up a tree and as she came by she looked at them and kept on going. It was not a big deal. But as fate would have it, some pictures were taken. They made it into the National Enquirer as a front page story. There was a picture of the plane crash on the front and a photo of a giant killer grizzly bear coming over the top of the mountain with the headline something like 'Thousand pound killer grizzly pursues its capturers.'

Bear #24 is everybody's favourite in the study because we caught her as a young subadult female. She was 175 pounds and had this incredible fur coat about 30 centimetres thick. She looked much bigger than she weighed. We suspected she had bred last summer because she was seen with a big male on a couple of occasions. She is still a protective mother and has put the run on a couple of people up at Ptarmigan Cirque—just bluff things, as if to say, 'I have cubs here and you stay away.' She is not afraid of people because she has been around them since day one. Last year she spent time around campgrounds like Boulton. She never bothered anybody, never touched food or anything like that. She goes on both sides of the pass, back and forth at different times of the year. She spends a lot of time right at Ptarmigan Cirque. We have another one like that, #47, who we just captured this year and who has two older cubs. She's the one who has always been up on Mount Indefatigable when it's been closed. She's never been aggressive toward anybody— not a mean bone in her body. We worry about them being too habituated around people and facilities.

Moose Study

The moose study started two years ago *(1994)* with Tom Hurd, who is the wildlife warden in Banff Park. He is looking at the state of the population in the Bow Valley, asking 'Where have the moose gone from the Bow Valley?' It could be related to the reintroduction of wolves in Banff Park, to moose deaths on railways and highways or to shrinking habitat because of development.

The reason we are doing it in Peter Lougheed Park is that Tom was looking for an area with a similar landscape, close to Banff, in which there is a good concentration of moose. Peter Lougheed Park, particularly the Smith-Dorrien area and the Lower Kananaskis Lake, fit that bill. The question to be asked is: What's different between Peter Lougheed Park and the Bow Valley around Banff?

We started the study in Peter Lougheed Park in 1995 and in the fall collared eight moose by aerial net gunning. We didn't use any drugs. We hired a group of Australians who came up from the States with their own helicopter and net guns. They take the doors off the helicopter and have a guy hanging out the door on a tether. They find a moose, get over top of him and shoot a net that goes right over the moose. The moose runs for a hundred metres or so, gets all tangled up in the net and falls down. The helicopter guy gets some helpers, who jump out of the helicopter and run down and tackle the moose. I got to do a couple of these last year and it's good fun—a regular rodeo. We put a hood over top of the moose's head real quickly so they can't see—that makes them calm down—then we shackle their feet together front and back so they can't kick. Although we don't weigh the moose, we take hair samples, a fecal sample, a blood sample and we put on a collar. We do all of those things with the moose while it is wide awake.

To release the moose, we leave the hood on the head and untangle it from the net and get everybody out of the way. One of the helicopter guys will pull the head piece off and release the belt that's on the shackle, then he runs like heck to get behind some trees. It usually takes the moose 10 seconds or so to figure out that it's actually free. Nine times out of 10 it will stand there for five or 10 seconds more, and then just take off. Once or twice it'll turn and take a run at you.

Surprisingly, of those eight moose four are now dead in the first year of the study. This really surprised Tom because that's a very high rate. One of them may have died as a result of us capturing him. He was an old bull, and not in very good shape to begin with. He was still alive for three to four weeks after we caught him, but there is a condition known as capturemyopathy that is stress related from the capture. We are looking at capturing again this year (1996/97), bringing back up to eight the number we have collared.

We monitor them and have full-time people doing telemetry four or five times a week. They go out, find the moose and mark down where they are. We have two people working for Tom this winter and they go out just about every day, four or five days a week each. Snowshoes are usually used because of the thick trees. They follow the moose and have set transects where they stop and count the amount of browse, how many times they bed down and what's around the bedding site, and exactly what they are eating. That goes into Tom's data base and will be analyzed over time.

The wolf study has switched into Carolyn Callaghan's hands. She is looking at human impact on wolves and the effects of trails and development. I suspect it will be ongoing for at least a couple more years, depending on funding. In 1989 we looked at how the wolves were recolonizing and put out several papers on that and on transboundary movement. The wolves were just coming back into the area after having been just about extirpated from this part of the Rockies. The grizzly bear study is in its third field season, and it will go at least five years, so there will be two more years and perhaps more than that if funding permits and the information is such that it's worth carrying on. This was our first summer field season with the moose study, and we are one year into it, although Tom Hurd is two years into the larger study. We anticipate at least two more years for the moose in Peter Lougheed Park, maybe more.

Endnotes
1. *McGuffin, W. C., 1975, personal communication.*

War Comes to the Valley

4

Prisoner-of-War Camps

Camp #130

A sign on Highway #40, at Barrier Lake, says "Colonel's Cabin Historic Site," but it is the rare visitor to the valley who knows the role prisoners-of-war played in the history of the valley during World War II. Internment camp #130 (sometimes called the Seebe camp) for civilian internees was opened on September 29th, 1939, at the site of the Kananaskis Forest Experiment Station. The first internees were suspect enemy aliens (including some Japanese civilians) and German merchant seamen whose ships were caught in Canadian ports or within the three mile limit that existed at the time. Among the civilians were Hutterite men who were conscientious objectors. Initially the camp was for these civilians and German nationals, but by late 1940 those internees considered minimum security risks, if they were risks at all, had been released and the hard core of security risks had been transferred elsewhere.

The camp was then enlarged, the fence rebuilt, lengthened and strengthened to enclose the whole area for security reasons. The camp was divided into two sections. One section was for the prisoners and one was for the Canadian troops guarding the camp. The Canadians were usually older men, ineligible to serve in active regiments. Some were World War I veterans.

In 1941 combat prisoners-of-war arrived and stayed until 1942 when it became a predominantly officers' camp. Early in 1945 the security arrangements were strengthened further in order to receive a group of officers from Grande Ligne, Quebec, where a breakout of officer prisoners-of-war was feared. Shortly before this group arrived, the men already at Kananaskis were transferred to the newly prepared Camp Wainwright.

This was the first prisoner-of-war camp in Alberta and it held 650 to 700 men. Most came from the African campaign and were transported by boat landing in either New York or Halifax. Their boat travel was very circuitous and often took six months to reach North America. They travelled by train across the continent and by truck from Ozada station, which was about 10 kilometres north of the camp. (The Ozada station was just north of the present Highways #1 and #40 junction.) The camp remained in operation as a prisoner-of-war facility until January 28, 1946, when the last prisoners left on their repatriation journey.

The camp contained several eight-man huts, all wood stove heated. There was a mess hall, a kitchen, a dentist's office, a doctor's office and a large hall where Rev. T. H. Lonsdale, the United Church minister in Banff, occasionally

risoner-of-war camp, 1942. Photo NA-4823-3: Hanns Walter Wolff. Courtesy: Glenbow-Alberta Institute.

gave slide shows. Camp security was enforced by normal prison camp methods, with double fence, illumination, guard towers and patrols.

The army headquarters was located across the road from the administration office and superintendent's cottage of the Kananaskis Forest Experiment Station at the site of today's Canoe Meadows day-use area and group camp. A gate and gatehouse were erected to monitor people going back and forth from the camp.

Internment camps in Alberta usually employed the internees in farming operations. As this was not possible in the Kananaskis camp, other forms of employment had to be instituted. Internees were therefore engaged in parole walks, woodcutting and garbage dumping detail.

During the time the German officers were in the Kananaskis camp there was competition for work in timber cutting for the Barrier Lake Reservoir. The men worked diligently on the dam project, moving soil with pick, shovel and wheelbarrow. Prisoners also worked in lumbering operations carried out at Marmot, Ribbon and Evan-Thomas creeks. The purpose was to salvage timber that had been burned in the fire of 1936 for use in the coal mines. Good behaviour was rewarded with the option to work on timber salvage and dam construction, and most of the men coveted these jobs. The attraction was not the small remuneration they received, but the opportunity to get outside the barbed wire and do some useful work. About 75 of the men in the camp would go out each day on timber salvage.

A small lookout cabin at the top of Sunburst Trail, in the Ribbon Creek area, is inscribed with the names and dates of several prisoners-of-war. One man wrote the number of the camp, which confirmed the assumption of the Department of National Defence that it was camp #130.

Leisure activities were playing football or cards, making liquor on the sly, gardening, or building models—mainly ships in bottles, which were sold to earn money for food. (There are a couple of these ships in the Colonel's Cabin.) Educational courses in areas such as agriculture, geology, animal husbandry, and animal and plant nutrition were offered to the men by professors who were living amongst them and by various universities with the help of the YMCA. The camp was very isolated and the prisoners saw few outsiders, although native people were sometimes seen passing on horseback. Animals were abundant; often moose, elk and bear could be seen looking through the barbed wire fence at the people inside!

Rev. T. H. Lonsdale, chaplain for the Canadian soldiers in the camp, arrived weekly from Banff to conduct services. For four-and-a-half years he made the trip on a Saturday night, held a service at nine on Sunday morning, then returned to Banff to hold his regular church service. During his time as chaplain he was able to meet some of the prisoners. Rev. Lonsdale remembered a man named Fritz well. Fritz was a humorous blacksmith who did all the ironwork in the camp; he may have been the one who forged the door hinges and fireplace grate in the Colonel's Cabin. Lonsdale also spoke to two German missionaries who were captured in North Africa. He frequently advised prisoners to speak up for their rights under the Geneva Convention.

Several escape attempts were made. One breakout of two prisoners was thought to be aided by an outside work party. Husmann, one of the two escapees, reached Vancouver before being captured; the other was captured locally.

The old fire lookout on Hummingbird Plume Hill, c. 1975. Photo: Ruth Oltmann.

Another two escapees were captured by Joe Kovach, the ranger. Three prisoners once followed the road to the Ozada railway station, where they asked the station attendants for food and directions to Banff. The mounted police caught up with them before they had gone far.

Sam Copithorne, a rancher west of Calgary, met a couple of prisoners walking down the Elbow River about 16 kilometres west of Calgary. They had been missing from the camp for 10 days to two weeks and by the time Copithorne came across them they had had enough of escaping. They knew where they were and where they were going, but their experience was tough and they believed that the rest of Canada was very formidable if what they had been through was any indication. Copithorne took them home and fed them, but thought they were "damn fools."

Fred Kennedy, in his book, *Alberta Was My Beat*, relates his assignment, in August 1942, covering the movement of over 500 German prisoners-of-war from the Kananaskis camp to a new one at Lethbridge. Among the group were some flyers from the German *Luftwaffe*, but most were from General Rommel's Africa Corps. Two incidents occurred with this particular group of prisoners. One was the discovery of a hidden shortwave radio set in the walls of one of the camp buildings, which enabled the prisoners to hear of the Canadians' 50th Battalion defeat at Dieppe before the Canadians themselves knew. The other was the disappearance of seven prisoners. The seven men had dug a tunnel about 20 metres long from the washroom building to the parade ground and had hidden there for about 36 hours before being discovered.

In the beginning the prisoners were easy to handle, but men coming into the camp later on tended to be arrogant. However, as the tide of war turned against Germany their arrogance subsided.

The prisoners were treated well. At the end of the war many immigrated to Canada, especially in the early 1950s. One such was Walter Schmidt, who worked for the University of Calgary's maintenance department for many years. He was a 17 year-old merchant seaman from the Pomona, docked in London, England, when he was captured at the outbreak of the war in 1939. He was interned in England until June 1940 when he was sent to Canada with other German civilian and military personnel. Schmidt landed in Halifax, and was sent to a clearing and screening camp at Nipigon, Ontario. In early 1941, along with 500 other merchant seamen, he was sent to the Kananaskis camp. Schmidt believed the selection of internees for the Kananaskis camp was on the basis of trustworthiness.

At the time of Schmidt's arrival, the Kananaskis camp was empty. Access was from Seebe, over the dam and down the road, which had been built in 1934, to the experiment station. Supplies for the camp were brought by train to Ozada, and taken by truck to the camp. Schmidt himself was moved from the camp to work on farms at Brooks. He said all the civilians were treated with leniency until Hitler's proclamation that all male Germans over 18 years of age were in the armed forces of the Third Reich. After this proclamation, civilians were treated as "second-class prisoners-of-war."

Painting of POW camp at Kananaskis. Photo courtesy: Dr. Cord Tietjen.

Another was Walter Wolff, who immigrated to Canada with his wife and two children in 1952, and while on a western Canadian holiday in 1970 visited the site of the camp. While touring the site his wife remarked, "I think this place is the reason we came to Canada." The mountain environment had captured Wolff's heart. His excitement was evident when he pointed out Mount Baldy and the explanation that he had climbed it once.

Dr. Cord Tietjen was another prisoner who returned to the camp site. He did so on May 4, 1976, while he and his wife were on a holiday from Bragnschweig, Germany. Tietjen had been a paratrooper in the Africa Corps and was captured in Egypt. He arrived in Canada in June 1943. The 60-day trip by the ship "Capetown Castle" brought the POWs from Egypt to Bombay in a strong convoy—they had difficulty avoiding German submarines—from there they journeyed via South Africa, South America, the Panama Canal, to New York, and finally by train into Canada. There they spent a few weeks at Farnham POW camp, together with officers of the navy. In the summer of 1943 these officers were moved into the Feller Institute, Grande Ligne, St. Jean, Quebec, an old agricultural school that was closed from 1942 to 1948 when used as a POW camp. After one-and-a-half years, in February 1945, a group of officers was sent by train to Seebe, Alberta, camp #130.

Tietjen recalled that during his time in the camp the prisoners were allowed beer and Pepsi-Cola; although they felt there was sufficient Pepsi-Cola, there did not seem to be enough beer! There appears to have been a shortage of food at one time. In order to earn money to help buy food they were encouraged to work at tree cutting, probably for the Barrier Lake dam site. When the food shortage was in effect the men were allowed 1,000 calories per day. If any of them lost too much weight they were put into hospital. In the beginning the men were too weak to work all day at the tree cutting, so they worked for only four hours. Eventually, with the increased amount of food, they were able to work all day long. One man, who was an artist, painted pictures from photographs of the guards and their families in order to make money for more food. When Tietjen came to Canada on his visit in 1976, he brought with him a photograph of a painting of the camp that was done by this artist.

Although there were many moose, elk and bear, the prisoners were not allowed to kill them for food because the Kananaskis Valley was a game preserve. The prisoners were never given the reason for this food restriction. The men operated a small chicken and rabbit farm for a while. In 1946, when they were anxiously awaiting news that they would be going home, they became concerned they would have to leave the chickens and rabbits behind. However, they were all eaten before they left.

Tietjen remembers two escapes while he was in the camp. One of the escapees left the camp in the truck with the laundry bags, but was soon found and returned. The other prisoner escaped after the war was over, but before being returned to Germany and, to Tietjen's knowledge, was never found.

Dr. Cord Tietjen

We arrived at Seebe in February 1945. We were a selected group of officers from internment camp #44, Grande Ligne, St. Jean, Quebec, where we had been since the summer of 1943. Two other groups of officers arrived with us, one group from the internment camp at Gravenhurst, Ontario, the other from the one at Bowmanville, Ontario.

There was a rumour the selection was done according to our political colour: black equals Nazi, white equals democrat, gray equals indifferent. The blacks were concentrated at Seebe. However, nobody asked us for our political attitude. These officers were from all three services: the army, the air force and the navy. There was a group of other ranks for kitchen and mess, tailor, saddler, cobbler, hairdresser and woodcutter for fuel. Two generals were the highest ranks, Lieutenant General Schmidt, taken prisoner in North Africa, and Major General Kreipe, captured on Crete.

There were very few changes in the number of prisoners. I remember the arrival of a man who pretended to be a paratrooper. After some weeks it turned out he was a member of Hitler's SS with the rank of sergeant *(Scharfuehrer)*. He finally disappeared from the camp without bidding farewell. He was a secret informer.

Door handle on "Colonel's Cabin."
Photo: Ruth Oltmann.

An artist, Erich Wesselow, not only painted the beauty of the camp surroundings, he was a prominent portraitist. I remember he also painted a portrait of the camp commandant. I think his name was Lt. Colonel Jackson.

We experienced another period of food shortage or reduced quality of food called Punishment Diet Number 2. This was inflicted by the camp commandant because of a disagreement between him and the camp community with regard to a member of his staff. Two high ranking officers were put into jail for 28 days. The POWs were punished collectively, a step that to a certain degree always strengthened unity and solidarity. The diet consisted of rough-ground corn, more than enough, but miserable food for our indulged taste. The first time we were caught by surprise, but following that we stored some food from the kitchen in our dwellings. If I remember right, this episode happened in the summer of 1945 during the 1,000-calories' period.

Rev. Lonsdale's comment that 'to escape … was more for something to do than anything else' is only half the truth. We POWs all knew the story of Hauptmann von Werra whose airplane was shot down in 1939 over the United Kingdom and who succeeded in escaping from a railroad transport in Canada. Von Werra returned to Germany via the U.S.A. before the declaration of war. Von Werra became a celebrated and decorated soldier. He was finally killed in action, but his successful escape was an idealistic stimulus for others to match him. Therefore, it was necessary to continuously collect as much information as possible about the country. Attending the meetings of Rev. Lonsdale gave us this opportunity. Among the private books in the camp was one that circulated with rather high speed from reader to reader. That was A. E. Johann, *Das Ahornblatt (The Maple Leaf)*. It gave plenty of detailed information on Canada. We held it in great esteem. During our stay at camp #130 only one of us made a successful escape, and I forget his name, and that was in the summer of 1946. It happened more than a year after the end of the war when we were embarking at Halifax for Europe. It gave us a feeling of satisfaction and triumph when we listened for his name to be called and the answer was 'Still missing.' The longing for freedom was inextinguishable. This did not exclude the admiration for the beautiful mountainous landscape and the enjoyment of the physical environment.

Another POW who returned to the camp was Ernst Riebenstein of Hamburg, Germany. He returned on August 5, 1976. Riebenstein had arrived in Canada as an 18 year-old prisoner-of-war on April 21, 1942, after having been captured in 1941 and interned in England. He recalled that the Kananaskis camp was clean and that the commandant and guards were very nice. While in the camp he helped cut firewood at Ribbon Creek and because of this experience made a reminiscent trip to Ribbon Creek during his visit and stayed in the hostel. Riebenstein recalled that the prisoners made their own booze on the sly, although the guards occasionally found it and drank it! One prisoner pretended to be insane and was so convincing he was returned to Germany, along with some prisoners who were seriously ill.

During Riebenstein's time in the camp he and some of the other prisoners found and made a pet out of a domestic cat that had gone wild. They also adopted a dog that may have come from the railway station. The dog proved to be a character. He would go with the men to cut firewood at Ribbon Creek and on the way back run alongside the truck all the way to the camp, a distance of 16 kilometres. Upon arriving, the hot, exhausted dog would lay in the small stream by the camp for 20 minutes, then gather himself up, go into the hut and sleep until the next day when he would repeat the performance!

Cabin from
POW camp, c. 1974.
Photo: Ruth Oltmann.

Riebenstein's stay in the Kananaskis camp was terminated in 1944 when he was sent first to a camp close to North Bay, Ontario, then to Chatham, Ontario. He went back to Germany in 1946.

Riebenstein immigrated to Canada in 1952 and for 13 years worked as a miner in the Yukon, Northwest Territories, British Columbia and Ontario. He went back to Germany in 1963 for a holiday, and while there met his wife, so he remained in Germany until his 1976 holiday visit.

When asked why he had returned, Riebenstein answered, "We had a good time and the treatment was very good. It was beautiful." He said coming back was not a disappointment; quite the contrary. Although everything else looked smaller, Mount Baldy was still the same. He often stated it was "a paradise."

At least some of the prisoners were cast under the spell of Mount Baldy. From time to time a man would ask to be allowed to climb the mountain, and permission would be granted on the condition he signed a paper promising, on his word of honour, not to escape and to stay on the trail. Competition developed as to how fast they could climb the mountain and be back at camp. One man claimed he did it in 90 minutes!

The Kananaskis Forest Experiment Station had, all this time, been operating on a reduced scale. Its labour force was comprised of men from the alternate service camp, conscientious objectors and men whose religious beliefs forbade them to engage in combat.

Bruce Ernst

As far as I know, my grandfather moved his family from the Russian Ukraine where they were German citizens, landing as immigrants in the Ukraine. They decided to get out of Europe a few years before the war broke out. They made the decision to come to Canada. The whole family came, and there were quite a few children. My dad was second oldest.

I believe when they came to Canada they were told they could go to the prairies, but when they got here they were told they had to stay in the maritimes. In those days all the farmers had guns and poaching deer was just another way of putting meat on the table. Everybody who lived in the country had guns. Grandpa had a lot of experience in Europe with the wars, having survived the Russian Revolution. Being a bit of a horse trader, he knew the Canadian government would come and ask them for their guns since they were expatriated German citizens. I guess once the war broke out, or immediately prior to it, being a sharp fellow he went out and sold all his guns. My dad always resented him selling the guns, because he felt when the RCMP came to the door to gather up the guns it was the fact this household didn't have any that made the RCMP think they were hiding them, therefore, the father of the house and the oldest son, which was Dad, were under suspicion and were interned.

I don't know how many people were interned or for what reasons. They were interned, he said, as political prisoners, not prisoners-of-war, and that's the reason why I suspect their loyalty was under suspicion. Grandma had to maintain the family. The next oldest brother would have been in his early teens, I think. In the course of those years, the farmhouse burned down and they lost most of their personal possessions. They, of course, were in dire straits just to make a living.

These are stories told to me by my dad—just bits and pieces—through the years of growing up, about his stay in Kananaskis. I think that in my dad's case it was three years and in Grandpa's case it was five years that they were there, but I am not positive about these numbers. I don't know if they both came out to Kananaskis at the same time.

Dad talked a bit about the trip over. I believe he was stopped in Ontario somewhere, at a place called, possibly, Escanada *(Espanola)*. It was a military base. Owing to some delays he was locked in a small cell for weeks with virtually nothing to do. He told me all my life that the hardest thing in the world was to do nothing. I would assume he was an 18 or 19 year-old man, sitting on a bunk talking to himself for two or three weeks. The trains they travelled on were blacked out, so they didn't really know where they were. I know that Grandpa and Dad had studied the geography of Canada before they came here, because Grandpa made a conscious decision whether to go to Canada or to go to Argentina. I talked to a caretaker who said he remembered the trains going by in Manitoba. Some of the POWs talked about escaping. He remembers discussions, and he always told them they had no idea how big this country was; they might as well forget about it. Europeans coming from Europe were used to being able to walk across a border in a day or two.

My dad always said those years he spent in the camp were the equivalent of going to university. He said he learned a great deal and the camp was really active in terms of sports. He talked about meeting all kinds of very qualified people. He didn't talk particularly about classes that he went to, or skills that he learned in the camp. However, he was very proud that he was qualified as a steam boiler. One time Dad got in trouble for scalding some of the prisoners the first morning he stoked the boilers. They had to get used to him stoking the boilers. It was a matter of pride that when he was in there the water stayed hot.

Dad also said that during the time he did his shift in the boiler house he sent away, I think by mail order, for an actual blueprint of the schooner Bluenose from Nova Scotia. He got the blueprint and built two models about two-and-a-half feet long, and the mast probably stood as high. It was an exact replica, as closely as he could using the materials at hand, which was firewood and a bit of lead for the keel from somewhere. He carved pulleys for the rigging out of a toothbrush handle and drilled them and made them to scale size, and they are minute. We still have the models. The sails were all hand stitched and the ropes were braided out of thread. The deck planks were all individually carved. It is a really elaborate model to make, which was likely indicative of the amount of time he had on his hands.

His favourite story, the one I most often heard, was when he spoke about a man who was great friends with my grandfather. He called him Mayor Hood. The man said he was the mayor of Toronto. I don't know if he was an ex-mayor when he was interned, or if he was an active mayor in Toronto. Dad said he was a huge man—way in excess of 300 pounds. Dad remembers him in the showers. He had a flap of skin on his belly that had to be lifted up to soap underneath when he showered. Dad also remembers him for his strength, because the prisoners built a skating rink and had contests about who could speed skate the most laps. Mayor Hood skated everybody else off the rink and then doubled the laps. He was just a powerhouse of a man, unbelievably strong. I guess he had legs like iron.

I remember that as a kid growing up in Quesnel, my dad always belonged to the Rocky Mountain Rangers, and I remember him going down to the Legion and drilling. Quite often for summer holidays we'd go down to Vernon, where they have a military camp, and he would go for two weeks of training. This went on for years and years and then suddenly Dad dropped out. One day he got around to telling me why he did it. I guess he was quite involved with the thing and aspiring to having a career in the army, but he said one fall they brought in a special military guy to train a group and Dad immediately recognized him as one of the guards at the camp. He felt the guy recognized him, too, and he decided right then that he had no future in the Rocky Mountain Rangers.

Views from the other side

Dr. L. A. (Bud) Smithers

In '45 and '46 I was the accommodation and fire prevention officer for M.D. 13, which came under the Army Engineers. I had under my charge and responsibility the maintenance of all the prisoner-of-war camps spread over Alberta. What we were doing at that time—of course the war was essentially over—was closing these places, declaring them surplus and putting value on them for salvage. Then people would bid on them and we would award them as crown assets. Of course, we were keeping them in repair and maintaining them until they were sold. I was all over the province and Kananaskis just happened to be one of the camps that I had to check into periodically.

By the time I arrived in Kananaskis I think there were still a few prisoners around, but they were virtually all gone. One of the main headquarters had two beautiful log buildings. When we first moved to Kananaskis from Ottawa, they turned the staff house over to Verna and I until we could get located. I don't know whether the paintings are still on the panels in the office and staff house, but the walls had huge wildlife murals. Apparently one of the German prisoners was a fine wildlife artist and he had asked permission to do some painting, so McLenahan thought it would be a good idea if he did some painting down in the staff house. McLenahan provided the paints and the wallboard for these panels to be painted on. There must have been, I guess, a good 15 of them, with mountain scenes and all kinds of wildlife. There was a great commotion about it afterwards because McLenahan felt, and rightly so, I think, that these were his paintings. He had provided the materials and the chap who had done the painting was long gone, so when McLenahan retired he went up and collected his paintings to take down to his ranch. Somebody reported this to Ottawa and there was great consternation. An investigative board came to me and, fortunately, I knew the story and said, 'Look, you are barking up the wrong tree, fellows. These belong to McLenahan. It had nothing to do with the government.' This cleared it up eventually. There was some beautiful work. I can't remember who the gentleman was who did the painting.

When we got rid of the camps, one of the interesting experiments was trying to figure out how to take down barbed wire. The compound in Seebe Flats *(Ozada)* was perhaps 10 acres, with tall poles (like telephone poles) stapled with barbed wire every six inches all the way up—massive lengths of barbed wire. So we cut the wire in one spot and hitched a jeep to it and started driving the jeep and the barbed wire flew off. It saved a lot of man hours.

Peter Roxburgh, Lucille Roxburgh
Frank Young was one of the engineers who was working at Barrier who had the rank of major. He had just come back from overseas, as had George Eckenfelder, and they didn't have any money or civilian clothes. They were still wearing their battle dress. Frank and George would frequently go to the mess at the camp and have a drink with the guards, the colonel in charge, and usually the dentist on staff. There would be two or three officers and some enlisted men who were all in the home guard. The home guard was World War I veterans—men of my father's age, who would have been in his fifties at that time, or older.

Lucille: Colonel Watson and his wife had a cabin on the bank of the Kananaskis River. We would go out in the evening or late afternoon and sit on the bank and watch the beavers. Also, the prisoners painted the floor to look like stones. It was beautiful, just like stonework.

Pete: That cabin was right on the bank of the Kananaskis River by Lusk Creek. *(Where the Widowmaker day-use area is today.)* The cabin was built by the prisoners for Colonel Watson. It was something for them to do before the days of the clearing contract—keeping them occupied.

Lucille: The prisoners kind of liked him *(Colonel Watson)*. He was fair. One thing that I remember in the cabin was a table made from a Douglas fir tree trunk. It was thick. He had polished and varnished it. It was the most beautiful thing.

Pete: The cabin that is there now *(the Colonel's Cabin)* was, I think, his office. I don't know what happened to the cabin at Lusk Creek.

The war was over in 1945. Germany had been defeated in 1944 and Japan in 1945. I started in the fall of '45 and hostilities had ceased everywhere. The prisoners were still there and they had no idea, at that time, when they would get back to Germany. Of course, shipping and transportation was devoted to getting supplies back to England and France to make up for the losses during the war. The last thing they were going to carry over in scarce space was prisoners, so they stayed in Canada. It was a full year after the defeat in Europe and they were still there, interned and guarded, although it was pretty low key.

We were kept busy doing the surveys around the reservoir and the prisoners cleared it. They sawed the trees off with a Swede saw. Cutting low with an axe was just the recipe for ruining your axe. They would cut the tree down to snow level and saw the trunk off later after clearing the snow. They had to cut the trees up into pieces anyway. Anytime we stopped for a smoke break, and if there was a bunch near where we were, they would flock around us. A lot of

Kananaskis Internment Camp.
— German Officer P.O.W.—
Reading of Proclamation of German Capitulation   May - 1945.

PROCLAMATION

The German Forces on land, sea and in the air have been utterly defeated and Germany has surrendered unconditionally.

The Allied Governments of the United Kingdom, the United States of America, the Union of Soviet Socialist Republics and the French Republic, acting in the interest of all the United Nations, have assumed supreme authority, including all the powers formerly possessed by the German Government, the High Command and all State, Municipal and Local Governments and authorities in Germany.

The Allies will make provision for the maintenance of order and the administration of Germany. All requirements of the Allies will be carried out unconditionally by the German authorities and the German people.

Ottawa,   *Major-General*
                                                                                              Adjutant-General

BEKANNTMACHUNG

Die deutschen Land-, See-und Luftstreitkraefte sind gaenzlich besiegt und Deutschland hat sich bedingungslos ergeben.

Die verbuendeten Regierungen Grossbritanniens, der Vereinigten Staaten von Amerika, Sowjet-Russlands und der Franzoesischen Republik haben, im Interesse aller Verbuendeten Nationen handelnd, die oberste Staatsgewalt uebernommen, einschliesslich aller Befugnisse, welche bisher die Deutsche Reichsregierung, das Oberkommando der Wehrmacht, sowie alle staatlichen, staedtischen und sonstigen lokalen Regierungen und Behoerden im Deutschen Reiche inne hatten.

Die Verbuendeten werden fuer die Wahrung der Ordnung und die Verwaltung Deutschlands Sorge tragen. Die deutschen Behoerden und das deutsche Volk haben allen Forderungen der Verbuendeten bedingungslos nachzukommen.

Ottawa,   *The Proclamation*   *Major-General*
                                                                                      Adjutant-General

Proclamation Series courtesy: Mrs. W. K. Jull.
Donated to Ruth Oltmann.

2 Camp Commandant entering Compound with Staff

3 Reading the Proclamation

iving Compound - Camp Leader marches off.

aising the Colours.

6 Three Cheers for His Majesty

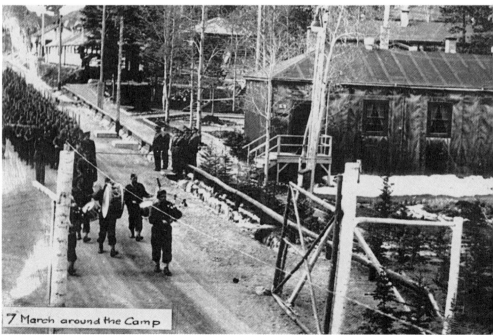

7 March around the Camp

them had been learning English and we were a fresh bunch of people, so they often gathered around and asked us questions and practised their English. There were a number of young people who were not much older than I was—I was only 17—who were concerned about their parents and complaining about the fact they hadn't heard from them in months. I remember one man said he hadn't heard from his wife in months and months, and I asked him where he lived and he said Frankfurt or Essen. Of course, I knew very well that both cities had been bombed out of existence by people like my brother, who was in the RCAF and was over there at that time, although he wasn't a bomber pilot. He knew the place had been bombed and that there was a high probability his family was dead. He was feeling sorry for himself. My feeling was, tough, you guys started it and we're just finishing up the job. I'm sorry you lost your family, but that is the way war works. My concern, of course, was my own brother, that he survived, which he did.

Anyway, we talked to these groups and there was more than one person who said that after the war they would come back. They preferred not to go home, they had nothing to go home to, but of course, that was not to be.

Dr. Patrick Duffy
I met some German-Canadians years ago, people who had come back to Canada after the war. I met at least one fellow who, when he was in the camps, said, 'As soon as I get out of here I'm coming back.' He became a construction contractor in Calgary.

After the Second World War the men who had been prisoners-of-war in Canada formed a group and called themselves *The Canadians*. Every five years they would have a reunion somewhere in Germany. In 1980, when Alberta was celebrating its 75th anniversary as a province, the man who was the German consular-general in Edmonton, and who had been a prisoner-of-war in Kananaskis, arranged for *The Canadians* to have their reunion in Canada. During their tour of former prisoner-of-war camps they came to the University of Calgary's field station in the Kananaskis Valley, where they were given lunch and a tour of the site. They said the only thing that hadn't changed "was the mountain."

I was the cook at the field station at this time and it was exciting to meet these men, who all had positive memories of their time in Canada. They were all given a copy of my book *The Valley of Rumours ... the Kananaskis*. I hoped they could read English, because most of them couldn't speak it.

Dr. Allan Legge
From 1975 to 1979 I was station manager. In the process I got to meet a lot of the ex-German prisoners-of-war who came back for visits. They were absolutely astonished at all the changes that had taken place. They told some interesting stories and some were about plays they had put on. I asked them how they got the materials for the plays and they said, 'Sometimes we would sneak out of the camp.'

'But that's escaping.'

'You can escape, but where to?'

'That's a good point.'

They said they had no idea Canada was so large. They would go over to Exshaw, take sheets off the line and bring them back to the camp to make costumes.

Dr. Gordon W. Hodgson
This reflects my wider world view of things. Seeing these guys, who were all well-to-do business and professional types, tumble out of the buses at the Kananaskis Centre and almost physically run all over the site, excitingly pointing out to one another where what was, it was such a graphic link to history. It made the whole concept of war so utterly stupid. I visited them when they were there for that short period of time. The scientific people amongst them were doing the same sort of thing we were doing. One guy was the director of a hydrology lab in Germany, yet 15 years before it was a period of insanity.

Ozada

A second military camp southwest of Ozada housed *Wehrmacht* troops taken in North Africa. This was only a temporary tent camp, which opened on May 27, 1942, and the men were soon sent to Lethbridge and Medicine Hat. The Ozada camp (#133) contained 14,000 men. For many years there was a big rock on the site on which 10,000 prisoners had engraved their names.

Peter Roxburgh, Lucille Roxburgh
What they called the Ozada camp, was actually a bit west of Ozada, just on the west side of what is now Highway #40. You can find the drainage ditches in the grass the prisoners dug around their tents, but at that time the fence was still there. This was in '46, I guess, and the guard towers were there, all the lights and the enclosure was a half mile square. It was out on the bald prairie with not a tree around it. Our survey went through the middle of it and of course the fence is barbed wire, spaced about three or four inches apart, and the barbed wire was not like farmers' barbed wire—it had great long barbs on it. It was terrible stuff. You didn't want to get near it, or even put your hand through—there was room to put your arm between the wires. We had to survey through it and we had to measure the distance, so we had to pass a steel tape through and work our way across. I drove a pickup truck around to the one entrance away at the far side and went through the gate, and then had to come back across the prairie to where Bill Gold was leading and, of course, in the grass you couldn't see anything, but it was the roughest trip across, because I couldn't find the spaces between the rows of tents. I was driving on the bias through all the tent locations. When the camp was set up they used circular bell tents, and in the spring the prisoners dug drainage ditches so the water drained away from the floor of the tents. I was driving through the humps and the hollows with this pickup truck.

Lucille: They unloaded the prisoners at the Ozada siding, and marched them over a couple of miles to where the camp was located. They used to come in small planes, Harvards, I think, and they circled around to make sure the men didn't go and hide behind one of the hills on the flats. One of the planes crashed and I think one pilot was killed. The prisoners all cheered when it crashed. Everybody was real mad because the prisoners had cheered. It was March and it snowed just after they put them in the compound. They didn't have any stoves so they cut food and oil cans and made themselves little stoves.

Pete: They were given tents and not much else. There were 10,000 to 15,000 prisoners in that little camp.

Lucille: Almost the population of Lethbridge at that time. It was a temporary camp. They were building a proper camp down in the Lethbridge area or near Medicine Hat. Eventually they were moved.

Pete: The remnants of the camp are still there. There is everything but the tents. There are a few buildings in the northeast corner where the guards and the Canadian Army staff stayed outside the fence, and then this half mile square of barbed wire with the towers, the lights and the big poles all around it.

Lucille: I remember one time we were riding along the Kananaskis River and were camping, when we suddenly came into a clearing from the big spruce trees and upon this bunch of prisoners dumping garbage over the bank of the Kananaskis River. *(You can see the rusty garbage cans on the slope today if you take the raft trip down the river.)* It was a real surprise to us and the prisoners, and, of course, the guards pointed their guns at us on our horses. We just stopped dead, and all these young guys were staring at us. The guards said, 'Get out of here.' We were actually on our way farther up the river to visit the wife of the officer who was camping in a tent along a bench of the river, just west and south. We thought she was pretty brave to be camping there—just in case the prisoners escaped.

The Canadian Armed Forces

While the British Army occasionally used the terrain on the west side of Barrier Lake in 1973 for tactical and training exercises, it was the Airborne Regiment of the Canadian Forces that was the most active military presence in the valley.

The Canadian Airborne Regiment Ski/Mountain School was opened in the summer of 1970. The regiment set up a camp where the present Kovach Pond is located, beside Ribbon Creek, after having been located for a short time a few kilometres to the north. The purpose of the camp was to teach basic mountain climbing and military cross-country skiing. The school operated for eight weeks during the first three winter months and eight weeks in July and August. Two courses of eight weeks per season were conducted, with 60 candidates each week. The basic techniques of free climbing, team climbing, installations and rappelling were taught in the summer school. Several climbing sites were used, all within a 16 kilometre radius of Ribbon Creek, two of the most popular being the cliffs along Wasootch Creek and King Creek. Both became extremely popular with sport climbers, although King Creek is presently closed to new developments, to preserve the cliffs from environmental damage.

The Ribbon Creek area trails were used by the army's ski school, where the students progressed from non-skiers to relatively competent cross-country skiers. Alpine skiing was taught but it was not emphasized.

When the army was at Ribbon Creek and I was houseparent in the Ribbon Creek Hostel, they used to pack all the cross-country ski trails so there wasn't any powder snow left. Being a powder snow freak, I quickly learned, after a fresh snowfall, to get out early in the morning and ski my favourite trails before they were packed down. I always tried to get on the Mount Allan Centennial Trail first because it was steep and narrow and was great fun to ski down when there was fresh snow, but was treacherous once it had been packed by the army. Some of the army men even broke their legs on that trail, and I'm not surprised, what with the gear they had, because they only had mukluks for boots!

The first year I was at Ribbon Creek Hostel (1972), the two fellows who were guides for the troops stayed at the hostel for a week with their families. I got to know them, and when they moved into the camp across the way they arranged to bring over their movies, which changed every week. On Wednesdays the army guys saw them and on Thursdays my hostellers saw the same film. They also showed me their *langlauf* films, which is the German word for cross-country skiing; used by the Canadian Forces.

The hostel was off limits for army personnel, but once I caught two men peering in the window. I opened the window and told them if they wished to see the hostel they could go to the front door, which was unlocked, and I'd show them around. They did that, but seemed rather hesitant. I found out later they were not supposed to be there.

The Airborne Regiment moved their school out of the valley after the summer school in 1973, and their buildings were dismantled and removed in September of that year. I was given some of their rations. This included a whole case of freeze-dried food. There was enough to feed three of us for three weeks of backpacking on a subsequent summer holiday. Likewise, when the British Army closed their camp, they also gave me some rations. I drank British Army tea for four years! It was great tea, but the fellows didn't like it; possibly because our mountain water is very unlike the water in England, giving the tea an entirely different flavour.

While the army was located near the hostel I never knew my cousin, John Johnsrud—whom I'd only met once in my life—was one of the guys in the camp. Life does take strange turns, because when he actually found out where I lived he came and visited me at Ribbon Creek Hostel some years later. It was a surprise to find we had been so close, but so far apart.

Sgt. John Johnsrud, C.D.
I went to Ribbon Creek with the Airborne Regiment. That was initially what we called the Mountain School. I was there in 1972 and 1973 for summer school and winter school. It was a pretty desolate area at the time, as there was only Fortress as a ski hill and the Ribbon Creek Youth Hostel, which was out of bounds. In the summertime we did all our mountaineering at Ribbon Creek. We didn't call it Ribbon Creek—it was just called the Canadian Forces Mountain School. All the areas around there were fair game for mountaineering activities. We could climb the mountains, chop the trees and ford the creeks. Sometimes we had to wash in them, too.

We had guides and instructors, but the instructions were: 'Here's where you are going to be, at such and such a grid reference, and be there by ten o'clock this morning.' It would probably be about 7:30 in the morning. They'd say, 'Be there by 10 and it takes four hours to get there.' We had two-and-a-half hours of running. There was never enough time to get somewhere. It was done that way on purpose. Our regiment didn't walk. Of course, we would then always have an hour to sit and have a smoke. We'd wait for an hour for the instructors to get ready to teach. It was one of those typical military 'hurry up and wait' experiences.

We did the Australian rappel: when we came off a cliff, face down. We'd throw the ropes over and then we leaned over the cliff, pointing in the direction we were going, and run. At the same time we'd have 80 pounds on our back, with machine gun blanks. It was so fast that we came down the face of the cliff running and shooting, and the idea was to totally surprise the enemy at the bottom. If we weren't careful when we put the brake on, we landed in the ground face first. The nice thing about that was then we had an opportunity to practise our field first aid, on each other! Your nose would be lying on the side of your face and your buddy would slap your face and put your nose back in place.

We had a first aid accident in Wasootch Creek. What happened was we dropped the litter in an evacuation. We had the guy about 30 feet up off the ground and let him go, and he was still tied into the stretcher. Fortunately it landed flat. There were supposed to be automatic brakes and other devices, but they didn't work. We had it hooked up and were pulling through some snap links that were supposed to lock as soon as it was slack. We let go and it just swooshed, and all this rope went taking off. Being soldiers we stood there watching the rope fly; 'Look at it smoke.' If we had grabbed it, it would have burned our hands.

And that was the other thing—how fast we went through leather gloves. I'm sure that was another reason they closed the whole operation. It was so expensive to run because a pair of leather gloves would only last two days when we were climbing.

A mountain range runs north and south where Peter Lougheed Provincial Park is, and part of our training was to go to the end of the road with all our packs and equipment (as engineers we carried all our engineering equipment with us), and get back to camp in three days. We had to climb the faces to traverse the mountain peaks. We came out at the lake just at the end of Ribbon Creek Trail, where the waterfalls are. We came down there and hiked back to camp, got in a truck, and went back to Edmonton.

The youth hostel was totally out of bounds. We weren't supposed to go near it or talk to the person who ran it, so being good soldiers we didn't go near it. At least I didn't because I was told not to, but I know two guys were charged for going over there and peeking in windows. It was intimidating because they were charged and confined to barracks for a couple of weeks in Edmonton.

What is ironic is that my cousin was running that hostel all the time I was there. We probably passed each other on the trail, but owing to the fact it was out of bounds we never met. 'Never mind the woman, keep walking.'

In the winter we came down for ski school. As engineers we cleared the slope where Nakiska is—one of the runs. It wasn't actually a ski run, we just cut it down so we had something to ski down without killing ourselves. It was the most gentle hill, perfect for skiing with our bangy boards. Bangy boards are two pieces of wood that look like a ski and have canvas straps on them. The straps are the binding, but it is worn with a soft mukluk, not a hard boot.

We figured we could have cleared the ski hill in about two days using explosives, instead of four weeks with chain saws. There were restrictions because of the nature of the place.

Before we started clearing the hill we used to ski on the area where the big hotel is. There were some trails up there that were pretty narrow at the time. We had to try and teach guys to ski down through that. There were soldiers piling into trees and falling off cliffs. It was a lot of fun.

The part I remember the most was Ribbon Creek *(valley)* because we often trekked up to the waterfalls. It was a day trip for us on skis and was always so nice. Even though I like to peddle my bike in there now, it's nothing like when we were there. Now there are bridges and a wide trail. We had one-way traffic only and it was whichever way you were going!

We seldom got to ride in army trucks. We either ran or marched everywhere we went. The only time we got to ride in trucks was when they took us to Norquay in Banff. We only had 'bangy boards,' because nobody had enough money to rent skis. Thirty-six of us piled out on top of the ski hill in our matching olive drab. The captain didn't like the attire as he thought we stood out too much, so we had to put on our all-white winter camouflage outfit. I remember standing at the top of the hill and not even starting to go down it, and thinking, 'I'm going to die!' Being the type of people we were, three of us stood together and said, 'Well, let's go.' Nobody fell down or got killed, but we skied straight down the hill. I knew if I tried to turn I'd die. None of us turned. I wasn't sure I wanted to ski anymore after that. I have never seen things go by me so fast. I've free-fallen out of an airplane and I didn't notice the ground rush by like that!

I don't know who got down to the bottom first, but once we stopped, a guy with a red cross on his jacket asked us if we would kindly get off the hill. So we did, but we went over to the day lodge and watched. We found out getting kicked off the hill had nothing to do with our skiing. They were totally amazed that we even lived, but that wasn't the concern, rather it was the white clothing. They couldn't see us coming down the hill and none of us ever thought of that.

Another nice thing about mountain school and ski school was we didn't have to shave. We were not the cleanest-looking people in the world, and I can honestly say most of us didn't bath that much, either. All we did was regularly brush our teeth. When somebody got too ripe someone would say something. We had to cook up the water ourselves for the showers and nobody was ambitious enough to do that. We always thought the cadre showered at the hostel across the road, but we found out later that they were going into Banff. They had a staff car, so they took turns going into Banff every night.

We built two Bailey bridges in Kananaskis. We did them in a day, whereas the Department of Highways would have taken three weeks because they did theirs with machinery. We did ours by hand, which is quicker. We can build one of those bridges silently. Our hammers were made out of leather, 'hide-faced hammers' is what they were called. All that could be heard when the steel pin was hit was 'thunk.' There was no talking on a bridge site. The bridge commander was the only person who spoke. Someone could stand within 20 feet of a bridge site and not hear what was happening, other than 'thud, thud, thud.' We could put up an 80- or 100-foot bridge in half an hour, with about 32 people.

I was a little bit disheartened when I returned and I couldn't recognize where the camp had been. I think it was one of the parking lots *(Kovach Pond)*. I was disappointed that there wasn't even a little cairn or something—a remembrance.

Managing the Valley

5

Administrators

The Kananaskis Valley has seen several changes in administration over the years. In 1902, when Alberta was still part of the Northwest Territories, the valley was made part of the Rocky Mountains Park (now Banff National Park). It was withdrawn from the national park in 1911 and put back in again in 1917. Finally, it was decided the national park was too large to manage properly, so the valley was taken out of the national park in 1930 and turned over to the province of Alberta. That same year the natural resources of the province of Alberta, which had been retained by the federal government when Alberta became a province, were put into the hands of the provincial government.

The Great Depression of the 1930s resulted in expenditures being drastically reduced by the province. Consequently, the Kananaskis Valley was left relatively unprotected. The reduction in forest fire protection was partially responsible for the extent of the forest fire in 1936.

With the change in administration, the valley became part of the Rocky Mountains Forest Reserve. The reserve was administered and managed by the Dominion Forestry Service, a division of the Department of the Interior. In spite of financial restrictions during the Great Depression, several developments took place: the construction of trails, telephone lines, lookout towers, stopover cabins, roads and ranger headquarters.

From 1930 to 1956 the valley was set aside as a game preserve. Unfortunately, the first few years after these regulations were lifted saw a large slaughter of animals.

The need for greater management in the eastern slopes was recognized in 1937, but because of the Second World War, little was done until 1947 when the Eastern Rockies Forest Conservation Board was formed between the federal government and the provincial government. The Eastern Rocky Mountain Conservation Act was passed by Parliament in July 1947. A similar act was passed by the Alberta Legislature in March 1948, and the Board became official on April 1, 1948.

The purpose of this Board was to "plan, advise, direct, supervise, and carry out the construction, operation and maintenance of the physical facilities of a forest protection program; the protection of the forest from fire, insects, disease and other damage; the conservation, development, maintenance and management of the forests with a view to obtaining the greatest possible flow of water in the Saskatchewan River and its tributaries."[1]

The Eastern Rockies Forest Conservation Board directed the construction of the forestry trunk road, which was begun in 1948 and completed in 1952, established radio sets at all the ranger stations, improved the fire protection program, improved existing forestry service buildings and built new ones, purchased new equipment and started a mapping program. Rangers were supplied with trucks and trail bikes for use in their patrols, and the use of saddle horses was discouraged or prohibited. Gordon Matthews retained his own saddle horses, but was the last forest officer to do so.

The Board was dissolved on March 31, 1973 when the Alberta Forest Service, which had been gradually assuming the Board's duties, was deemed capable of administering the forest reserve.

In 1975 Premier Peter Lougheed eliminated the Department of Lands and Forests and placed the Alberta Forest Service under the jurisdiction of the Department of Energy and Natural Resources; thus, once again changing the administration of the valley.

Late in 1975 Premier Lougheed announced the creation of Kananaskis Provincial Park (changed to Peter Lougheed Provincial Park on January 1, 1986). The park, centred around the two Kananaskis Lakes, covered an area of approximately 208 square kilometres and bordered on Elk Lakes Provincial Park in British Columbia and Banff National Park. The dedication took place on September 22, 1978, at the Pocaterra Visitor Centre. When the present visitor centre was built the building became Pocaterra Ski Hut.

In October 1977 the creation of Kananaskis Country—a multi-use recreation area—was announced by Premier Lougheed and J. Allan Adair, the minister of Recreation, Parks and Wildlife. The Alberta Heritage Fund provided funding for the development of this 4250 square kilometres of foothills and mountains in the eastern slopes of the Rocky Mountains, of which the Kananaskis Valley is only a part.

The Alberta government's coal policy, which allowed no exploration or commercial development in the Kananaskis Valley, set the stage for recreational development. In

Ribbon Peak and Mount Bogart centre, Mount Allan and coal mine scar on the right.

preparation, one of the first projects was the reclamation of the coal mine scar on Mount Allan. This commenced on August 28, 1976 (the reclamation, which was done at the close of the mine in 1952, was very rudimentary). The 1976 reclamation project was filmed as a documentary to assist coal companies in similar projects.

Dave Nielsen

Originally, Improvement District No. 5 was part of Improvement District No. 8, it was all the same municipality. I believe after Kananaskis Country was formed, they decided to make a municipal entity with the same boundaries as Kananaskis Country for ease of administration. So they created a separate municipality called I.D. #5 for administering the municipal services portion of Kananaskis Country. The improvement district was then able to collect taxes and provide municipal services like fire and ambulance, along the same organizational lines as Kananaskis Country. Later I.D. #8 became the Municipal District of Bighorn.

What has happened recently is that I.D. #5 had no advisory council or advisory committee like other I.D.s had within the province. The managing director of Kananaskis Country, now the director, was also the I.D. manager. Early in 1994 there was an interest expressed by certain local residents and ratepayers to have more say in how their municipal taxes were spent. An interim advisory committee was established by the minister of Municipal Affairs in August of 1994, consisting of seven members. Its purpose was to make a recommendation to the minister of Municipal Affairs and the minister of Environmental Protection on an appropriate local government's model for their Improvement District. They have done that and the model has been accepted.

I.D. #5 became the Kananaskis Improvement District (they are in the process of getting rid of numbers and all municipalities now have a name). It is now under the authority of the minister of Environmental Protection and they have just completed the elections, by sector, for what will be called the Kananaskis Improvement District Council. It will consist of six representatives: four drawn from local residents and ratepayers groups and the other two members will be the citizens representatives on the Kananaskis Country Interdepartmental Committee. It is four groups representing the interests of local residents and ratepayers and two members representing interests of Albertans at large with respect to Kananaskis Country. There was concern by all that they didn't want the tail wagging the dog when it came to making decisions on things.

It wasn't an election where you have ballot boxes and polling stations, returning stations, and people go to the ballot boxes and everybody votes for the person in their ward as in a typical municipality. It was something that was developed that was unique to Kananaskis Country. We don't have a ward system. We have sectors: big business, small business, non-commercial residents, ratepayers, cabin owners' associations. From within those sectors it was select and vote for a member to sit on the K.I.D. Council.

The Kananaskis Improvement District Council reports to the minister of Environmental Protection. They will not get into approving subdivisions or development permits or making municipal development plans or anything like that. Those powers will remain with the Department of Environmental Protection because the department wants to make sure it controls and continues to guide what is appropriate and not appropriate development in Kananaskis Country, because it is for Albertans at large and not just a small group of people who happen to reside there and pay taxes there.

Kananaskis Country and Peter Lougheed Provincial Park

Robert (Bob) Reynolds

Initially, Kananaskis Country was part of Alberta Provincial Parks and at that time was, more or less, under the direction of Jim Acton, who was director of Parks. The planning process started in 1975, but prior to that time there had been an initial inspection of the sites by a fellow called Archie Landals. He looked at what is now Kananaskis Country and one other site northwest of Edmonton in the Grande Prairie area. The Alberta government wanted to have a mountain-type park, similar to Banff and Jasper national parks. Kananaskis was picked, primarily because it was in Peter Lougheed's home ground.

When I came out to Alberta it was with the knowledge that Kananaskis Country would be part of my responsibility. I came out to Rimbey in 1975 when Kananaskis Country was in the planning process, and spent about three days a week all through that winter in Edmonton with the planners. We spent one week roaming around on snow machines; just getting an idea of what the terrain was like and what would be possible. This was just for Kananaskis Provincial Park as there was no Kananaskis Country involved at that time. Kananaskis Provincial Park was officially dedicated in September 1978, but as far as the planning process was concerned, it started in 1975.

I had three rangers in the park in 1976, and we officially took over all the campgrounds from the Alberta Forest Service. We operated the campgrounds in much the same way, doing maintenance, minor cleanup and ranger patrols. We did a lot of hiking and climbing in '76 to get an idea of where campgrounds might be located.

There were lots of discussions about what road to use as access. Should we use the TransAlta Utilities road, or go farther up the Forestry Trunk Road, beyond the TransAlta road, and cut across country to make a new entrance to the park? I felt it would be a waste of money, and also would make another scar in the Kananaskis Lakes area if a new road was cut. One planner wanted to cut across the present information centre and join the TransAlta road there, but there was a 75-foot cliff in the way. Other ideas were to tunnel through the cliff to get up onto the ridge or make a suspension bridge.

After that we settled down and decided to use the TransAlta road. We varied it slightly and took out some of the straightness where it followed the powerline. We curved it to access things like campgrounds and the visitor centre. There were several good places where we could curve into facilities.

At that time we were also dealing with Alberta Transportation, working out the centre line of the road. We had to persuade Alberta Transportation that this was not going to be a major highway and we didn't want the large right-of-ways and shoulders that they usually had, because they felt it had to meet highway standards. Fortunately, at that time, we had a good local superintendent and we were able to convince him that we could curve the road and reduce the shoulder, and also keep the speed down, and still maintain the aesthetics without having 20 or 30 feet of shoulder on both sides of the road.

We had a forestry campground at Boulton Creek and a little day-use area, and there was a campground at Interlakes. That, basically, was all we had.

Photo: Ruth Oltmann.

We tried to decide where we could put other campgrounds and Elkwood Campground came up. This was a relatively easy site because it was flat and there weren't any archaeological problems. There were numerous archaeological sites throughout the park area, but not many interfered with campgrounds or other facilities. Boulton Creek Campground was probably the last one we planned. The planners felt it was too undulating, had too much variation in terrain. To me, that was one of the best sites for building a campground because the sites were broken up, and the campers wouldn't feel they were right next door to each other. All we Operations people had to do was convince Planning that it could be done.

Past the end of the old forestry cabin at Boulton Creek and up onto the next bench the road went through an archaeological site. It was a camping site, but not a permanent one. Artifacts had to be dug out and catalogued, and then taken to Calgary. This caused some delay and rerouting of the road, which wasn't a major problem. We created what is probably the nicest campground in the park area, other than the original Interlakes Campground, which is still the most popular. People like to get close to the water, if they can, so the Lower Lake Campground is also popular, with about 10 sites that are actually adjacent to the water.

One of the humorous things that happened with the Planning people was discussions about the old Forestry Interlakes Campground. They wanted to cut off access to the peninsula between the two lakes altogether at the Upper Lake day-use area, and create a parking lot with people walking to a picnic area. I couldn't see why anybody would want to walk a distance to a picnic site with their coolers or whatever they would have. We had quite an argument and it lasted about a year. I asked my staff if I was being reasonable, but they agreed with me. Finally I spoke to the deputy minister and told him the problem, and he came down with the planner and stood at one of the nicest sites in the campground and asked the planner to explain his reasoning. Within half an hour he stipulated that it would be left a campground. It was redeveloped so we could put in more sites and make them a little bigger.

For the Lower Lake Campground, we were thinking of just developing the old Forestry site, which was on the north side of Boulton Creek. That was kind of wet, because there was a lot of loam in the area, and there were old trails throughout from people camping everywhere. We converted it into a day-use area, and on the south side of the creek we created a campground on drier ground.

We spent a good deal of time in 1977 looking for a site for a visitor centre. One day I took off on the TransAlta road and walked over to the cliff that overlooks the fen below, which runs right from Pocaterra Cabin (we had developed Pocaterra as an interim visitor centre). I went farther south and then cut back to the TransAlta road, coming onto the upper fen where the present visitors' centre is located. It was a fantastic, sunny day, and I came out of the lodgepole pine onto the edge of this fen, which at that time of the year had ponds in it. The ponds come and go, quite often they are there in the first part of spring and then they dry up by July and August. They looked beautiful because of the reflection off the mountains, so I had lunch there. Later the staff interpreter and I made a presentation to the planning team for this to be the spot for the visitor centre. That, in fact, is where it was built.

We were also scouring the area for trails. There were a few old, cut trails that we decided to use. Don Gardner was hired to look at ways of joining what is now called the Pocaterra Trail with the Lookout Trail. We wanted him to examine ways of creating loops that would appeal to a variety of hikers and skiers, so they would have a choice of lengths.

That was a pleasurable time, because I spent a lot of it with Don Gardner walking the trails and discussing how they should work. We also looked at the old fire road at Upper Kananaskis Lake and the trail into Three Isle Lake and Maude/Lawson lakes. We wanted to improve them and build them up to standards that would accept more people. We also wanted to put a trail right around Upper Kananaskis Lake. At Three Isle Lake and Maude/Lawson lakes we decided to create backcountry campgrounds that were set back from the lakeshore in hardier areas, not in meadow, which could be destroyed by too many people camping. We were able to build platforms for the tents and fly in material that was better than the mud and loam that was there.

I came from Ontario and had spent a great deal of time in the Ontario bush; hiking, road locating and timber cruising—where I had to constantly rely on a compass because we were in dense bush. When I came out here I found it was next to impossible to get lost if I had a map because of all the landmarks, mountains and creekbeds. The rangers, who were good people, had come up through the ranks in Alberta Parks and had to test me to find out how a flatlander from Ontario could manage in the mountains. I knew they were doing this. They were so obvious it was kind of ridiculous, but we had a lot of good times. Jim Ridley was one, Rod Jaeger was the other one.

I worked with Sharon Bowie, Ray Andrews and Dan Brunton in visitor services. The four of us sat down and worked out a five-year plan. From that time, going up to and including 1979 and 1980, we worked out the number of staff, trucks and so on, we would have to have each year for the budget. Once we put that together, from then until 1981, we had virtually no budget problems because all Treasury asked us each year was: 'Is this according to your five-year plan?' Treasury found it acceptable, so each year we would add maintenance staff, ranger staff and clerical staff, to accommodate our five-year plan.

Snowmobiles were not allowed in Peter Lougheed Park, so it was decided to put them in McLean Creek, which wasn't the best as far as planning is concerned because snow conditions are marginal there. They were also allowed down in the Highwood, which gave them a fair amount of terrain. There was a lot of bitterness over the snowmobile club having to leave the Smith-Dorrien and Spray area. They lobbied the government to change this policy, but the politicians, fortunately, backed up the plan. We also used Kananaskis money to develop snowmobiling up in the Waiparous area of the forest reserve that was not part of Kananaskis Country. It was a way of providing the snowmobilers and the all-terrain vehicle riders with more terrain.

In 1979 or 1980 Peter Lougheed decided to make Kananaskis Country a separate division within Parks. It was primarily a political decision, having something to do with the Olympics. Barry Mitchelson was the deputy minister of Parks, and I was reporting to Jim Acton who was assistant deputy minister and no longer director of Parks. Ed Marshall was brought in as the director of Development and as a liaison person between the various government agencies involved in Kananaskis Country, which were Alberta Forest Service, Fish and Wildlife, Public Lands, Transportation and Parks. Also, Ed Marshall was chairman of an intergovernmental group called the KCIC *(Kananaskis Country Intergovernmental Committee)*, made up of people from all these government agencies. When the planning was done and the construction was underway, the need for a person like Ed Marshall or the committee was not that important any more. So Peter Lougheed decided that Ed Marshall would then be the managing director of all of Kananaskis Country, including Development, Operations and so on. My title changed from regional director to operations manager. I was doing basically the same thing, but I would be reporting to Ed Marshall instead of the assistant deputy minister in Edmonton.

At that point we broke off from Parks and became a separate division with an office in Calgary. I was the operations manager, responsible for every day park maintenance, and Fred Wilmot was the manager for major maintenance and construction. There was also a director of Planning and an administrative section. That was the structure until Fred Wilmot's retirement in 1994 when they reassessed all of Kananaskis Country. *(Wilmot had followed Ed Marshall as managing director.)* Partly because of the reassessment and partly because of budget cuts, they decided that Kananaskis Country would be brought back in under the Parks' umbrella and then answer to, and work under, the Edmonton office. Now they are closing the Calgary office and moving the staff to Canmore. *(The office moved to Canmore on April 1, 1995.)*

After a while we changed our interpretive program. Joel Christensen came on staff—he had been working for us under contract—and developed the interpretive program (live shows) for which Kananaskis Country became famous. The only other park that was doing live shows, which is using costumes and interpreters as actors, was Dinosaur Provincial Park. Their head interpreter, Ron Chamney, came to Kananaskis Country and worked with us. My main enjoyment was watching the shows and listening to the audience. We wondered whether we were entertaining them or educating them, so by listening to the people when they left we could tell they were remembering all of the information about ticks or bear problems, or whatever was presented. It turned out to be an excellent way to get a message across, and it was far superior to standing in front of an audience and showing slides or giving a talk.

The audiences grew to the point where we had to build the Elkwood Amphitheatre, and even it was overcrowded on the long weekends. It was the biggest amphitheatre built in Alberta. We surpassed the capacity of it by the quality of the shows and the desire of the campers to get to them.

Bob Wood was the district superintendent of Kananaskis West and he came to us from national parks. He had a lot of good background in building parks, developing trails, and so on, but he was from what I would call the 'old school' of park superintendents, which is provide a campground, trails and firewood, and keep them clean. Why waste your time doing anything else, like interpretive programs?

We used to run the interpretive programs out of the old forestry cabin. The interpreters would change their costumes inside the cabin, and use the deck and the flat ground in front of the cabin for their performances. Bob Wood saw one of the programs, and part way through the evening a guy dressed as a squirrel came barrelling out the window into the audience. Bob wasn't sure about this. He came out with a few choice words about a staff person coming out dressed as a stupid squirrel, and queried whether it was necessary or worthwhile. But by the time Bob retired he was thoroughly convinced the interpretive programs were excellent and worthwhile. Taking an old school fellow like that and converting him to live drama in the park was a real success.

The other key thing was that by 1979 we had rangers, and from 1976-79 we had developed trails and backcountry campgrounds in mountain areas, so we had to have a safety and rescue program. In the first two or three years our rangers trained with Peter Fuhrmann and the Banff National Park wardens. In fact, in those days, for major rescues the Banff Park wardens helped us out. We didn't have the necessary expertise or equipment.

Our budget was drafted in 1979 to include the hiring of an alpine specialist. I consulted with Peter Fuhrmann on his recommendation. He suggested I not interview anybody and just look at hiring Lloyd Gallagher. Lloyd worked for Canadian Mountain Holidays at the time, but he was at the point where he wanted to get out of it. He liked it, but both he and Fran were tired of him being away so much. He decided to take the job, so it was up to him to organize mountain rescue. He was so enthusiastic and, to this day, that hasn't changed. I told him the job was his to make, that I would just watch and work with him to see how it developed and, if necessary, recommend changes. But I didn't have to. Lloyd was so good that he not only developed, probably, Canada's best rescue system, he branched out into search and water rescue.

Lloyd worked with the rangers and Jim Davies, who was the premier helicopter pilot in those days, in using helicopters for water rescue, as well as for mountain and cliff rescues. Lloyd and the rangers, and George Field now, have pulled off some very spectacular rescues with good pilots.

In the initial stages we bought rescue equipment, like slings, from Switzerland, but then Lloyd found manufacturers in Edmonton and Calgary who would do the same thing. He changed the design so that we could get it cheaper. He had trackers come up from the United States to teach our rangers how to track. He even dealt with psychics. He will not leave any stone unturned in a search if there is a chance of it being productive. He has imagination and initiative, and has done such an excellent job that now he is looked on as the search and rescue, and mountain rescue specialist for the whole province. Working with Lloyd for, say, 16 years, was a highlight for me. Getting the Bill March Award for Excellence at the Banff Film Festival was the culmination of all the work Lloyd has done.

For the Olympics in Kananaskis Country, the government built Nakiska and the Canmore Nordic Centre. Public Works coordinated the construction of both areas, but I had more to do with the Nordic Centre because we knew that would be an operational program for us, more than Nakiska. My role with the Nordic Centre was with Don Gardner, whose involvement in the trails was excellent, because I think our trail system is one of the best in any park system. I was amazed at the way he could ski on skinny skis. He showed me the skis he was using. They had been broken, I don't know how many times, and glued back together. He was an amazing character in the development of K Country.

William Watson Lodge, for handicapped people and seniors, was Jeanne Lougheed's idea. It was made for Albertans first and if there was any room, people from other provinces or countries could use it. Initially there was a lodge and four cabins. The four cabins were big enough that they could be divided in half and each half had a washroom—one with a shower, toilet and sink, and the other with a tub, toilet and sink. The lodge was designed so that if a large group came out and took two or four cabins, instead of cooking in the cabins, they would cook as a group in the lodge where there is a big commercial kitchen. When it opened, it was so popular that within three years there was a need to either build another one somewhere else or expand, so we built four more cabins that were a little more luxurious.

Visitors can leave the lodge in a wheelchair and go to Elkwood Amphitheatre on a paved trail. They can go anywhere without using a vehicle via the bike trails, but they can also drive throughout the park and use the facilities. It is a world-class facility for the handicapped and people have come from New Zealand, Australia and from all over North American to see it, with the possibility of building something similar in their country.

Ross Watson, the manager, is blind and he is phenomenal the way he gets around. He does cabin inspections when people are through by checking dishes, pots and pans by feel. He walks the trails. Each intersection is marked with Braille markings, so he knows where he is. He has been there almost from the start. George Szwender was the first manager and Ross was his assistant. When George got a promotion and went to B.C., Ross became manager.

I retired June 1991. I don't think a Parks' person in Canada has had the experience that I have had. To be able to start a project like Kananaskis Country right from the planning stage, go through the development and the operations, and end your career that way is very fortunate. I could never leave Kananaskis Country even though I've retired.

Kananaskis Country development included the placement of a number of visitor information centres. Initially there were two temporary information centres in the Kananaskis Valley: the Barrier Lake Information Centre, which was a trailer, six kilometres south of Highway #1, and Pocaterra Hut in Peter Lougheed Provincial Park. The permanent provincial park visitor centre was opened in 1980 and the interpretive displays were completed in 1982. The centre has two theatres with a variety of shows related to the park. The Barrier Lake Visitor Information Centre's permanent structure was opened in

February 1982 and was initially operated by Travel Alberta, the tourism arm of the provincial government. The Kananaskis Village Centre also has an information centre in conjunction with a franchise post office. This centre opened in 1987. Initially it was operated by the Kananaskis Village Resort Association, a not-for-profit organization. It was taken over and operated by Kananaskis Country management in 1992.

I started to work as a travel counsellor for Travel Alberta at the Barrier Lake Visitor Centre in October 1981, while it operated out of a trailer. In the job interview with Barb Spencer and Jackie Grant, I was asked a lot of questions, but none of them dealt with how I would react if confronted with a bear between the outside toilet and the information centre trailer! I remember being asked what I would do with my time when I wasn't busy in the centre. We are a long way from that scene now, being kept busy with more than 60,000 visitors in the summer season alone.

During my first few years with Travel Alberta, I was given the opportunity to supervise two seasonal information centres, Grand Centre/Cold Lake and Canmore, but I always came back to the Barrier Lake Visitor Centre in the winters. Then in 1988 the Barrier Lake Visitor Centre was turned over to Kananaskis Country management and my position went with the transfer, so I went back there permanently as Supervisor of Information Services. However, nothing remains the same in the Alberta government, and in no time I was supervis-

Ruthie at work at Barrier Lake Visitor Information Centre, 1982. Photo: Dennis Jaques.

ing anywhere from one to four information centres throughout Kananaskis Country. It's been the most challenging job I've had in my long career and the best job I've had. I've been stretched, squeezed and poured, and I hope I stay until retirement.

Meeting the needs of Kananaskis Country visitors has been exciting. They ask simple questions like where to go on a short hike (I often recommend Troll Falls), to complicated questions like where to find their friend who is camping in Kananaskis. With 63 campgrounds this is a tricky one, but we can often answer it. Questions about the history of the valley are easy, but where to find some obscure frozen waterfall mentioned in the Calgary Herald can be more difficult. It once took me a whole year to find the answer for one visitor who wanted to know the names of the two mountains between which she could see the setting of the summer solstice from her house (Mounts Romulus and Remus). There are always lots of questions about hiking trails, so I try to hire staff who know the trails. Campers come in droves, and we help them find campground space based on their wishes. A whole new brand of visitor came to the valley when the Kananaskis Village hotels were built, including lots of conference people looking for something to do in their spare time.

There are two major questions people ask. In the summer it is, "How are the bears?" In the winter it is, "What is the avalanche hazard?" We try to be as informative as we can and yet not scare people to death. Both queries are valid concerns. We get reports on trails with closures or cautions owing to bears and the avalanche hazard. I'm glad I'm a backcountry skier and know where the hazardous terrain is on major trails. That makes my job easier.

I've met a lot of interesting people, some of whom have become personal friends and hiking buddies. I thoroughly enjoy seeing my regulars during the cross-country ski season (the Norsemen Ski Club, for example). In the summer of '94 I was particularly lucky when several people who came into the centre informed me they had worked in the valley many years ago—those people are now in this book! It is interesting how the origins of the visitors have changed from largely Calgarians to people from all over the province and around the world. There are lots of friendly Americans.

The Kananaskis Country information centres play an important role in satisfying visitors' information needs and directing them away from potential harm. It has been very fulfilling for me to be able to use my extensive knowledge of the Kananaskis Valley, Kananaskis Country, the mountain national parks and the province of Alberta. It is a joy to share with visitors and help them have a good time.

Cabin at Lower Kananaskis Lake. Photo courtesy: Forest Technology School, Hinton.

Rangers

Rangers have been part of the valley's history since the valley was included in Rocky Mountains Park (now Banff National Park). At that time the Rocky Mountains Park gate was about one-and-a-half kilometres west of the hamlet of Kananaskis on Highway #1A, where a Canadian Pacific Railway station and water tower used to be located.

The first permanent park warden, Arthur Tom Staples, patrolled the Kananaskis Valley on horseback, a trip of approximately 64 kilometres. A cabin at Lower Kananaskis Lake was used by the wardens, and later by the forestry rangers, until Lower Kananaskis Lake was flooded. The site is now under 18 metres of water.

When the Kananaskis Valley was removed from the national park in 1930, the District Forest Ranger, operating out of Canmore, was put in charge of the valley. Summer rangers were installed at the Kananaskis Lakes. Joe Champion was the first summer ranger, and he worked there for about 10 years. Joe Kovach became District Ranger at Canmore in June of 1940 and remained until September of 1953 when he retired.

Ranger duties involved forestry work, land administration, fisheries and wildlife management, and enforcement of fish and game regulations. By 1950 the emphasis was on predator control, and a poisoning program commenced to control coyotes, wolves and cougars. During this time a bald eagle was shot.

Ranger responsibilities have changed over the years. In the 1950s they were responsible for everything that took place in their district, in some cases their powers exceeding those of the police. They were expected to deal with every crises, from finding lost travellers to supervising fire fighting. A chief ranger could have one or more small towns in his area and a lot of administrative duties connected with local affairs. They were also responsible for maintaining and supplying the fire lookouts.

When the Kananaskis Ranger Station was built near Ribbon Creek a ranger was installed on a year-round basis. This was at the site of the present Kananaskis Emergency Services Centre, where the rangers' Boundary Cabin was situated. Boundary Cabin still exists and is periodically used as sleeping accommodation for helicopter pilots. In the 1980s the Kananaskis Emergency Services Centre for Kananaskis Country was built and consists of a firehall, RCMP office and space for Forestry Service personnel.

In the spring of 1961 Gordon Matthews and his wife Ida arrived in the valley and took up residence at Kananaskis Ranger Station. They had previously been at the Ghost and Elbow ranger stations. Matthews had also worked for outfitters in the Banff area so had many years of experience in the backcountry. The Matthews saw many changes take place from the spring of 1961 to the spring of 1975, at which time Gordon retired having worked for 25 years with the Alberta Forest Service.

At the time of their arrival the Matthews were the only permanent residents south of the Kananaskis Forest Experiment Station. Although Elmer Smith spent a lot of time at his rock quarry on Ribbon Creek, he was not a resident. During the winter there were times the Matthews were snowed in, because Calgary Power only plowed the road when it was necessary for their work. It was an isolated life, particularly in the winter, but the Matthews were happy. This was what they were accustomed to. Previously they had lived without electrical power, with outhouses and with water hauled from the creek. Ida, a resourceful woman, had at one time canned half a moose.

One of the most noticeable changes the Matthews observed were the number of people coming into the valley. They had one particularly hectic episode. It was in 1963, on the July first holiday weekend. A big snowstorm blew in, washed out the Evan-Thomas Creek bridge and caused a mud slide off Mount McDougall. Sixty people were stranded between the bridge washout and the mud slide. At the time of the catastrophe Gordon was up at the Pigeon Fire Lookout. When he came down he found he could only drive as far as the mud slide. From there he had to walk three kilometres to get home. When he arrived at the ranger station it looked like a sport's day! Ida was in the office with the phone in one hand and the radio in the other and 20 people were asking questions!

Carving by Jack Fuller in live tree at Lower Kananaskis Lake Ranger Cabin, 1922.
Photo: Elizabeth Rummel.

For three-and-a-half days the Matthews coped with the emergency. The Matthews' salvation came in the form of a magnificent woman who was a good organizer. She took charge of the people who were being housed in the storehouse, putting a tarp up to divide the building in half, and scrounging food and distributing it to everyone. Ida, who is an extremely capable woman herself, looked after the people staying in the house. Together these two women brought order out of chaos.

One man in the group was a diabetic and one woman had a small baby. As both were dependent upon supplies that were unavailable, they were taken north as far as the mud slide, where they walked across to a waiting vehicle that took them into Calgary. The rest had to be content to stay on at the ranger station until the slide was cleared. A number of other people were stranded on the south side of the Evan-Thomas Creek. Because they were mostly campers, they looked after themselves or went south over Highwood Pass.

The Matthews saw many changes in the valley's environment. When they first arrived few people used it for winter recreation. Gordon noted that human traffic affected the wildlife population and estimated the ungulate population had decreased to half what it was on their arrival by the time they left in 1975. Also, when Matthews first started in the forest service all patrols of the forest reserve were done by horse. He saw this aspect of his work evolve until it was exclusively a four-wheel drive patrol. He was the last ranger to patrol by horseback and this was limited to the Evan-Thomas Creek valley; more from a personal desire than as a requirement of the job.

Gordon Matthews

I was probably the last guy to use horses for forestry work because I was the last person on top of Black Rock, which is in the Ghost area, to pack the stuff out with horses and I was the last guy on Moose Mountain to pack out with horses. When I moved into Kananaskis I brought my horses. When they issued me a four-wheel drive truck I thought I was King Tut.

Every month we had to take our reports into the office in Calgary, and every month the trucks had to be checked. The mechanic used to say, 'You've got less miles and burn less gas than anybody we have, why?' I said, 'I still do a lot of work with my horses.' That's when they didn't have established campgrounds. People camped wherever they wanted to and most of them would have a fire. Consequently, Monday morning was always a busy morning for we rangers because we had to see if people had put out their fires. I covered the Kananaskis River valley from the ranger station south for 25 miles to the lakes. Instead of leaving a truck out on the road and walking into all these campsites, and coming out and finding the truck was back a mile or two, I used to go on a saddle horse. That's why my truck had so few miles on it.

What I miss more than anything is the stopover place with the teepee poles and the tea pail hanging on a tree. Or the ability to catch a few fish for supper while on patrol. There were many places like this and even the horses knew them and would quicken their pace. Now the road goes through with dust and cars, and you remember these little places and miss the way it was. It was yours and nobody else ever went there.

I got into a few jams. The one that sticks in my mind most occurred with Mike Lawler the timberman. We had to go into Marmot Basin to do something for the

Dominion Forestry when they were going to start setting up some gauges. We had had a real wicked lightning and thunderstorm with a lot of rain. I had never seen Ribbon Creek so high. It was coming straight over the road instead of making the bend. *(Ribbon Creek used to flow under the Ribbon Creek Road.)*

We'd got half way when I got a call from my wife Ida saying there was a big smoke up on the slopes of Bogart. So we came back, but when we took a look at the creek I realized there was no way we could get in there with the truck. There's a prison camp stationed down about four or five miles, so I went down and got hold of the guard and said I wanted at least six men. If they could walk into where that fire was I could pack what equipment we needed with pack horses. Anyhow, I got this camp established and took a portaphone, tent and some grub with me. The guard said, 'I'm not going to leave six prisoners all by themselves overnight.' I said, 'I'm really in a bind, so I'll leave these guys a portaphone and they can check in with Ida at the station every hour, then we'll know if they're still there.' He went along with it.

These guys were having a ball. It was something new for them. There were two Indian boys in the group. I came in there one night and they had a camp fire all set up with tripods and a rod to hang their tea pails as usual, but before I got in I could smell something cookin', and it smelled good. One of these Indians had killed a big porcupine, skinned it and had put a stick through him and was roasting it!

We put the fire out. After we returned the prisoners to the prison camp, I went in to make certain the fire was out for sure. I took another horse, a beautiful bay I had got from Bill Bagley, a cowboy who worked for Brewsters. As I rode in I noted that because Ribbon Creek was running so high and fast it had undermined some of the banks. I should mention that the first issue of our uniforms were different to the uniforms they have now. They were made in a western way so that we had a western riding boot, what they call a gaiter, and we had a Stetson hat.

I had fought this horse so much in the water going in that I thought I'd try something different coming out. I had a portaphone strapped on my left-hand side inside a wooden case and an axe in my scabbard where I used to carry a gun. I'm coming out and instead of going down in this deep hole I decided to go up on the top of the bank and ride along it. Well, the water had undermined it. I got about half way over when six feet of bank broke off. The creek had big rocks down below and it flipped the horse completely upside down and threw me out into the creek. I landed on the portaphone and it just about broke my ribs. I can see this horse yet coming down all upside down with four feet in the air. My hat had come off and landed on a big white rock. That horse came down on top of that rock and the saddle horn cut a hole through that hat just like if you had cut it with a pair of scissors!

I could see the horse was hurt. I had to lead him the four miles from there to the ranger station. Ida saw me coming under the yard light and thought there was something wrong. We got hold of Bill Bagley, who was as good as a vet. He came down and said he's hurt in the back, and that we would just have to see if he gets over it. He never did and I lost that beautiful horse. It really bothered me.

The piece of the old hat that was cut by the saddle horn didn't fall out completely, but it was perforated. I kept it as a souvenir for a long time. Finally I made wads with it for the partition between the shot and the powder in my shotgun shells. Of all the different scrapes I've been in, I'll always remember that one.

Another incident I remember well, although I don't want to remember it, happened in the '60s—maybe '65 or '66. It was the 1st of September and in those days sheep and goat hunting season opened on the 1st of September and game like deer, moose and elk opened the 1st of November. Well, I was making up these reports when a knock came on the door. When Benny opened it I could hear this man speak in a deep, gruff voice in very broken English. I said to Benny, 'Ask the man in.' Benny said, 'He won't come, you'd better come out.' I didn't know what was up when I walked outside. Here was this huge man—he must have been six feet six and probably weighed 240 pounds. He had a half ton truck with a little camper on the back. I said, 'What is your trouble?' He was dressed in a red jacket, so I knew he was a hunter. He said, 'My boy has been hurt, he's in the back of the truck.'

I went around to the back of the truck and saw blood running out of the corner of the box! I opened the two little doors and crawled in and here lay this boy, dressed in a red and black jacket with both of his hands folded over his face. When I pulled his arms they were stiff. He was dead and had been dead a while, otherwise his arms wouldn't be that way. When I got his arms pulled back there was a great big blood splash on the front of his chest and the blood was coming out of a hole in his back—that was what was running out of the truck box. I knew he'd been shot because I could see where the bullet had come out, and I knew he'd been shot from behind because a bullet makes a bigger hole where it comes out than where it goes in. I had worked with game as a game guide and I knew right away.

I got out of there and said, 'Your boy isn't hurt, he's dead.' 'No, no,' he said. 'I take him back home to Calgary and put him in his bed and get a doctor.' I reached in the truck and took his keys and said, 'You're not going anywhere.' I stepped into the office and asked Ida to phone the Mounties at Canmore. 'Tell them to get an ambulance and a doctor and to be at the station as quick as they can.' I went back out and said, 'Now look, you better get everything straight because you are going to have a lot of questions to answer when the Mounties get here. Where did you come from?' He said, 'Calgary.' I said, 'Did you come straight in?' 'No, we crossed at that lake.' He meant Barrier Lake. They had driven up the powerline and come out at Ribbon Creek bridge. The boy was driving and he was the passenger and being that they were going south the boy was on the left-hand side and he was on the right-hand side. The boy's name was Bruno. He said, 'Stop Bruno, I see a deer.' He told me, 'I saw a deer standing on this hill right where you make a quick dip.' I knew the exact spot. 'I tried to keep the truck between me and the deer and I snuck around and came into the river where I crawled through a bunch of little bars.' He was talking about one of Soapy Smith's old wild horse corrals. He came up the hill from the river to where the deer was, heard a shot and hollered for Bruno. He said there's no answer. 'I look over and here's my boy lying on the side of the hill.' Well, I had it all in my head—I didn't jot any of it down. He just sat on the doorstep and started to cry. We had a little Basenji dog and he was licking the tears off this fellow's face.

After they put the boy in the ambulance and went back to Canmore, the Mounties took me aside and said, 'What do you think really happened?' I told them the story he told me and said it didn't jive. The country was tinder dry. I was one of the rangers preparing to have the road closed, so you can imagine how much dust there would be on an old trail. He said to me, 'When I went to pick my boy up I see a car with big taillights, a green car going real fast.' I thought, with all the dust on that road I don't know how you could tell if it was green or black or what it was.

I waited for this fellow to come in with a huge black police dog, then drove to the spot—I knew exactly where to go. When we came to the sharp hill on this little knoll you could see where the boy had lain because the blood was in the grass. Then the Mountie and the tracking dog, using something belonging to the guy, followed the man's scent. When he returned he said, 'That's where he went.'

He then asked, 'Has he got any rifles?' I said, 'Yes, there are two big rifles in the back.' We wanted to see which one of those guns had been fired. We took the bolts out of the guns—one was a Remington and the other was a Winchester—and we looked through the bores. They were both as clean as the day they were bought. I suggested he could have used a pull-through cleaner. I had it figured that he was in the best position to shoot. The boy was higher than he was, and the bullet went in just at the bottom of the ribs and came out of his right breast, so he was shot at an angle. Anyway, the Mounties took the guy in.

The inquest was in Canmore. The guy was a Hollander called Potsema. When they brought him up on the stand to give his statement he could speak English as good as I can! I got up on the stand and told the judge exactly what he told me. Potsema got up and said, 'That guy is lying, it didn't happen like that at all.' The judge picked up two pieces of clean paper and said to me, 'go over to that room and you draw the trail in, where the mountains are and where the river is and make dots like you do on a map of where this man told you he went.' I did that and the judge laid a book on it. Then he gave one to the guy with the tracking dog. He said, 'I want you to do the same.' When the judge saw our two maps were the same he knew the guy who was lying was this Potsema guy. They charged him with manslaughter.

This is a hard thing to believe, but he had a $50,000 life insurance payable to him from the boy and the boy was to be married in two weeks. Whether he and the girl had anything going or whether he just had a crush on her, I don't know, but he had it figured two ways: he kills the boy, he gets the insurance and he also gets the girl.

When he got out on bail he skipped back to Holland where he got in with a gang that held up a bank. A picture was taken of him with a machine gun, which was shipped to the Mounties in Canada. The Mounties said he would get a bigger sentence in Holland for robbing a bank than he would if he was brought back here for manslaughter, so the department decided to let it go. It was a real trial for me because we were talking about a human being, not a dead moose that somebody had illegally shot. To think that a person could be like that. His own boy!

Our hunting season continued into December and one year the deadline was the 10th of December, a Saturday. If there are going to be any game violations it generally happens more frequently on the last day than any other day. The guys think, 'This is the last day I've got. I haven't filled my licence,' and they will take a chance.

I came out of Kananaskis Lakes late that night, about nine o'clock, and it was dark. I saw a fire down by the river, so I parked my truck and walked down and this guy's got a fire going, trying to keep warm. Hunting had been over for a couple of hours, so I said, 'Are you in trouble? Why are you here at this time of night?' He says, 'I'm waiting for my partner. He crossed the river and saw half a dozen elk go over the ridge and he crossed after them. He's been gone

Gordon Matthews with a cougar
he shot and his dog Goldie.
Photo: Ida Matthews.

four hours.' I said, 'If he gets in trouble he'll probably shoot.' I stuck around for a while and then said, 'Fire three distress shots and see if he will answer.'

He came to the station about an hour and a half later when it was getting colder, around 10 below. He said there was no word or sign of him and I said, 'I'll get in touch with the Mounties in Canmore.' We all went back that night and it was starting to snow and was getting colder, and of course the river had come up. Calgary Power used to turn it up. The Mounties wanted to call off the search until morning.

The next morning I arranged to get a helicopter. What had happened was there was this little creek coming down into the river south of Galatea. Up higher it has a few flat spots so that the water gathers where it is deepest. When we flew in we could see footprints. He must have been pretty near played out, fighting his way through the fallen timber, and when he hit the creek he decided it was better walking on the ice than fighting his way through the snow. All of a sudden we saw a big hole in the ice. It looked like he had fallen through and probably got soaking wet. He had got out of there and kept on going and when he came to the river it must have been up. Probably if he hadn't been wet and if it hadn't been around 10 below he might have waited, but he decided to cross when it was still high and it knocked his feet out from under him and off he went down the river. We found him lying on a gravel bar just one cake of ice.

When I first went to Kananaskis we didn't have a TV. TV reception was crazy. It bounced from one mountain to the other. I had one of the old camp tables they made for the campgrounds on our front yard. I had tried a television antenna up on the roof and I had tried it everywhere. Finally one day I set it up on the table and Ida said, 'You know, it's best there than anywhere.' So I bored a hole in the table and shoved it down. There was still a lot of snow and stuff like that. One night we were watching television when all of a sudden the picture cleared up and it was the best we'd ever had. Our dog ran to the front

161

door like she was ready to tear it down. I looked out and saw that a big black bear had knocked the table and antenna on the ground, which resulted in the best reception we ever had! We left it there.

One day I was up at four am and returned home from Calgary about seven. The phone rang and it was a fellow on the night shift at Calgary Power. He said, 'Gordon, I've had a few calls from the house at Lower Kananaskis Lake. There's this man there in bad condition and his three children are stranded up on High-wood Pass.' It was 17 below at the station, but I didn't think he could be in much in trouble because he could get a fire going and had food and bedding. I guess he was worried about the kids. I took an old International truck, put my chains on it and started for the lower lake. I don't know how many times I broke those chains and wired them up. I got there and he had just got a big log and battered the door and tore a great big hole out of the side. His nose was frozen and he had got his boots off, of all things rubber boots cut part way down. They had been full of snow, I could see his toes were frozen. He'd started from Calgary in a new four-wheel drive Toyota truck with three boys aged 12, nine and six. He was an interior decorator and didn't know beans about being out in the sticks. He went through Longview and up the Highwood, then started up the Highwood Pass. Of course, the higher you get the deeper the snow. Why the stupid ass didn't turn around and go back before he got in trouble, I don't know. When he got to the top of the pass the drive shaft on the truck broke. If it was 17 below at the ranger station it probably was 27 below on that pass.

So there he was, stuck with three kids and a broken truck and he could see a light at the Calgary Power house over at Lower Kananaskis Lake. So the nut started over there on foot and left the kids in the truck. He made it, but he was completely played out. The thing that saved those kids' lives was when the little guy started to cry that he wanted to go home and the older boy told him the only way was to clear the snow around the vehicle so they could turn around. They had a shovel and they all took turns clearing a space, which kept the kids warm.

There was no way I could get in there because the road wasn't plowed. From that corner to the Highwood Pass is 10 or 12 miles. I got hold of Ida on the radio and asked her to get Hi Baker at the Highwood Ranger Station and find out if he'd got a skidoo to get up to the pass. I guess the guy in the filling station had a skidoo and they had one at the station, so the two of them went in with the skidoos and brought the kids back to the Highwood Ranger Station. They saved those kids' lives.

I wrapped the guy's feet in blankets and gave him some coffee laced with rum. I said, 'Get in the truck and I'll take you back to the station.' He figured I was going to try and get to the kids! An argument ensued, but I insisted I would take him to the station and then do something from there. What was bugging him was he had $250 in his wallet he had dropped behind the seat in the truck so he wouldn't lose it. I think he was more scared of losing that money than he was worried about the kids.

Anyhow, I got into the station and his feet were hurting bad. I got in touch with the Canmore rangers and asked them to get a doctor to advise me what I should do. The doctor told me to put two or three pair of wool socks on him and wrap him in a warm blanket and he would come and get him. I said, 'You'll never get in to Kananaskis from the highway because it's blowing snow, I'll bring him to the highway and you have the ambulance and doctor waiting there.' I gassed up again and went out to the highway and when I returned home it was six o'clock in the

Boulton Creek forestry cabin, 1975. Photo: Ruth Oltmann.

Old Kananaskis ranger station. Photo: Gillean Daffern.

morning. I had been up 26 hours! They took the fellow to the Canmore hospital and he lost all his toenails, but they fixed his face up. The next time we saw the Calgary Herald there was a picture of this joker sitting up in bed in Canmore. He made himself out to be a hero instead of a jackass!

By the time Gordon Matthews retired, it was felt a permanent ranger was no longer necessary and a summer-only ranger was installed at the ranger station.

With the development of Kananaskis Country the role of rangers has changed. The Kananaskis Country rangers, who look after the Kananaskis Valley, operate out of headquarters in Bow Valley Provincial Park and Peter Lougheed Provincial Park. Their duties include law enforcement, administration, public relations, safety (including mountain rescue), minor maintenance (both frontcountry and backcountry), trail patrol and resource management.

James Stomp

I came to Kananaskis in the summer of 1982, as the supervisor of the Elbow area. I moved into my present role in January 1995. My title is the Outdoor Recreation Coordinator for Kananaskis Country. Basically I supervise all the field delivery of operations programs, particularly outdoor recreation programs. I am classed as a ranger.

When I first started, even when I started seasonally in 1967, it was around the time the change was taking place. In '67 I still worked with a lot of old-timers. When Parks first started rangers were very much a jack-of-all-trades. In a lot of cases they were the only people who were employed in the park on a year-round basis. They did all of the standard things they still do today—like protecting the resources of the park. A lot was public relations work—they didn't really charge anyone. They did a lot of maintenance work. They were the ones who would clean washrooms, cut grass and do maintenance on buildings. They were the people who hired the equipment to build roads, and they were the carpenters who built the buildings. There were a lot more caretaking type of duties and less technical work. There wasn't as much administration work to be done and certainly not as much resource management, and very little public safety work, although they were there for that purpose. I would imagine they looked for lost people and people who were in distress. They were much more isolated and much more the only person on the scene who was responsible for everything in the park.

In the olden days communications were very different. There was no such thing as park rangers, forest officers, fish and wildlife officers. One person did all of those jobs. Parks was one part of it. They actually put up telephone poles and lines and had the old ring telephones, which they had to maintain for the towers and the park offices. They had to horse ride the lines to be sure the line was up, and when things went wrong with those old telephone systems, they had to fix it.

When I started in '67, resource management was coming into vogue. People were planning parks instead of finding a nice grove of trees to build a campground. There was a lot more design taking place. They built things for the future as opposed to 'right now.' The whole clientele has changed. Now transportation and communications are so quick the number of people visiting these areas is phenomenal.

What rangers do today is constantly changing; particularly now with budget cuts and downsizing of government.

Generally speaking, you could divide our work into a number of areas. The big one is administration—park rangers do far more administration than they ever did before. Such things as supervising large numbers of staff involved in all kinds of activities takes a lot of administrative procedures, like doing the payroll and dealing with camping permits and revenue collection. Supervising seasonal rangers, radio operators and maintenance staff—who cut grass and clean washrooms and buildings, is something rangers have always done. With the downsizing and budget cuts a lot of that is changing. We still have to do that same work, but we are accomplishing it in different ways. Now, of course, we are going with the privatization route so a lot of the campgrounds are switching over to private operators.

The job through the years has involved more park enforcement work, because of the ever increasing number of people. Conflicts arise when people recreate and sometimes do it in a manner that isn't exactly according to the laws of the land. Such things as liquor abuse, noise and highway traffic problems come into it. Enforcement rangers do two things: they protect the natural resources, and they intervene in conflicts involving people. There are special constable appointments to enforce a number of the provincial statutes that occur in parks. Park rangers will inform people, give written warnings, charge them, evict them, and if the case warrants, sometimes arrest them. This is done in concert with the local RCMP. In Kananaskis Country we probably lay upwards of 600 charges a year, resulting from about 3,000 occurrence reports.

A lot of our people conflicts occur in campgrounds. Contractors will take first action, but the rangers are still the ones who have to come in and do the legal end of the job. That job has certainly increased a lot through the years and is continuing to increase.

Public safety is something rangers have been involved in from the beginning, but with increased people and more types of recreational activities, public safety incidents are more frequent with well over 300 incidents a year. For example, we assist people involved in vehicle accidents, lost people, and people who do not have a significant skill level to keep themselves out of trouble in hazardous types of recreational activities such as mountain climbing, backcountry travel and canoeing. General first aid is something we do. We get everything from people cutting their finger with an axe, to falling on a firepit and burning a leg, to getting bitten by an insect and having an allergic reaction. Then, of course, there are the normal health things that occur in the city—a weak heart, heat exhaustion from high temperatures, or overexertion. Other kinds of crises include airplane crashes, which result in injuries and searches, people being thrown from horses; mountain biking injuries; and people going at high speeds on terrain that isn't designed for it, or slippery conditions, whether that be snowmobiling or cross-country skiing.

The Parks mandate is turning more toward preservation of park areas, and Kananaskis has a lot of significant natural places that need to be protected. This requires scientific study—documenting and taking inventory of areas to see if they are significant, whether from a local, national or international point of view. Park rangers do the tasks themselves, or they hire people or get volunteers to do the studies. They also do a lot of technical measuring by tagging animals and monitoring their activity or patterns.

In the very old days rangers came from the armed services; especially after the war. If they had an outdoor bent, they might gravitate to that kind of job.

The education part of it wasn't as important as their background. Of course, the education standards were a lot lower. Today, it's very different. Right around '67 was when it started to turn all across Canada. Two year technical courses in resource management were developed, some in forestry, some in wildlife management and fisheries. Very few of them were in park management. By the mid-seventies the norm was a two year technical diploma. By the early eighties we were already getting park rangers in the field with university degrees. By 1991, it would not be unusual for us to interview people with a technical diploma in some form of resource management—park management specific—plus a bachelor's degree and maybe a master's. In 1996 there are no jobs! Today, for a Ranger II job we would be looking for a technical diploma and over eight years experience directly related to parks. Many people we would interview would have a technical diploma, a degree and nine-plus years.

Our seasonal rangers have to have at least the first year of a two year technical program before we will look at them. That, and at least four months related experience. Related experience can be varied—everything from fighting forest fires to working in a campground selling permits. St. John's standard first aid is the basic requirement for first aid.

A permanent ranger must have taken, at the very least, something called a Wilderness First Aid course. This is a week-long program, very similar to the Emergency Medical Technician course an ambulance person would have, but in an outdoor setting. All of our people have that and advanced CPR training. Our permanent people have taken other safety training—everything from advanced backcountry skiing courses, to major search and rescue courses. Search and rescue includes using computer programs to aid in detecting where a lost person might go and what they might do. We take advanced climbing training in order to retrieve people from rock faces like Yamnuska. We also work with the Calgary City Police on a swift water rescue course that is designed to get canoeists and kayakers out of tricky swift water. We have public safety vehicles in Kananaskis that have all kinds of ambulance type of equipment: oxygen and suction units, lots of first aid supplies, and stretchers. We practise how to get people out of backcountry environments, whether through the use of slings with helicopters or other means.

When I first came in 1976 there were no women seasonal rangers. We weren't getting applications up to that point in time, but then we started getting them. The first permanent women park rangers started in 1978/79. In the Kananaskis Valley the first permanent female was Donna Schley. She started seasonally in 1982, and full time in 1984. Mona Kronberg was the second and then Nicki Lepage. Now our seasonal ranger complement is probably two-thirds men and one-third women in an average summer. Our permanent complement is not that high—we only have two year-round women: Donna and Nicki. That is out of a staff of 25.

James Stomp, David Hanna
Jim: Just prior to the Olympics when Mount Allan was being developed as an Olympic site, there was a great deal of consternation about the impact that would have on the bighorn sheep herds in that area. Alberta Fish and Wildlife started some projects to monitor that sheep herd and get a feel for it. One of the biologists assigned that task was Orval Pall, who worked out of Calgary. He had two projects going on at the same time: a bighorn sheep project and a cougar monitoring project that was located in the Elbow/Sheep/Highwood valleys. He tradi-

tionally went out in a fixed wing aircraft to monitor the tagged sheep and to pick up his tagged cougars. One day he got into some difficulty when he was surveying sheep in the Nakiska area and his plane did not return. Orval travelled with a number of pilots, but commonly used the same ones. When he and the pilot didn't return, friends of the pilot went looking for them. This was probably five or six o'clock at night. That plane didn't return at dark. So we then had two planes missing. The military became involved looking for these lost planes and we became involved in the search that night.

Dave: I was in one of the helicopters flying around before the second plane went down. We had been called in and were requested by the military to do helicopter fly passes in the area. It was extremely turbulent and scary because we had these fixed wing aircraft going over top of us. Somewhere through this they realized that a second plane was missing.

Jim: The second day was when the real search started and again it was led mainly by the military people with their search aircraft. No beacons were located from either aircraft, so it was pretty well hit and miss where these planes were. The flight plan that was filed by the first plane was a very broad plan that could have been anywhere from Water Valley in the north through the Kananaskis Valley, perhaps into the Sheep/Highwood depending on which of his animals he was monitoring at that time. It was a large search area, although it was thought the Mount Allan area was where he should have been.

The first plane found was the second one to go missing—about two weeks into the search. It was found on top of Mount Lougheed, on the backside. It seem that it hit trying to get up over Mount Lougheed. It hit the middle of the mountain and broke in two pieces. One piece went down the north side and one piece went down the south side. There wasn't a lot left of it. Three people were killed in that one: the pilot and two spotters. That, of course, was a tragedy. A ground team found that plane.

Because the search area was so large, all the Kananaskis Country personnel were involved in searching all parts of Kananaskis Country. We had a good contingent of volunteers involved and the military became more heavily involved right around when that second plane was found. Large military groups were brought in to search areas like Sibbald. About the two-week mark people were getting weary of searching, having searched almost every portion of Kananaskis Country with various means: helicopter, intensive ground searches, interviews with people who had any kind of information. About halfway through the search, I would

Cairn at Memorial Lakes.
Photo: Gillean Daffern.

167

say the third week, the military had a search plane with seven people aboard crash in the Cox Hill area and kill everyone aboard. It was in a search mode at the time. I was in a plane myself at that time and we were ordered to return to the ground immediately.

Things at that point started winding down a bit. I think it was felt by the government that a lot of resources had been committed to this search. We had lost even more people than were originally lost in the first place, and it was starting to become very costly lives-wise and cost-wise. There was then a resurgence from relatives and friends of Orval Pall to continue the search, so a political decision was made to continue for a while longer. About the end of that last week the plane was finally found. It was almost a month after it had gone missing. It was found quite by accident by a fire crew who were going out to do their morning fire protection patrol at Ribbon Creek.

Dave: They found the plane on Mount Kidd.

Jim: The plane had apparently crashed against the hillside in some type of a bank situation in the steep valley. It was smashed up and burnt and had fallen underneath the canopy of trees.

Dave: Forestry spotted it because they saw the orange trees and thought it was a lightning strike and then they saw some wreckage. Jim Lapinsky, from Cochrane, was the pilot who found the plane.

The Cessna 182-R with Orval Pall and pilot Ken Wolff crashed on June 6, 1986. It was found on the south face of Mount Kidd, east of the Guinn's Pass Trail. The second plane was a Cessna 185 with pilot Bruce Pratt and spotters Rod Harradence and Hayden Evans aboard. It crashed in the evening of the same day on Mount Lougheed. The third plane, a Twin Otter 807, crashed on June 14, three kilometres south of Highway #68, a little east of Highway #40. The three military people in the plane were Capt. Wayne Plumbtree, Capt. Ted Kates and Sgt. Brian Burkitt. The other five people were volunteers with CARES in Calgary: Patricia McLean, Jerome Schindler, David Hall, Carl Grant and Charles Mazur.

A memorial cairn was subsequently erected on the shore of a little lake nestled between Mounts Bogart, Sparrowhawk and Lougheed at the headwaters of the north fork of Ribbon Creek. This lake is one of three that were named Memorial Lakes in honour of all 13 people killed. The cairn overlooks the highest of the lakes.

Endnotes
1. Hanson, W. R., ca. 1974, *History of the Eastern Rockies Forest Conservation Board 1947-1973: Calgary, University of Calgary, Kananaskis Field Stations, (unpub. ms.).*

The Growth of Tourism

6

Routes into the Valley

Initially, the Kananaskis Valley was reached via a trail that was first established by native people. Later the early explorers forged a trail that was frequently covered in deadfall. By George Pocaterra's time the trail was kept open by the ranger service and guided fishing parties.

Back in 1867, the ratification of the terms of confederation by British Columbia and the establishment of the Dominion of Canada was taking place. One of the terms of confederation was for a transcontinental railroad to be built. Within a year, Sandford Fleming, later the chief engineer on the Canadian Pacific Railway until William Van Horne took over, was in the mountains searching for a pass to the Pacific Ocean. The North Kananaskis Pass was surveyed in 1881, but was felt unsuitable for a railroad. Major A. B. Rogers had no faith in the Kananaskis route and declined to even visit the survey party working there.

Remains of log bridge on 1934 truck road between Seebe and KFE station, 1975. Photo: Ruth Oltmann.

170

Picnic shelter along
1936 trunk road, 1975.
Photo: Ruth Oltmann.

By 1883 the railroad being built across Canada had passed within sight of the Kananaskis Valley. It contributed to the white man's development of the valley. This was the year Colonel James Walker started his logging operations and shortly before the Eau Claire group commenced theirs.

For an undetermined number of years the Canmore Trail had been used from the Bow Valley, over what was locally called Pigeon Pass, now called Skogan Pass, to the Kananaskis Valley at Ribbon Creek. In 1936 this trail was widened and a telephone line ran along it on trees from the Dead Man's Flats ranger cabin to Boundary Cabin, then to the Kananaskis Lakes Cabin and Mud Lake Cabin.

In 1934, the relief camp at the Kananaskis Forest Experiment Station constructed 20 miles of road from Seebe to the experiment station headquarters. In 1936, the first Forestry Trunk Road was built. Sections were often in bad condition and necessitated constant repair. In spite of this, the first automobile entered the valley in 1936. "Leaping Lena," driven by Bob Bell and owned by Calgary Power, plied her way up and down the valley with many a hair-raising incident. The Model T Ford wasn't much more than a motor, a seat and four wheels, with a box on the back for supplies and antlers mounted on the front. The high clearance of the car enabled it to travel the rutted road when nothing else could get through. In 1946 Leaping Lena was replaced by a four-wheel drive Dodge power wagon equipped with a winch but lacking the character of its predecessor.

The portion of the road from Seebe to Ribbon Creek was improved during the time the Kananaskis Exploration & Development Company was operating the mine on Mount Allan. Norman Holt, who had the contract for hauling coal from the Ribbon Creek mine, maintained the road from the Forest Experiment Station south to Ribbon Creek. This section was not well engineered and minor accidents did occur. Truckers continually warned each other not to meet on the one-lane bridges. In spite of these warnings, two trucks met on a bridge and wiped out the rails. The road over Barrier Hill, at that time, was much steeper than it is today, as there was no rock cut to lower the grade. During the winter months coal trucks had to be winched up the hill. A truck was maintained at the top for this purpose.

The road from Ribbon Creek south to the Kananaskis Lakes was continually in need of repair. Joe Kovach, the ranger, spent a major portion of his time maintaining the road just so he could use it. It was difficult to negotiate at the best of times and proved to be a hazard for many years.

There are many places where one can find sections of the old roads into the valley, but I have never been successful in finding the early trail.

The Alberta government commenced construction of the new Forestry Trunk Road from Coleman to Seebe in about 1948. It officially opened in 1952. The road took a higher route than its predecessor, thus avoiding wet sections. It was a good gravel road and was instrumental in opening up the valley to tourists. Upon completion, the road had the distinction of being the highest engineered road in Canada where it crossed the Highwood Pass summit. At 2206.3 metres (7,239 ft.), it was only 92 metres (300 ft.) below timberline.

The completion of the trunk road was followed by the establishment of a permanent ranger station in 1952/53, near the site of Boundary Cabin, which had been in existence at the junction of the Kananaskis River and Ribbon Creek for many years. The ranger was, essentially, a support to the recreationists now entering the valley in much larger numbers.

During Gordon Matthews' tenure as ranger, the rerouting of Ribbon Creek took place. Originally the creek flowed under the Ribbon Creek Road (currently known as the Nakiska Road), which for many years was subject to flooding. The Alberta Forest Service decided it would be advantageous to divert the creek away from the road. This diversion took place in 1963 or 1964. Two caterpillar tractors dredged a channel south of the Ribbon Creek Road. The old channel eventually became clogged with silt, rock and debris, but was enhanced during the development of Kananaskis Country and, in particular, during the building of the day-use area called Kovach Pond. In the 1990s part of the creek was diverted back to its original creekbed for runoff from Kovach Pond.

When the Matthews came to the Kananaskis Valley, the bridge over the Kananaskis River on the Ribbon Creek Road was the old log bridge built by the Eau Claire and Bow River Lumber Company. This bridge sagged badly and was, therefore, closed to public traffic. As enforcement there were two gates on the bridge, one at each end, but foot traffic was allowed. The bridge was replaced with a timber bridge painted blue. As the development of Kananaskis Village and Nakiska Ski Resort progressed, a new road was built, slightly rerouted, and a modern bridge installed, clad with Rundle stone.

The Kananaskis Country planned development was evident in 1972 when clearing of the right-of-way was begun for Highway #40 (Kananaskis Trail), which was to replace the Forestry Trunk Road. Construction began in 1973.

The Forestry Trunk Road from Highway #1 took a more westerly route than the present Highway #40. It turned off the Trans-Canada Highway at Fort

Chiniquay where there was a service station and restaurant. I understood the owner of the service station wanted more money than the Alberta government was willing to pay for his property, so the new highway was built farther east.

During the initial work for Highway #40 a number of concerned individuals formed the Kananaskis Action Committee to protest the design of the road. The committee felt the road design would allow for too high a vehicle speed, and it was felt the province should pave the Forestry Trunk Road rather than build a completely new highway. It was also felt there would be less damage to the environment if the

Picnic shelter on 1936 road before Barrier Lake existed.

width of the road was narrower than 60 metres. Their efforts resulted in a narrowing of the right-of-way through the Stoney Indian Reserve and from mile 15 south from the originally planned 60 metres to 36 metres.

Lusk Creek

There are interesting stories about some of the places along Highway #40. Driving south one passes Lusk Creek, which, it is assumed, was named after Tom Lusk, one of the more colourful characters to leave his name in the valley. Lusk, from Morley, was head packer for Nordegg's outfit on his 1907 trip to the Kananaskis and Brazeau coal fields. Nordegg's own words portray a graphic picture of this interesting man:

> And while we partook of some more cool beer in the cellar, somebody stumbled down the ladder. In strutted an old cowboy, dressed in buckskins. He was properly introduced as the famous Tom Lusk, our head packer. He had spent his life in Texas and had come north only a dozen years ago.
>
> Tom squatted on the floor. The factor offered him a glass of beer, with a knowing grin, but Tom declined with a shudder. He pulled from his chaps a large bottle of whiskey, took a very long drink interrupted by gurgling, and then smacked his lips. When he took the bottle out of his face I saw that the contents had dwindled to nearly half. He wore a Stetson hat, and a red bandanna decorated his neck. The silver spurs on his high Strathcona boots tinkled like bells. His leather belt was studded with silver nails. He looked like a figure from a Wild West show.
>
> As long as we were at Morley, his eyes appeared to me glassy, and I began to believe that this was their natural appearance. But when I noticed the copious drinks which he took so frequently, I had doubts and asked Dowling. He replied that Tom never took a drink on the trail for several reasons. Bottles are too fragile, and the weight of many cases had to be taken into consideration, as they would have required several more packhorses. But at the finish of the season's work all these reasons do not exist any more; then he invests his hard-

earned wages in liquor and retires with many cases to his cabin near Morley. The Indian agent and the neighbours watch the smoke from his chimney. When that stops they pay a courtesy call to see if they have to relight the fire or just prepare a funeral. Tom is very methodical in his habits. He divides his cases and bottles into the six winter months, and allows himself double quantities only on holidays such as Christmas and New Year's.

Tom had been put on a horse already as a child, and he was safer in the saddle than on his feet. Once he visited a friend and drank his host's liquor, was therefore not subject to his own regulations and got consequently very full. When he left he wobbled like a ship in a storm. His friend preferred to put him in the saddle, and he galloped home as if he were quite sober, unsaddled the horse, filled its crib, and went to sleep for two days.

Tom Lusk became a good friend of mine. He was in his late sixties. He carried two revolvers and a large bowie knife. On the revolvers he showed me with great pride several notches, indicating the number of men he had shot, as he said. Dowling thought this possible, because Tom had had to leave Texas very suddenly and never wanted to go back there.

O'Shaughnessy Falls

O'Shaughnessy Falls has its origin at a spring. Originally there were no falls, only a little creek with determination. The creek was determined not to go completely through the culvert and under the road, instead some went over the road. When the Forestry Trunk Road was in existence this was always a difficult spot to cross. If the weather was warm the creek would cut a little ditch across the road and if a car did not creep across, its axle was liable to get broken. If the weather was cold there was 20 feet of ice to slither across.

During construction of the new Kananaskis highway, this little creek was determined not to be deterred! Fortunately, there was one person the creek did not count on having to deal with, and that was John O'Shaughnessy. O'Shaughnessy was the engineer for the highway construction. He had heard of a plan to put a large pipe along the stream and under the culvert in order to control the flow. Since this did not appeal to his aesthetic nature, O'Shaughnessy decided to try another approach and constructed a waterfall, hoping to control the stream. His creativity progressed into landscaping around the waterfall and building a wishing well. The roof for the wishing well was made from a long-defunct sign on the Forestry Trunk Road. All the hard work and late hours on the site came out of O'Shaughnessy's spare time. Someone in the Canadian Forestry Service named the falls and it was some months later when John O'Shaughnessy learned it was named in his honour.

Some time in the 1970s or '80s, someone in Kananaskis Country decided to tear down the wishing well. Warren Harbeck, who was working for the Stoney Indians, got wind of this and started a petition against the demolition. He acquired 400 names and when the petition was submitted, it had the desired affect and the wishing well was rebuilt.

O'Shaughnessy himself was an interesting character. He told me he was born in Ireland with a silver spoon in his mouth. At the age of 16 he was a celebrated tennis player and went all over Europe and Russia playing competi-

Drawing of O'Shaughnessy Falls, 1979.

tive tennis. He spent a week living in the palace in Denmark and played tennis with the King of Denmark. After coming to Canada he worked on the Alaska highway in the Yukon Territory and got buried by a blast of rock. When he was rescued his face was badly crushed and "looked like spaghetti." He had surgery at the Mayo Clinic in the United States and afterwards one would never have known he was injured. He died in September 1986 at the age of 58.

Mount Lorette Ponds

The ponds are natural, originally part of the Kananaskis River where an oxbow was formed. When Highway #40 was built the engineers didn't want to put in two bridges over the river as they are very expensive to maintain. They dug a new channel for the river, west of the road, and lined it with big rocks. This diverted the river in a straight line, leaving the beaver to maintain what was then named Mount Lorette Ponds. The site was subsequently developed by Kananaskis Country for handicapped people in wheelchairs and limited mobility so they could fish. Today it is one of the most popular picnic spots in the valley and is not restricted to handicapped people. There are pleasant trails around the ponds and a couple of bridges. The beaver have built some small dams and a big lodge for themselves, and can still be seen at dusk or dawn.

$\mathcal{E}$arly $\mathcal{T}$ourists

$\mathcal{R}$ecreation did not play a major role in the valley's history until around the turn of the century when packhorse trips were made from Banff, following the Spray River to the Spray Lakes and through the Smith-Dorrien Valley to the Kananaskis Lakes. These lakes had earned a reputation for unusually large fish because of stocking and outfitters were taking advantage of this and bringing in fishing parties.

Claude Brewster established the Kananaskis Dude Ranch (now called the Kananaskis Guest Ranch) at the confluence of the Bow and Kananaskis rivers in June 1923. He also saw opportunities at the Kananaskis Lakes. Subsequently Floyd Smith, one of his wranglers, took fishing parties to the lakes and later, when the game preserve regulations were removed, he led hunting trips.

The Kananaskis Lakes were also a popular holiday destination for people from the Millarville-Turner Valley ranch lands. A number of Belgian people had immigrated to the Millarville area in the early 1900s, which probably resulted in a Belgian military official, who was on an emigration promotion tour, making a well-publicized trip into the Kananaskis Lakes in 1911.

Elizabeth Rummel often spoke to me about the 12 consecutive holidays she, her sisters, their spouses and friends spent at the Kananaskis Lakes. They were

Highwood Pass, 1937. Photo NA--33-555: R. M. Patterson.
Courtesy: Whyte Museum of the Canadian Rockies.

Belgian military official pack trip at trapper's cabin near Kananaskis Lakes. Seated centre is Belgian military official and his wife behind him, George Pocaterra seated right, men at doorway: seated left and standing right are the Ford boys, 1911. Photo NA-2158-1 courtesy: Glenbow-Alberta Institute.

fascinated by Jack Fuller's remarkable carving of a naked lady on a live tree near the Lower Kananaskis Lake ranger cabin. She talked of the beautiful waterfall between the two lakes and the wonderful fishing. Lizzie and her family spent two days making the 60-mile ride from Millarville. The usual route was to follow the Sheep River to Burns Mine, climb the steep trail over Rickert's Pass to Mist Creek, then follow Storm Creek over Highwood Pass to Lower Kananaskis Lake where their favourite camping spot was located. The first night's camp was on the Sheep River. In her ongoing effort to lose weight, Lizzie's sister, Jane Fisher, used to run in front of her horse for the 60 mile trip! The return route was via Elbow Lake and Elbow Pass to the Sheep River. Portions of this old trail can still be found between Highway #40 and Elbow Lake and beyond the lake to the present Sheep Trail.

Lizzie's family started visiting the Kananaskis Lakes around 1920 or 1922. The summer of 1932, they discovered Calgary Power was felling trees at Upper Kananaskis Lake and building a dam. They were heartbroken. The beautiful wilderness they had all come to love and enjoy was shattered. With bitterness in her voice, Lizzie said, "We never went back again."

When the first proper road was built in the Kananaskis Valley in 1936, picnic shelters were erected on the Kananaskis Forest Experiment Station lands for the use of travellers. One of these shelters is still standing; hidden in the woods south of Mount Lorette Ponds. It was the completion of the Forestry Trunk

177

Upper Kananaskis Lake, 1922. Left to right: Elizabeth Rummel, Johnny MacGregor, Nina Rogers, Jane Fisher. Photo: Elizabeth Rummel.

Kananaskis River between Lower and Upper Kananaskis Lakes, 1922. Photo: Elizabeth Rummel.

Fishing at Upper Kananaskis Lake, 1922. Left to right: Paddy and Nina Rogers, Elizabeth Rummel, Gayla Archipenko, Johnny MacGregor. Photo: Elizabeth Rummel.

Camping at Kananaskis Lakes, 1922. Left to right: Nina and Paddy Rogers, Bob Carry, Jane Fisher, Bobby McKay, Dorothy Thomas, Elizabeth Rummel. Photo: Elizabeth Rummel.

Road in 1952 that was responsible for bringing in a different kind of person: the modern-day tourist. People started to look at the valley as a place to camp, hike, climb and fish on a much larger scale than what occurred previously. The Eastern Rockies Forest Conservation Board set up a road registration system upon completion of the new Forestry Trunk Road. The system was instituted to establish responsibility for forest fires, to estimate annual use of the road, to ascertain visitors' reasons for travelling and to track down stranded people.

In the 1960s, the incredible rise in the city of Calgary's population started to have an effect on the valley. Over the years Banff National Park has become increasingly more crowded, and with the rise in park entrance fees in the 1990s the result has been an increase of visitors to Kananaskis Valley and Kananaskis Country as a whole. Nineteen ninety five alone saw a 12 per cent increase.

Flatbed scow on Lower Kananaskis Lake, 1922. Left to right: Margery Glaister, Elizabeth Rummel, Johnny MacGregor. Photo: Elizabeth Rummel.

Enjoying the Valley

7

Introduction

Tessy Bray

My parents immigrated to Canada in 1956 from Holland. What my parents loved about Canada was the wilderness. Although we lived in various places, when we lived around Calgary my parents discovered Kananaskis. I first remember going there when I was quite young—preschool or just starting school. It would have been in the late fifties or early sixties.

We always went to the same spot, which not until years later did I discover was Lusk Creek. I remember that after leaving the highway we travelled on a trail, which went through numerous cattle guards and gates. It was an adventurous expedition driving out there because the road was winding and rough.

My parents built a firepit with rocks at an open area with big conifers by Lusk Creek. That was when my dad first taught me how to gather little twigs off the spruce and build a fire. We always had a picnic supper and would sometimes stay until the stars came out. This would have been 10 or 11 at night, so it was a big deal.

My dad loved fishing and he had a hole that was close to our little spot. We mostly played in the creek, but not far from there—this is behind the Tim Horton Ranch—there was a big hole, like a big spring or pond. It wasn't part of the creek. That place was great for hours of exploring, but it made me nervous because the bottom was really slimy. We used to catch bugs and play around the edges.

My sister and her friend found a baby robin with a broken wing that had fallen out of a nest in some apartments in Calgary. My sister adopted this little thing and took it home. We fed it milk with an eye dropper, and when it got a little stronger we fed it cat food. My dad fashioned a little cage out of an orange crate with a stove or firepit grill. We started taking the robin out to Kananaskis with us in his little cage. We thought it would be great if he could fly free, so we would let him out and he would sort of hover around us. Sometimes he would disappear for part of the day, but it never failed that when it came time to go home and we were packing up the car, back in his cage he would be! Eventually the robin was comfortable and would go away for longer times, until finally one time he didn't come back to his little cage when we went home. Sometimes when we went back there we thought he might be around, but I don't recall ever seeing him again.

My mom wanted to be cremated after she died, and I wanted to sprinkle her ashes around that special spot, but I didn't know exactly where it was in relation to how things are now. My husband *(John Dupuis)* and I decided to explore one day to see if we could find it. We searched for about an hour and were successful! The old firepit was in the same place that I remembered. I looked up at the horizon and saw the exact same view that I had always seen. You can't see that view from the highway—only from that spot.

I started getting into hiking, backpacking and cross-country skiing with friends around 17 years of age. I used the national park, because Kananaskis was unknown and completely undeveloped. And being a much less experienced outdoors person than I am now, I wouldn't have thought to go off trail or cross country. I began using Kananaskis again in my twenties with Alf Skrastins. Alf was a died-in-the-wool user of Kananaskis Country, and he did lots of things off trails. That was in the late seventies, early eighties.

John Dupuis
I take kids from Bishop Pinkham Junior High School and do trips, like skiing from the Ribbon Creek Hostel or wherever there is snow. We also do a trip where we cycle up Highwood Pass from the Highwood River side to the pass. I like that excursion because the highway is closed at the time, and it eliminates a big variable I can't control, and that is flaggers on the road.

Last year we did a white water trip with the grade nines. We worked out of the Pocaterra Group Camp and paddled on the Bow River and the section of the Kananaskis River below the race course down to the Bow River.

We go up to Fortress Mountain and north of the parking lot three or four hundred metres we have a snow shelter evening where the kids spend a day building shelters. We dig in and spend the night. If they don't do a good job and I've got cold kids, I can just pull them down to the parking lot and send them home or put them up in the hotel.

$\mathcal{F}acilities$

Campgrounds

Although camping was allowed anywhere on Alberta Forestry Reserve land, the Kananaskis Valley held five official campsites by 1970. Two of the campgrounds were located at Kananaskis Lakes (by Boulton Creek Campground at Lower Kananaskis Lake and Interlakes Campground between the two lakes), another at the old lumber campsite of Eau Claire and Bow River Lumber Company (Eau Claire), one at Ribbon Creek and one at the mouth of Evan-Thomas Creek (Evan-Thomas). A group campsite was situated about half a kilometre south of the Kananaskis Ranger Station. For some years the Church of Jesus Christ of Latter Day Saints operated a summer youth camp along Pocaterra Creek where the Pocaterra Group Camp is today.

When Kananaskis Provincial Park was created in 1975 it began a period of facility development. The Evan-Thomas Creek Campground was expanded and upgraded in 1984 into the present Mount Kidd Recreational Vehicle Park, which has been privately operated by Barry and Philip James since it was developed, through their company Mount Kidd R.V. Park Ltd.. It offers everything from full camper hookups to a hot tub, convenience store, snack bar, showers and other amenities.

Param Sekhon

Construction started on Mount Kidd R.V. Park in late '82 or early '83. When we looked at the facility it was a Class-A campground, but in summer it can get warm and dry and all the roads in the campground were gravel, so it could get very dusty. I remember that on the 27th of August, which is my birthday, we met in Kananaskis to do the inspection with the managing director of Kananaskis Country, Ed Marshall, who wanted all the main roads to be paved immediately. For budget reasons it had to be done before the end of March of the following year, but paving cannot be done between November and March because of our winters. We put together the complete tender package within about two weeks, which amounted to about half a million dollars worth of work. We had to public tender it, which could take two to three weeks. The contract was awarded the beginning of October and by the first week of November every road was paved. As I recall, as soon as we finished the snow started. It worked out well.

The campground at Ribbon Creek was closed and the Eau Claire Campground was upgraded. New campgrounds were built in what is now Peter Lougheed Provincial Park: Canyon, Elkwood, Boulton Creek, Lower Lake, Mount Sarrail, Interlakes and William Watson Lodge for special needs camping. All became extremely popular.

Group campgrounds are available in the valley: Lower Lake Campground and a walk-in one at Pocaterra Creek, both in Peter Lougheed Provincial Park, as well as a basic one at Porcupine Creek just off Highway #40. Plus there is Canoe Meadows, which is for river users only.

Alberta government budget restraints resulted in the valley campgrounds being turned over to private operators in 1995. Kananaskis Camping, owned by Ken and Judy Nichol, operates all the campgrounds in Peter Lougheed Provincial Park, as well as Eau Claire Campground. Sundance Lodges, owned by Brian and Sheryl Green, opened in 1992. Authentic Canadian-made teepees give visitors a unique camping experience.

Ribbon Creek Hostel

The history of the Ribbon Creek Hostel goes back to late 1959 when the Canadian Youth Hostels Association (CYHA) started looking outside the national parks for a hostel site. The Kananaskis Valley seemed more promising than another possible site near Canmore. Fred Daw, one of the hostellers, told Ray Marriner (then president of the Mountain Region of CYHA) about the mining village schoolhouse at Ribbon Creek. All attempts to purchase the building failed until Jim Cunningham saw a legal notice for tender in the Calgary Herald for the purchase and removal of the schoolhouse. It was being sold by one of the local school districts. Upon checking with the school district assistant superintendent, Marriner was informed someone from Canmore had offered $100 for the building the previous year. The CYHA put in a bid for $105! They acquired the building on October 11, 1960, as well as a miscellaneous lease for the land from the Department of Lands and Forests on October 24, 1961.

In 1963, Jim Lisoway, the new president of the hostel region, in a "classic example of hostel enthusiasm, decided to turn the structure into an A-frame."

Ray Marriner

We started by dismantling the roof, then sawing the side walls off about three feet from the ground. We then used the completely inadequate lumber from the old rafters to make the A rafters. A properly constructed A-frame building is one of the strongest structures, but our new hostel was anything but! By the time the shingles were applied to the roof the whole building was so unstable the sides of the roof would flap in and out in a strong breeze.

Fortunately for everyone, Neil Worley arrived on the scene and put his draftsman's knowledge to work. With the help of volunteers, internal partitions were added and the structure was divided into two floors, thus "preventing the whole building from collapsing."

The demand for a larger and better hostel was evident by 1969. The A-frame building had deteriorated considerably and become overridden with pack rats. On one occasion Mary Campbell insisted her husband, Don, set up their tent outside the hostel as she was certainly not going to sleep with the pack rats!

Neil Worley again put his pen to draftsman paper and designed a new building, starting first with two dormitories and a kitchen-dining room. Don Campbell, in another classic example of hostel enthusiasm, acquired some books on the Calgary Stampede and a number of eager hostellers tramped door-to-door in Calgary selling them. The $1,000 that was raised through this project was the first money put toward the new hostel building. After acquiring more financing, the executive committee of the association took the building plans to the Cee-Der-Log Company who delivered the construction materials to the site. Hostel volunteers erected the building during a succession of work parties.

This basic building of two dorms and a kitchen-dining room was officially opened on July 20, 1970. The work was truly a "Worley Enterprise." Not only did Neil Worley design the building, but he was the main power-drive behind the construction.

It was not long before an addition to the building was necessary. In the spring of 1971, a large common room, four family rooms and a houseparent's quarters were added. The addition of these rooms proved to be an asset. Families were soon beating a path to the hostel. Two more construction projects took

Construction of the A frame youth hostel at Ribbon Creek, 1963. Photo NA-2468-14 courtesy: Glenbow-Alberta Institute.

185

Ribbon Creek Hostel, c. 1975. Photo: Ron Hopf.

place soon after. The fireplace that had been built in the common room had been improperly constructed. It smoked so badly that it required replacement with a metal unit that was overlaid with rock. That was in the fall of 1972. The fireplace was again reconstructed in the 1980s.

During the summers of 1971/72, with the benefit of a Local Initiatives Program grant (LIP), volunteers also dug under the building for a basement. This was suitably dubbed "the pit" by the diggers. The last development took place in 1987 when a portion of the basement had sleeping rooms and showers added.

Demolition of the A-frame structure, which had been used for storage since completion of the new building, improved the appearance of the hostel grounds. In the summer of 1975 Spud McCormac, the operator of the nearby stone quarry, donated 12 yards of topsoil for flower gardens and lawn.

Initially the hostel association employed a summer houseparent (now called hostel managers), who was in residence during July and August. With the building of new facilities it was felt a permanent houseparent should be installed. Therefore, in the fall of 1971, Alex (a New Zealander) and Phillippa (Pip) Buchanan (a Tasmanian) assumed the duties. This interesting couple had travelled in South America and acquired a monkey, which they brought with them to Canada and to the hostel. This monkey proved to be infamous, as he was tied up in a corner of the hostel and would bite anyone who came near.

The Buchanans were replaced in the spring of 1972 by Sylvia Hassett who received a proposal of marriage from her future husband while at Ribbon Creek Hostel. In September of that year I took over the management and stayed until the end of 1978. Since that time the hostel has seen a succession of hostel managers.

One such was Heather MacLaurin who spent two years there in 1979/80. She added to the romantic flavour of the Kananaskis Valley, when, after having moved on to other things, she came back to Ribbon Creek to get married in Hay Meadow, a kilometre along the Hay Meadow Trail from the hostel.

When MacLaurin was the houseparent she had a cat named Tiger. At one point she decided to wean Tiger off cat food so it would catch more mice. However, this didn't work too well. One day, while she was having tea with a friend, the cat came around a corner of the building with a spruce grouse in its mouth. It deposited the grouse on the step and went away. Another time it caught a couple of short-tailed ermine and a Steller's Jay who ended up in Alberta by mistake. (They are rarely found east of the Continental Divide.) The rangers were coming around to see this jay, until the cat got it! After that MacLaurin bought more cat food rather than see the bird life decimated.

Gerry (alias Clogs because she is Dutch) and Tim Dormain arrived at the hostel in 1989 with their two children, and as of 1996 they are still there. They have educated their children through home schooling for several years. History may be repeating itself as they call their home school the Ribbon Creek School.

I moved to Ribbon Creek Hostel on August 1st, 1972. My duties commenced on September 1st.

During my time at the hostel it never had a telephone. The nearest one was at the University of Calgary research centre, 16 kilometres down the road. Gordon and Ida Matthews were living at the ranger station, where the Kananaskis Emergency Services Centre is today, and there was a fellow who acted as custodian at the bankrupt Snowridge Ski Resort (the present Fortress Mountain Resort). He used to leave his car at the bottom of the Snowridge road and snowmobile up to the lodge in the winter. Occasionally he'd come down to the hostel for a visit. The four of us were the only people living south of Barrier Lake at that time.

I received my mail in Seebe. Whenever they were coming down the valley the staff from Calgary Power would bring it to the ranger station along with mail for the Matthews. I would walk over and combine a visit with my mail pick-up. That was how I inadvertently learned how to preserve fruit. I went over one day when Ida was in the thick of canning, so I just pitched in and helped her. It was the greatest way to learn and after that I got about three cases of fruit every summer and canned like crazy.

As soon as I arrived at Ribbon Creek I wandered around the trails and old roads. I found all kinds of interesting things; a couple of dynamite sheds, old dumps (I still have two big pots and a coal scuttle I use for flowers), bits of old buildings and lots of old roads. I helped Don Gardner map the best ones for cross-country skiing and hiking trails. I also contributed to the naming of the trails we found, but it was Don who named Ruthie's Trail. When I go back to hike them, it's like visiting old friends.

I had my own favourite spots. On Mondays, the day I washed the hostel floors and things like that, I usually finished my work about 2:00 pm. I would make a thermos of tea and then either ski or hike, depending on the season, up Barclay Trail to Stump Meadow, and sit on a stump for afternoon tea. Barclay Trail is now called Coal Mine Trail. Sometimes I took my tea break on Terrace

Trail where the Kananaskis Village is today. Both places gave me a wonderful view of Mount McDougall and the valley.

The hostel wasn't very busy on week days, except in the spring and fall when school groups came in droves. The weekends were very busy during the cross-country ski season. In those days, summers were quiet as hostellers often camped, so I would get a hostel-sitter and take three weeks off to go backpacking with friends. By the time I left we were getting around 4,000 overnights a year.

When I arrived at the hostel in '72, I had a cat called Kitty. I was only at the hostel a few days when Kitty disappeared. She showed up many days later in the army camp office, along with the army cat, and came home pregnant. The cat had four kittens and I named one Ribbon, after the hostel, and the others after the mountains. I gave three of the kittens away, but kept Ribbon and the mother.

When the coyotes got Kitty, someone offered me another cat, and suggested the name Creek. So I ended up with Ribbon and Creek. The little children who regularly came to the hostel could often be heard prancing through the building singing: "the Ribbon Creek cats, the Ribbon Creek cats." They loved the double meaning. Creekie was a very mild cat, but Ribbon was a real character. Every night, about ten o'clock, he would go into the common room and start howling at everyone. He was telling them it was time to go to bed as 10:30 was curfew! Ribbon lived to be 15 years old and I buried him near the hostel, even though I was no longer living there. Creekie lived to be 17 years old and is buried in Exshaw near my house.

Ruthie's trail, 1984.
Photo: Barbara Snyder

One time Don Gardner and John and Kathy Calvert were snowed in at the hostel. They had come out to Ribbon Creek from Calgary for a day of cross-country skiing, but with the -20°F temperatures they weren't able to get their car going, and ended up staying the night. It had been snowing all day and by morning there was a metre of fresh snow on the ground. Of course, we ran out of propane fuel at the same time, so we had no heat! We spent our time sitting in front of the fire trying to keep warm. The next day it was still snowing and Gardner was desperate to get back to Calgary as he had something important

Creek and Ribbon.
Photo: Ruth Oltmann.

to attend to, so he and I skied over to the ranger station so he could make contact with the outside world via the Matthews' forestry radio.

Skiing in a metre of snow is difficult—difficult for me, that is, but not for Don Gardner. He just skipped over the top of the snow with his skis going like crazy. I had to double kick every step behind him! I don't think he hit bottom once in that light, fluffy snow. He was a cross-country ski racer at the time, on one of the national teams.

The second night of the snowstorm we were all sitting around the fire, when suddenly John jumped up and went outside. He came back in and stated that a chinook had blown in and the temperature had risen to +33°F. It took about one hour for the temperature to change 53 degrees! Then it started to rain, and it rained for two days and two nights. All the snow hardened and the poor animals had a terrible time getting something to eat.

During my time at the hostel the Forestry Trunk Road (today's Highway #40) was not plowed regularly. It was just two lanes and narrow, with no shoulders. Calgary Power would bring in their V-shaped plow when they couldn't get through with their own four-wheel drive vehicles, and plow the road the whole width at once. I remember one time when Ida Matthews and I were going to town. Driving up the road in my little car in one foot of snow, we were breaking trail, when suddenly the Calgary Power plow came around a corner, right at us. I headed straight for the ditch, which, fortunately, was not deep at that spot. The plow stopped and pulled us out.

Another time I was coming home with Don Gardner and Dave Smith and a car full of a month's worth of groceries. It was snowing very hard. In those days the road did not go up Barrier Hill through the rock cut, but around the hill where the upper Barrier Lake picnic site is today. I got halfway up the hill, breaking trail in at least a foot of snow, and I couldn't get any farther. I had to back down the hill with my head out the window to see where I was going in the blizzard. We went back to the university's field station. I left my car there, stuffed me and my groceries into Don's car, and eventually arrived back at the hostel. When I went back to get my car a few days later it had two feet of snow on it and a flat tire.

In those days the hostel was closed from 10:00 am to 5:00 pm to encourage people to participate in outdoor activities. Hostels around the world had this policy and they also had unique ways of getting people out of bed. In Scotland, for instance, hostellers have been awoken by bagpipes! I developed my own unique way when Jean Kensit gave me a recorder for Christmas and a book on how to play it. Eventually Marj Stakenas taught me a tune she had composed called Wake up Snowdrop. In the mornings I would walk through the hostel and play this tune. Some people made snide comments, but many others thought it was great and still remember me doing this.

One time I had two young fellows, about 15 years old, who went off for the day and returned in the afternoon with several sticks of dynamite in their hands, wanting to know what to do with them. I was horrified, and told them to carefully put them back where they found them. Fortunately, nothing horrendous happened. They had found the dynamite shed used by the man who operated the Rundle stone quarry at the end of the road. The shed is still there, buried in a man-made hill and very secluded—with no dynamite in it!

The same weekend these same fellows went hiking up Mount Allan. When they got up high, above treeline, they heard several gunshots. They were so scared they raced down the mountain, worried they were being shot at, and in the process fell. One of the boys scraped his thigh badly, and the other injured his leg and limped his way back to the hostel and me for help. I had to nurse them until their parents came.

I think that same hunter was the one I came across when I was taking a short ski up the lower part of Mount Allan Trail. There was snow on the ground—not much—but enough to see tracks of people or animals. When I came upon the hunter he had his gun pointing up the trail. I suggested it wasn't a good place to be as there were 30 school children in the area, as was evidenced by the tracks in the snow. Unfortunately, the hunter didn't seem at all concerned.

I was paid $75 a month when I started running hostels in 1970, and when I moved to Ribbon Creek I got a raise to $85 a month. By the time I quit running hostels eight-and-a-half years later, I was making $215 a month. I didn't pay rent, but I paid everything else. Because the pay was so low, I had to have a part-time job somewhere else. After a year at Ribbon Creek Hostel I realized I was living beyond my means, so I went to the University of Calgary's research centre and got the part-time job I mentioned earlier. After I finished my history book (*The Valley of Rumours ... the Kananaskis*), I started weaving wall hangings and table runners, which I sold to hostellers as a way of increasing my income. Weaving was all the rage then. I had a built-in clientele and I always had orders ahead of time.

All my hiking led me to writing the first trail guide to the valley. I came to know so many beautiful places that I wanted to share with others. That little book came out in 1978 and was called *The Kananaskis Valley Hikers' and X-C Skiers' Guide*. It's been out of print for many years now, but Gillean Daffern has an excellent and much better replacement covering all of Kananaskis Country.

Top: Dave Savage, Mike Youso, Pete Wallis at Ribbon Creek Hostel, 1978. Photo: Ruth Oltmann.
Bottom: Phill Oltmann, *Ruthie* and Kelly at hostel, 1978. Photo: Warren Harbeck.

In my six-and-a-half years at Ribbon Creek Hostel I spent 528 nights alone. People used to think I was crazy, but I loved it. I never felt I was alone. I had my hostellers and I could never feel alone in the mountains.

In spite of my saying this, one terrifying incident happened May 1977. I woke up at 3:30 one morning. I sat on the edge of the bed and heard the floor in the hall outside my door creaking, and the creaking was coming toward my door. I was kind of dazed and just sat there in a stupor. A clear, strong voice said, "Put on your housecoat and slippers," which I immediately did. There was a deadbolt lock on the door and it was locked. Again a voice said, "Hold the lock on the door." I walked over to the door and held the deadbolt in the closed position. As I stood there all was silent, then I heard a hand slowly move across the door. Something sharp went into the lock and the lock turned! Immediately I turned the bolt back to the locked position. I didn't say a word as I didn't want anyone to know there was a woman on the other side of the door.

Creekie, the cat, started scratching at the door. My legs were shaking so much I couldn't stand on one foot to push her aside with the other. "I've got to get out of here," I thought, "before he goes around to the back door and I'm trapped. There may be more than one person." My hiking pack was on a stump near the door, so I reached for it and put it on the floor against the door, thinking it might slow him down. I held the bolt with one hand, but hesitated, because I realized if I let it go I would be in a very vulnerable position. This was probably the scariest moment of my life. All those solo hikes and backpacking trips were nothing compared to this.

I said a big prayer and carefully let go of the lock and walked to the back door. I peered around the window blind and couldn't see anybody, so I unlocked the door and gingerly stepped outside. Since I didn't want "him" seeing the door open if he came around to the back of the building, I quietly closed the door behind me.

Slipping, sliding, falling, picking myself up and scrunching my toes in the ends of my moccasins to keep them from falling off, I ran through the woods and shallow snow to the highway construction camp, where Kovach Pond is today. My pace slowed a little in my relief. I ran through the lighted construction camp kitchen, and finding no one there continued on to the first bunkhouse. Opening the door, I screamed in terror. The fellow whom I woke grunted, staring at me in shock. I started babbling my story and he said he would get the camp foreman. I started to close the door to give him privacy to dress, only to realize I would be out in the dark all alone. So I went back in and sat in the next cubicle, babbling.

I waited in the camp kitchen while he and the foreman drove over to the hostel.

Kelly. Photo: Ruth Oltmann.

They returned and reported that no one could be found, and that my hiking pack had not been moved from beside the door. The camp cook gave me tea while the men drove up the valley to the top of Barrier Hill, the nearest radio contact. The only police were in Canmore, about 62 kilometres away. By the time they arrived it was six in the morning and too late to find anything.

After that Don Campbell put special locks on the doors and I got a dog—a big German Shepherd I called Kelly. He was a great comfort to me and we went everywhere together after that, both summer and winter.

While I didn't see a lot of wildlife around, the area did have lynx. I saw four during quiet times at the hostel. One time I encountered a bobcat no more than five feet from the building. He looked at me for a few seconds and then quietly walked down the trail. Later, Ida Matthews told me there were no bobcats in the valley. I checked all the animal books I had, as well as the ones at the research centre, and I concluded positively that it was a bobcat. Finally, to be real sure, I went to the Calgary Zoo and looked at a live one and compared it to a lynx.

I regularly saw what I called Mrs. Moose in different places. And one morning I woke up to something walking on my back deck. It turned out to be a bear just out of hibernation and looking rather gaunt. We didn't have garbage outside, so we were not usually troubled with bears. When Ida and Gordon Matthews went on their October bird-hunting holiday, their horses, Peanut and Tiddlywinks, would hang around the hostel as they were lonely for people.

One night when the hostel was empty and I was sitting in my quarters reading a book, two bats flew down the chimney and came through the building into my room. They landed on the wall above the outside door. I jumped up and opened the door and turned out the light. One bat flew out, but the other clung to the wall and wouldn't budge. Suddenly someone knocked on the front door of the hostel, and when I opened it there was a gentleman asking for directions to some place in the valley. I gave him the directions and was going to close the door, but on second thought asked him if he knew how to get rid of bats. This man, whom I'd never seen before, put a little box over the bat, against the wall, and slid a flexible piece of cardboard between the wall and the box and very nicely got the bat in the box. He then let it go into the great outdoors and went on his way.

When I left the hostel on January 1, 1979, all I had was $62 to my name after eight-and-a-half years of running hostels. But the money wasn't important as I was working for the love of it. Those years were very important to me. I made many wonderful friends, learned a lot of lessons and developed a lot of skills that enhanced my life. In a way, Ribbon Creek has followed me ever since. Some years later I rented a little house in Exshaw where, I discovered, three of the houses across the street had been moved from the village at Ribbon Creek! In 1992 I was asked to supervise the Kananaskis Village Information Centre. Even though I love all the valley, Ribbon Creek still has a big place in my heart. Going there is always like going home.

Kananaskis Village under construction, 1986. Photo: Param Sekhon.

Kananaskis Village

Set amongst some of the most awesome scenery in the Canadian Rockies, the Kananaskis Village provides hotel accommodation to the tourist. Construction of the resort commenced in 1986. In 1987 it was largely completed, and two of the hotels opened in June of that year.

Today the village consists of two Canadian Pacific hotels (The Lodge at Kananaskis and Hotel Kananaskis), one Best Western hotel (Kananaskis Inn) and the Kananaskis Village Centre, a day lodge open to the public. The village centre provides various amenities, including the Charlie Beil Room with its cozy fireplace and Charlie Beil sculptures inlaid in the rock on the fireplace. In the forest surrounding the hotels are tennis courts, picnic and athletic facilities, and the Village Rim Trail, which gives a panoramic view of the valley.

The Kananaskis Village location is, pictorially, very dramatic and was one of my favourite haunts when I was at Ribbon Creek Hostel. In June 1987, when I was the dinner speaker to 300 conference people in The Lodge at Kananaskis, which is the largest hotel, it gave me a very strange feeling to be sitting at a white linen table with first class food instead of sitting on the ground with a sandwich and thermos of tea.

Param Sekhon
The whole project was referred to as the Alpine Village, and there were three alpine village sites proposed. I'm not able to say where these sites were, but Kananaskis Village, the present site, was chosen for economic reasons, and it seemed there was only one village economically viable at that time. The reason

194

this site was chosen was because there was a lot of existing infrastructure. There was the golf course and Mount Kidd R.V. campground, which is a world-class camping facility. In 1984 Nakiska was started. The utilities—the water and sewer systems—were there too. The announcement of the Olympics was also a catalyst.

The Kananaskis Village master plan had been floating around for a number of years. The problem was finding developers who were willing to come to the site and invest their money. It was a long process, but in approximately 1985 something must have happened, because all of a sudden three developers were willing to build the three hotels. The project was supposed to take three years to finish. When the developers became involved and heard about the World Cup being staged in '87 and the Olympics in '88, they wanted to open for these events. Development did not start until early '86.

Public Works *(of the government of Alberta)* was responsible for constructing the day lodge and completing the infrastructure, landscaping, utilities, maintenance building and things like that. We were almost 70 to 80 per cent complete for the World Cup. Some of the inner courtyard areas were not finished, but we had the roads done, and all the access roads to the hotels and the entrances, so that at least people could come and stay at the hotels. The whole project was finished in '87. It was a very, very busy period for us.

Cottages

In 1961, the Eastern Rockies Forest Conservation Board leased 70 lots on Lower Kananaskis Lake. Each applicant paid a $5.00 initial fee and a $30.00 annual rental fee, agreeing to build a cottage to government specifications within two years' time. There are now 75 cottages, most of which are used during summer months, although more and more winter usage is taking place. The owners of these cottages formed the Kananaskis Association, whose purpose is to provide a united representation to the improvement district, and negotiated to have the cottage road plowed in the winter.

Over the years some of the cottages have changed hands through sales, and some are seeing use by a second generation.

A Lower Kananaskis Lake cottage, 1975. Photo: Ruth Oltmann.

Boundary Ranch

Boundary Stables was the original name of Boundary Ranch, the only dude ranch in the valley. It is owned and operated by Rick and Denise Guinn who set up the business in July 1987. At that time the site was just willow trees and bush, so the Guinns lived in tents. They received permits to build in the fall of that year. The house and office were built first, then Elkhorn Hall. The hall was originally supposed to be a barn, but the film company Lorimar Productions wanted to use it as a set for their movie *Dead Bang* starring Don Johnson, so another barn was built for the horses. The barbecue business grew quickly, and in 1991 a second hall, Kiska Lodge, was built to accommodate about 350 people. It is unique in that it is octagonal, with plate glass windows and a Rundle rock fireplace. The ranch offers visitors day rides and backcountry riding adventures. The ranch also offers hay rides and sleigh rides at Kananaskis Village in the winter and they operate the Tim Horton Children's Ranch riding program. This is a great opportunity for both the ranch and the children's program.

Rick Guinn is the son of Alvin Guinn of Guinn's Pass. He was raised on Rafter Six Ranch—probably on the back of a horse—which his father owned at one time.

Tim Horton Children's Ranch

The Tim Horton Children's Ranch was officially opened June 22, 1991, as the third camp of the Tim Horton Children's Foundation. Their aim is, "to help children whose circumstances are more difficult than most was conceived after his untimely death in February 1974. The foundation is a non-profit, charitable organization committed to providing a summer camp environment for children from local communities who come from monetarily under privileged homes."[1] The children participate in a wide variety of activities, including white water rafting on the Kananaskis River, rock climbing at Mount Yamnuska and Wasootch Cliffs, and horseback riding at Boundary Ranch. The children's camps run for 10 days each during July and August.

Fortress Mountain

In 1966 the Eastern Rockies Forest Conservation Board approved the development of the Snowridge Ski Resort in the Kananaskis Range. The Snowridge Ski Development Company was formed in April 1967, with Arnold Choquette, a Calgary geologist, as president, and Al Compton as director. The brothers Reed, Evan and Bruce Bullock obtained an interest shortly thereafter. The development was built high above the valley floor below Fortress Mountain at an approximate elevation of 1950 metres. The yearly snowfall had been calculated, according to a 10-year observation, at five to seven feet per year. Construction began in 1968 and was completed in 1969. The ski area provided a hotel as well as day-use facilities, and was equipped with two T-bars and a chair lift. Access was by a eight kilometre-long gravel road off the Forestry Trunk Road (now Highway #40).

Dr. Floyd Snyder

The story Bernie Woods told me about Snowridge was about when the army was there and the sarge led the troops down the hill. I forget the configuration, but there was a fairly steep bowl in the centre somewhere, not a very big bowl. The sarge skied down and made some kind of a corner and hid underneath a cornice or something like that. Most of these people couldn't do very decent turns, and I guess the rest of the troops would come whipping around, fail to negotiate the corner, and go flying over the lip. I don't know how many bodies there were, but a pile of them ended up on the other side in the snowbank.

Another time they were supposedly going up the chair on the backside and just before the sergeant and his partner dismounted, the sergeant looked over his shoulder and yelled at the pair behind him to jump, so they would know how to disembark off the lift. He and his partner got safely off and slid down and made the corner, but the pair on the chair behind him turned to pass the message on to the pair behind them before they jumped—that must have been a few feet down. Then the pair behind them passed the message on—they were even higher off the ground—and so on, continuing down the whole chair lift line. They all disembarked right where they were! Some of them apparently broke bones. Some of them fell a long ways. I guess the ski patrol had more injured people than they had sleds and patrollers to haul bodies out of there.

The point of that story is to understand the importance of being a mindless follower of your leader when you are in the army! Oh, and they had suicide bindings, so you can understand how some of them broke themselves up.

By 1970 Snowridge had come under the direct control of Greyhound Leasing and Finance Company of Canada, a subsidiary of Greyhound Bus Lines. Greyhound assigned the responsibility of the physical operation of the ski lifts and the 140-bed lodge to Brewster Transport Company Ltd. of Banff, also a Greyhound subsidiary at that time. Approximately a year-and-a-half after it opened the development went bankrupt. A caretaker remained on the site but all the facilities were closed down.

The venture was not totally abandoned. In the fall of 1974, while still in receivership, the lodge and ski area were brought back to life and reopened for the 1974/75 ski season. Humat Management and Consultants of British Columbia became the manager, and the area was renamed Fortress Mountain Resorts. Hugh Smythe managed the ski area and Dave Matthews operated the hotel.

In June 1975, the Federal Business Development Bank sold half its interest in the skiing facilities to Aspen Ski Corporation. During the summer of 1975, $1,000,000 was invested in staff housing, a maintenance garage, a ticket wicket trailer and a triple chair lift. On October 1, 1975, Fairmont Hot Springs Resorts obtained a lease to purchase the hotel, renaming it Fortress Mountain Lodge. Toby Nakamura was appointed general manager, and his wife Rosemary and Carol Wilder were his assistants. Renovations and redecorating took place prior to the opening of the hotel.

The Fortress Mountain Ski Resort then became a viable operation. During the 1974/75 ski season, skier visits totalled 37,000. A year later this figure almost doubled to 70,000. Increased patronage was attributed to the new highway and the triple chair lift. Three Thiokol snow cats and other modern equipment were added. The Aspen Skiing Corporation further expanded during the summer of 1976, with the addition of more staff housing and an administration building that housed first-aid quarters and a ski shop.

Locke, Stock & Barrel Co. Ltd. obtained a half interest in the resort in 1986, and a full interest in 1991. The company has long-term development plans for upgrading the accommodation, and plans for cross-country ski trails and snowmaking facilities.

Fortress Mountain has a reputation for allowing almost anything that other ski areas do not allow. For instance, it is the only ski resort in western Canada to have a homologation speed skiing run (the Third Chute) and a paragliding with skis program. It also offers cat skiing. The resort was the first to host freestyle skiing competitions and is now the only permanent training facility in North America for aerial, mogul and ballet freestyle. The freestyle community considers Fortress Mountain "home." It was also one of the first ski resorts to allow snowboarding and is now a snowboarding mecca. Springtime sees snowboarders trudging up the mountain, long after the lifts have closed for the season.

Nakiska

Like Kananaskis Village, Nakiska was built between 1985 and 1987, initially for the alpine events of the 15th Olympic Winter Games in 1988, but also as a training facility and as a recreational ski resort. The government of Alberta built the resort at a cost of $25.3 million. It opened for the 1986/87 ski season as some ski competitions had to be held before it was viable as an Olympic venue. During the games, people were mostly bussed from Calgary for the events, but large parking lots were also available in Hay Meadow beside the Kananaskis River from where shuttle busses moved people to viewing locations at the base of the ski hill. People from all over the world came to Nakiska to see the slalom, giant slalom and downhill events. The Olympics were a huge success and the world discovered the Kananaskis Valley in the process.

Nakiska comes from the Cree Indian language and means "to meet." This name, along with the names of the ski runs, depicts the association with people of the past. The appropriateness of the name related to the 15th Olympic Winter Games in 1988 when athletes from around the world met at Nakiska.

Ski Kananaskis Inc. was the original leaseholder of Nakiska (the company later changed the name to Rocky Mountain Skiing Inc.). This company managed the resort from 1986 to 1995. In July 1995 a numbered company, in which Charles Locke has an interest, acquired the assignment of the lease.

Dr. Patrick Duffy

I don't know how many people—I don't expect it's many—know that it was in 1957 when the Calgary Ski Club, including Bob Reed, Ed Davis and a few other people, thought it would be possible to hold a Winter Olympic games at Banff and Lake Louise. That winter we all went by train to Revelstoke to the Canadian Ski Association's annual meeting to ask for permission to carry the bid past the ski association to the Calgary Olympic Association, and if they approved then go to the International Olympic Committee.

Since then our mind-set on how we use our national parks has changed considerably, but at that time it was seen as a reasonable thing to do. We did go

Construction of Nakiska Lodge. Photo: Param Sekhon.

Snowmaking on Mt. Allan. Photo: Param Sekhon.

on to bid for the 1972 Olympics and during that four-year period, or maybe it was even longer than that, the lobby from park lovers and environmental groups was such that we were not successful in the next round and Sappora, Japan, got the Olympics. The irony was that the Olympics were held in a national park in Japan.

From that experience another group in Calgary decided they'd like to try for the Olympics at Nakiska and Canmore and they were successful in 1988.

Robert (Bob) Reynolds

Bill Wilson, who was with Travel Alberta, and Lloyd Gallagher looked at various areas for a downhill ski course for the Olympics. They looked at Mount Shark, Mount Sparrowhawk, the area by the gypsum mine in Peter Lougheed Park, the Mount Odlum area and Mount Allan. They also had a consultant doing studies on all the areas. They proved statistically that Mount Allan was the best area to develop, better than all the other ones. So Mount Allan became 'Nakiska at Mount Allan.' The snow reports coming out of there were excellent, regardless of the criticism.

I think the upper hill is limited, both wind- and icing-wise. After a big dump of snow it is fantastic, until it gets skied off. Then it tends to get icy and a little bit dangerous. I find the lower hill at Nakiska one of the nicest ski areas for my age and ability. I don't think the criticism of Mount Allan was that well founded.

Param Sekhon

When I got involved with Nakiska I was working with Public Works (of the government of Alberta) in the development of a number of campgrounds, the golf course clubhouse and a few other major projects. Nakiska came along and, at that time, the Department of Tourism was the group spearheading the project. This group did not have a lot of expertise in technical matters, such as construction costs, what type of construction, scheduling and things like that. They were asking a lot of those kinds of questions, and I remember working late in the evenings preparing information for them. This was on top of our regular work. Eventually some of the senior people in government found out who was preparing all this information. That was the first time it was thought Public Works should be involved, as they had the expertise to handle this project.

The government was still interested in going with a private developer, but none of the private developers had the money for the project, so that's why the government had to step in and develop it themselves. At the same time OCO '88, which was the group looking after the development of the Olympic venues, endorsed Mount Allan as the site for the alpine events. At that time a consortium of consultants was picked to do a master plan. The main consultant was Ecosign from Whistler, B.C., and there was also Land Plan Associates (landscape consultants and planners), Mountain Planning and Management (architects), Stanley Associates Engineering Ltd. (infrastructure) and the Delta Environmental Management Group (snowmaking system). The lifts were by Doppelmyer.

The plan was prepared and the departments made their input as the planning process went along, especially Forestry and Fisheries regarding the environmental issues. Once the master plan was completed, which I believe was in February 1984, the project was passed on to Public Works for implementation. I started looking at it in 1983 for the first time. There was the will on everybody's part to get the project moving as fast as possible. If you look at ski hill development, they are built in bits and pieces generally, but this was the first time a complete development was going to happen in one shot.

We had a lot of interest from ski writers who wanted to come and look at the mountain. I remember a hundred of them came. We gave them a tour of the mountain and told them what the development was going to look like. I remember one of the local writers—it always seems the local writers give you more of a hard time than others—asked me if I knew what the word 'Kananaskis' meant. I had heard the story about an Indian fellow whose name was Kananaskis and that he had met Mr. Palliser's party when he was exploring the region. So I told him this was the guy who survived a wound from an axe and that's how the valley was named. The guy seemed to be very upset. He said, 'No, no, that's not true. Kananaskis means fast flowing water.'

Initially we were not very well set up to handle the project in terms of public relations. One day I was in my Calgary office when we got a call from the federal government that the sports minister, Otto Jelinek, wanted to visit the site and land near Mount Allan in his helicopter around noon. I rushed out to meet him and prepared a pot of coffee in our trailer on site. I was a klutz with that coffee maker, and made coffee that you could float a horseshoe in! When Mr. Jelinek arrived, I asked him if he wanted to look around on the mountain or go to our office and look at the plans. He wanted to look at the plans. I offered him and his two executive assistants coffee, and, of course, the two assistants wouldn't have any when they looked at it, but Mr. Jelinek had some and drank it all!

The ski hill was completed in two years, partly because we got a lot of support from the minister, Tom Chambers. He used to visit us once a month and because he was so actively involved with the project he understood the issues, thus we could get decisions at a high level very quickly.

Activities

Movie-Making

Film companies have taken full advantage of the variety of terrain in the Kananaskis Valley, along with its spectacular scenery. Initially several animal movies were filmed. *Nicky, Dog of the North* was filmed in 1958 by Disney Productions. Art Krowchuk, an animal trainer from Banff, worked on this film, which was a story about a trapper, his husky pup and a bear captured as a young cub. The story, which covered a period of a year in the bear's life, took two-and-a-half years to film. The shooting could not be completed before the original bear's size conflicted with the script, so filming was delayed a year while another bear the proper size was secured. Krowchuk did most of the bear training on location.

The movie's set was built on the west side of Kananaskis Trail (Highway #40), where Canoe Meadows day-use area is today. The big fort was handbuilt by Alvin Guinn, Walter Morris and a few of the cowboys who lived on the Rafter Six Ranch. The teepees were constructed on skids so they could easily be moved with a truck, and all the props and hides came from the Hudson's Bay Company. Don Haldane was the producer and Emile Genest, a Canadian, was one of the actors.

Dr. L. A. (Bud) Smithers

The Disney people came up to make a film, which I think was *Nicky, Dog of the North*. Basically the story related to MacKenzie delta huskies. They are a distinct variety, very long-legged, big, and they stand very high. This young couple had been raising and mushing them up in the Yukon, and Disney hired them to look after these dogs and to rear dogs, because they needed dogs at every stage. At one time they must have had 50 or 60 dogs. Somewhere I have a picture of Alvin Hamilton, he was minister of Agriculture, I think, in the Diefenbaker government. At any rate, he was also minister of Forestry at one time, and he came out to visit the Kananaskis, so we took pictures of him posing with these huskies.

Some of the episodes in the film were extremely interesting. They hired a chap to train black bears and part of the film involved the bear going down the Kananaskis River on a log. The handler was sitting on the rock at Lusk Creek, and the bear had gone down the river and they took him out of the river and brought him back up to Lusk Creek. I guess the bear was pretty annoyed at his handler for the treatment he'd been receiving going down the river, so he walked up and put his mouth on the trainer's shoulder and chomped down! The trainer turned around and hit him with his fist, right on the snout. The poor bear yelped and yowled and jumped back about 20 feet.

The bear was supposed to be a grizzly bear and they'd also gotten a young grizzly from the Calgary Zoo, a two year old. One of the sequences in the film

Alvin Hamilton with Nicky, star of the Disney film *Nicky, Dog of the North*.
Photo: L. A. Smithers.

was the bear chasing the young dog. The dog was to run through a hollow log and the bear was to follow him and get stuck in the log, so the dog could get away. They had this enclosure, perhaps 100 feet across, and they had this cotton-pickin' bear in the enclosure. They'd made this hollow log out of plastic and it was the most realistic Douglas fir log you'd ever seen in your life. The trick was to get the dog to run through first and the bear to run through afterwards. Well, they kept fooling around with different sizes of logs, because they could get the dog to go through, but the bear wouldn't follow. He'd get stuck before he got into the log. They kept getting bigger and bigger logs. Finally they got a log that was big enough for the bear to get through, but then the bear wouldn't get stuck, he could go right through after the dog. This was getting rather hard on the dog!

Some bright character said, 'Let's take an inner tube and put it inside the log and attach a CO_2 cylinder, so when the bear goes through we'll trip the CO_2 cylinder, the inner tube will inflate and he'll be stuck in the log.' This worked marvelously. The dog ran through the log and the bear charged after him and somebody fired off the CO_2 cylinder. The inner tube inflated and the bear was stuck and started to roar. It managed to get up on its hind legs and was charging around the enclosure with the plastic log wrapped around it, roaring. Every time the bear dashed into the fence it would almost fall down. We were all trying to figure out what we would do about this bear if it ever got out of the enclosure. Fortunately, the enclosure held up and they managed to calm the bear down.

It was quite an experience to watch these Disney people work. They would decide they wanted to shoot a fall scene and it would be spring, so they would paint fall colours on all of the foliage. They turned it into a magnificent fall scene. They would go to tremendous lengths to get just what they wanted, when they wanted it.

In one of the scenes the dog had to attack someone. They trained one dog to attack on command and it was the most vicious-looking thing you ever saw in your life. The bear was nothing compared with the husky. The trainer could handle it and had it on a chain. They were taking close ups of the dog's face and this actor was in front of it. They would catch reverse shots (*back and forth from the dog to the actor*) and then shots of the dog snarling and snapping and lunging, and then the chain broke! I don't know who the actor was, but he got well worked over. That dog was just mad.

In 1971, a movie called *Grizzly Adams* was filmed in the valley by the company, Adanac Films. Adanac Films camped on the site of the *Nicky* film's fort. Art Krowchuk again worked as an animal trainer for the film.

Art Krowchuk was also the animal trainer for a movie about Siberian tigers, *Snow Tigers*, filmed in the valley in 1974. Bruno Engler, a Banff photographer, worked as a cameraman. The film featured wild pigs, Japanese deer, wolves, a large Alaskan brown bear, two Siberian tigers and a white tiger. Scenes with the white tiger were shot above timberline on Mount Allan. When a snowstorm blew in, Bruno had visions of trying to get a film crew off the mountain in winter! He didn't want to spend the night on the mountain with a tiger. The white tiger used in the film was one of five in existence, and was worth about $150,000.

Rugged valleys, frozen rivers and plains were all settings needed for the filming. A village scene was shot in Banff, but the main portion of the movie was filmed in the Kananaskis Valley, at Barrier Lake, where a fishing scene was shot (the tiger was actually afraid of the fish), and at locations as far south as Fortress Mountain. I remember seeing the tigers on the riverbed at the junction of Ribbon Creek and the Kananaskis River.

While filming was in progress at Barrier Lake, a snowmobiler happened to see one of the tigers, but not the film crew. He returned to Calgary and told the Mounties what he had seen. They asked him, "How many drinks did you have?" Subsequently, they found out from the local ranger about the filming.

Superman II also used Barrier Dam with the backdrop of Barrier Lake, as well as the Stoney Indian Reserve, for some of the scenes. I didn't know they were filming in the valley when I was driving home to Ribbon Creek Hostel one day and passed the dam. As I drove by and glanced at Barrier Lake I saw a chain link fence across the dam road, a small guard tower-type structure and a great big sign saying "Danforth Missile Base," with an American flag flying beside it. Well, I saw red! "What are those Americans doing in our valley?" I said out loud, and immediately made a U-turn on the road and drove over to the chain link fence with fire in my eyes. I rolled down my car window, but before I could say anything the man at the fence said, "It's okay, lady, we're only making a movie."

Last of the Dogmen was filmed in 1994. Some scenes were shot where King Creek crosses under Highway #40, at the junction with the Kananaskis Lakes Trail. The film crew wanted to drive a vehicle off the road in this area and tear up the ground, but the Peter Lougheed Provincial Park officials wouldn't allow it.

> Calgary Herald: To find the secret Cheyenne settlement in the movie *Last of the Dogmen*, the characters must pass through a mountain cave whose entrance is hidden by a towering waterfall.
>
> In reality, stars Tom Berenger and Barbara Hershey, other actors and horses walked through a fake cave—complete with controlled cascading water—constructed by set builders inside the high-ceilinged Goodstoney Rodeo Centre on the Morley Reserve west of Calgary.
>
> A second fake had to be fabricated outdoors for the moment when the characters emerge on the other side. 'They come out and they see this beautiful valley.... You look down the valley on the Elk Range Mountains. That was done in the Kananaskis near Grizzly Creek.'
>
> A bus wreck, seen in a helicopter shot early in the movie, was created at King Creek in Kananaskis.

In March 1996 the movie *Silent Tears* was filmed near the Barrier Lake Visitor Centre. This was a non-commercial film being made for the professional development of the artists. It had a trapper's tent, partridge flying and shots of children walking. Two dogs, two children and two adults were in the cast.

Wild America was also filmed in 1996. Canoe Meadows was one of the locations.

There are approximately 10 movies and films made each year in Kananaskis Country. The government charges the film companies a fee, which varies, depending on what is required.

It looks like the celluloid will keep rolling on and on!

Ruthie at Ribbon Lake, 1972. Photo: Arnold Hartford.

Hiking

Trails have been around for a long time, but with the creation of Kananaskis Country they were upgraded and developed more for hiking. Later they were used by mountain bikers when that sport became popular. For example, the Ribbon Creek Trail, one of the oldest trails in the north end of the valley, now has bridges for the creek crossings, so one is no longer challenged by the scree slope and its narrow, precipitous trail. For Dennis and Betty Falconer, who hiked Ribbon Creek in the seventies, this scree slope was the terror of their lives and they still talk about it.

Ribbon Lake was originally called Hidden Lake, but at some point in the 1970s it became Ribbon Lake. This is probably because the nearby creek was called Ribbon Creek and you can only have so many hidden lakes before you are totally confused. The route to the lake involves climbing a cliff. When I first came to the valley there was a rope hanging down the cliff. It was attached to a long, iron pin that was stuck in the rock in such a way that when you were lower down and hanging on to the rope it was very secure. If it was pulled from the top it would come out. It was as safe as any old hemp rope can be after hanging exposed to the elements for many years. I always needed the help of the rope for one handhold, but when my friend Arnold Hartford was visiting from Toronto he didn't require the use of the rope at all as he was six feet six inches tall and could reach all the handholds. Today the handholds are all worn away from so much use and one needs help to get up.

The rope was replaced with an iron chain after an accident in the 1970s. A couple of families went up to the lake with two 12 year-old boys. They camped overnight and in the morning the boys started back down the cliff on their own. Subsequently, one of the boys fell. Fortunately, he had a backpack on and when he fell he landed on the big ledge on his back and the pack protected him. He

205

bounced off this ledge and plummeted down the cliff and once more landed on his back in the scree at the bottom. Then he rolled down the slope. Altogether he fell about 46 metres. He received a lot of bruises, but luckily no broken bones. His friend, the other 12 year old, ran down the eight kilometre-long trail to the hostel for help. When he knocked on the door and couldn't get a response, he ran another 1.6 kilometres to the ranger station. A helicopter was brought in and the injured boy was flown to hospital.

Immediately after the accident the Calgary Mountain Club was asked to put a chain on the cliff and keep their mouth shut as to who did it.

Galatea Creek Trail, prior to the upgrading, was always an exciting adventure. The Kananaskis River had to be forded, but this could only be done when the Pocaterra Dam on Lower Kananaskis Lake was closed, otherwise the water was too high and too fast. Many times people would hike up Galatea Creek to Lillian Lake, only to come back later in the day and find they could not cross the river. It was common to see a fire burning on the west side of the river, indicating someone was stranded and waiting for the morning to arrive so the river would go down.

Galatea Creek had 10 logs for bridges, and they were not big logs, so it was a precarious hike to Lillian Lake. Once I was with a party of hostellers led by Don Campbell, when we hiked the trail and went over what is now called Guinn's Pass to Ribbon Lake and down Ribbon Creek. There was no trail over Guinn's Pass and the trip took nine hours. Alvin Guinn cut an eight foot-wide pack trail from Spray Lakes up Buller Creek, over the north Buller Pass to Ribbon Lake,

Hostellers clearing trail in 1974. Photo: Ruth Oltmann.

Upper Kananaskis trail, 1974. Photo: Ruth Oltmann.

over Guinn's Pass (named after him), down Galatea Creek, up Rocky Creek to the Evan-Thomas Creek and thence on to Bragg Creek, in the 1930s. There was no evidence of his trail on the pass when we hiked it.

Prior to the formation of the provincial park, the trails in the valley and around Kananaskis Lakes were very rugged. There was a lot of deadfall, there were no bridges across creeks and no trails were marked. And of course, there was no such thing as a trail guide until 1978 when my little book came out, followed a year later by Gillean Daffern's *Kananaskis Country Trail Guide*, which covered all of K Country.

The first time I tried to go to Lawson Lake and the North Kananaskis Pass was in August 1974. Some friends were going to come with me, but they didn't show up, so I went by myself. I had a 40-pound pack as I was going for five days, and was planning on returning via the Palliser River and Three Isle Lake.

The first challenge was to ford the Upper Kananaskis River not far from the present Point backcountry campground. There was a log jam that one could use, but being alone I preferred to trust my feet rather than take the chance of falling in, so I got my feet, knees and thighs wet. After I crossed Three Isle Creek—and it had to be forded as well, I got lost following someone's orange flagging and spent a fruitless hour wandering around.

I passed what is now the Forks backcountry campground, then followed blazes paralleling the Upper Kananaskis River. I had a topographical map, but no one had told me the trail on the map was not accurate. The willow bushes on the avalanche slope had overgrown the trail, so I never did see where it climbed uphill. I continued following the blazes and the map until I came to a rockslide, where the trail quit and there were no more blazes.

I consulted the map again and figured out exactly where I was. I decided to go up the rockslide, making the assumption that it would have a run out at the top, and hoisted my heavy pack on my back once more. Upon nearing the top of the rockslide I was horrified to see it was a gully with a headwall! It was about 800 feet back down the slope with no place to camp, so I went higher and found three slightly sloping rock ledges on the left-hand side of the cliff.

To make a long story short, I had to climb the first two ledges without my pack on, and then knowing where the foot placements were, go back down and get my pack and carefully climb it all over again. I couldn't climb the third ledge with the pack on as I had to put my foot up around my chin for one move and haul 40 pounds at the same time. Because I only weighed about 115 pounds this was an impossibility. I tried hauling the whole 40 pounds on my rope, but couldn't do it, so I carefully took out my sleeping bag and ensolite and cautiously climbed the cliff with them, depositing them in a safe place so they wouldn't roll back down the slope. Once more I tried hauling the pack. The pack got caught on the cliff, so I had to go back down and put on the pack. With less weight in the pack I was able to make it. When I got to the top I checked my hands and discovered I'd rope burned my fingers when trying to haul the pack. The whole episode was like a living nightmare.

When I finished my first-aid treatment it was seven o'clock at night and I was worn out. All I wanted to do was find some water so I could camp. Walking uphill through the forest I suddenly tripped over the trail! From that point I knew it was only 10 minutes to Lawson Lake. At the lake I found a wonderful little campsite with handmade benches around a firepit. I quickly threw up my orange tent and when I did someone hollered from across the lake. "Wow, I'm not alone," I thought. I cooked up some dinner and afterwards fell into my sleeping bag and slept for 12 hours!

The next afternoon I wandered around the lake to see who had hollered at me the night before, and found a young lad from the Wilderness One YMCA camp, whose companions had gone climbing. He pointed me in the direction of Turbine Canyon. Turbine Canyon is one of the most spectacular canyons I have ever seen. It is narrow and deep and a waterfall drops into the canyon at a wide crack, one end of which you can jump across.

By the time the second morning came around, I had given up on the idea of doing the circuit to Three Isle Lake. That morning two friendly fellows stopped and said hello on their way back to Upper Kananaskis Lake. They had gone over South Kananaskis Pass and Palliser Pass, and up to Leman Lake in the Spray Valley, and back over North Kananaskis Pass.

Unfortunately, the Wilderness One leaders were not as friendly. When I asked if I could follow them back to Upper Kananaskis Lake, one of them made comments on my equipment, right down to the toe caps on my well-worn boots. This made me feel uneasy, even though they said yes to my request. The next morning when they passed by my campsite they didn't say a word. I had the distinct impression they didn't want me along, but since I was determined not to get lost again, I ignored their coolness and hiked along behind. No one spoke to me for the longest time, and when they did the guy who had been assessing my equipment tried to get rid of me by telling me to go on ahead. Still not wanting to get lost, I ignored him until I arrived at Three Isle Creek and knew my way.

Peggy Magee and I tried to go to Aster Lake in August 1976, on another one of those unmaintained trail excursions. We started off from what is now Upper Lake day-use area, but there was no trail along the lakeshore. At first the shoreline was easy to follow, but eventually we had to climb and crawl over huge piles of driftwood. This took about three hours. When we finally got to the "white bottle" tied on a tree as a marker for the turn-off to Hidden Lake, we found the underground stream that came out of Hidden Lake was above ground and everything was flooded—trees, trail, the whole bit!

Since we were a determined pair, we bushwhacked for 45 minutes to get to Hidden Lake where we camped (it can be done in 10 minutes when it's dry). The next day we spent two hours bushwhacking around Hidden Lake as the shoreline was flooded. To make matters really exciting, it was also raining. The bushwhacking was so bad we had to crawl over logs, on top of logs and under logs, as well as grubbing through the bush. We finally gave up and went back to our campsite.

I never did get to Aster Lake until 1992, and then I had to go by myself. By that time the Upper Lake Trail had been built around Upper Kananaskis Lake, and there was a good trail, albeit unmarked and unmaintained, into Aster Lake. I'm glad I finally got there. I had a great time in this wonderful place.

In 1967, Canada's centennial year, people all over the country were celebrating with centennial projects. The Rocky Mountain Ramblers' Association in Calgary received permission to cut the Mount Allan segment of what was to be called the Eastern Rockies Trail. It still exists today. It climbs the southeast ridge of Mount Allan, passes the old coal mine site and follows the ridge of the mountain right over the summit of Mount Allan at 2846 me-

tres, before dropping down to the Bow Valley at Dead Man's Flats. The trail is now called the Centennial Ridge Trail, and is the highest maintained trail in Canada. Mount Allan is a great place to see bighorn sheep and to find wood ticks. Fortunately, the trail is closed each year during the lambing season, from April 1st to June 21st— prime wood tick season.

Mt. Allan, 1970.

Mount Allan was named in 1912 after Dr. John A. Allan. He was the first professor of geology at the University of Alberta, and was with the university for nearly 40 years. Jack Charlesworth, who worked at

Ruth Oltmann.

the Kananaskis Lakes in the thirties, remembers Allan as a wonderful, energetic person who was liked by everyone.

Mount Collembola is the northeast spur of Mount Allan. In 1973 or 1974 Jan Sharp was studying Collembola on Devon Island in the Arctic for her Ph.D. thesis. Because she couldn't be on Devon Island all year-round, she, or her assistant, walked up Mount Allan to the 2600 and 2800 metre level, which was equivalent to her Arctic location, to take soil samples. For one year, every three weeks, one of them would hike the mountain. At the time, Dave Smith and Don Gardner were working at Ribbon Creek Hostel. They were so impressed by her tenaciousness they named the northeast spur of Mount Allan after the microbe in the soil that Sharp was studying. Jan would always check in at the hostel to tell me when she was going up on the mountain, so if she didn't come back I would get a search party to find her (or her assistant).

Alf Skrastins

I don't remember when I first went into the Kananaskis, because I went with my parents to fish and hike in the Kananaskis Lakes area. I do remember the long and tedious road—we lost a lot of mufflers on cars on the trip in. That must have been when I was between 10 and 13.

I seriously started doing a lot of stuff in Kananaskis around 1972/73. I'd done a lot of the hiking trails in Banff and Jasper; the ones that were in the hiking guidebook Patton and Robinson put out. I made a pact with myself that I was not going to repeat a hike for five years and not do any hikes that I'd already done, so that excluded most of the national parks. I looked around and one of the first places I saw was Kananaskis Country. It was nearby, very accessible and good terrain for hiking. I hiked existing trails and off-trail routes.

I remember the struggle getting into Lillian Lake with all the deadfall. It was an interesting time because there was also a sense of discovery. In many places I got the impression that either there had not been very many people there or nobody had gone there. For example, the North and South Kananaskis passes, Aster Lake, Rawson Lake and unnamed lakes. One interesting adventure was the first time I skied to the top of Mount Joffre. I can't recall what year it was. It struck me as remarkable that a place with some real ski mountaineering flavour was so close to Calgary.

In the early development stages of Kananaskis Country, there was an ongoing discussion as to whether it was a good idea to pave the way into the Kananaskis Valley. My attitude was that if nothing else the paved road would keep those people who were four-wheel driving and snowmobiling out of the valley, because there is a psychological break that happens when you go from pavement to off-road as opposed to dirt road to dirt road. In effect that happened. We ended up getting a lot more wilderness out of it.

The interesting thing about that whole seventies time period was how difficult it was to travel. Trying to get around the south shore of Upper Kananaskis Lake was dreadful. I was lucky if the main lake level was low so I could walk around the shore most of the way. In some places I would hit a game trail and suddenly it was a lot easier. When Kananaskis Country came to be, there had been a lot of trial and error from people like Tony and Gillean Daffern. Now there are well-worn paths all over the place.

Some of the things I enjoyed about the area were the longer backpacking trips we did, connecting trails together. In fact, they are hard to do now because Kananaskis Country doesn't let you camp in a lot of the places. For example, going from Mud Lake over Burstall Pass, over Palliser Pass and down the Palliser Valley and from there over North Kananaskis Pass, across the Haig Glacier and the French Glacier and completing a loop to Mud Lake.

Walking in the summer is still my favourite activity in Kananaskis. It's hard to beat places like Mount Allan for scenery. I can get a late start from Calgary and still be up in the alpine with incredible views and lots of wildflowers. The first time I went up to the snow research cabin in the Marmot Creek Basin was in the fall and discovered this huge basin of larch trees. Like many people, I had the impression the only larch trees to be found were in Larch Valley and a couple of places in Banff Park. I thought, 'Maybe there are a lot more places like this,' and I went on to find them in the Kananaskis, like at Fortress Lake, and in places tucked in behind the Opal Range.

One trip that I still think is one of the hardest, but most fascinating trips from the wildlife point of view, is to go from Little Highwood Pass parking lot—going between the Opal Range and the smaller range, over the passes all the way to Rocky Creek. There are bears in there, and goats, sheep, deer and elk. Just an amazing amount of wildlife.

I'm still finding new pockets of places—new ski touring routes. Two or three weeks ago I went off the ski runs at Nakiska and found chest-deep powder in late April!

Climbing

In the early days of the valley's history mountain climbing was not a major sport, although A. O. Wheeler's boundary survey in 1916 climbed many of the mountains along the Continental Divide, such as Mounts Jellicoe, McHarg and Beatty. Mount Joffre, at 3450 metres, is the highest peak in the Kananaskis Valley and was first climbed in 1919 by J. W. A. Hickson and his guide E. Feuz Jr. It was probably climbed at that time because of it being the highest peak between the United States border and Mount Assiniboine. Katie Gardiner was guided up a number of peaks around the Kananaskis Lakes in 1930, as part of her extensive climbing career in the Rockies.

Mountain climbing in the valley increased in the 1950s, owing to better access. The mountains in the Opal Range saw activity during this time, with Mount Hood first ascended in 1953, Mount Evan-Thomas in 1954, Mount Blane in 1955 and Mount Brock in 1956.

Part of the pictorial drama rising high above the Kananaskis Village and the Kananaskis Country Golf Course is Mount Kidd (2958 metres). This mountain was probably named after John Alfred Kidd, the first white Stoney chief. Kidd was born in Ontario and came west in 1890 to teach school in Saskatchewan before moving to Calgary. In 1902 he moved to Morley, where he remained until 1907. While there he outfitted survey parties, one of which was headed by D. Bogart Dowling, the geologist, who probably named the mountain for him.

Dr. Patrick Duffy

Because we are mountaineers we can appreciate how the Calgary section of the Alpine Club and other people said, 'Hey, we have a whole new area to go and climb in.' I think my first climb was probably within a week of my arrival in Kananaskis, in May 1953, when we went up Barrier Mountain *(Mount Baldy)* and had a look south. Later that summer on a Saturday Ross Waldron and I had worked our normal five-and-a-half day week and were on Wasootch Flats, doing some work. From there we hitchhiked to the point immediately east of Mount Kidd. I remember these people were very nice and gave us a ride, and we told them we were going to climb Mount Kidd. As I got out of the car and slammed the door, I slammed it on my thumb. I tried to contain my outrage at my foolishness, but I walked around for the rest of the day with my hand over my head. We waded the Kananaskis River and climbed up through the big cirque that forms the eastern part of the mountain. It was basically a climb for which one didn't need a rope—just a matter of scrambling around some ledges. We arrived at the top and found to our surprise we were only the second party that had been up there. I think Bob Hind and some people from the Alpine Club had climbed it by another route just before us. *(The first ascent was June 1947 by R. C. Hind and J. F. Tarrant via the NNW ridge.)*

In 1954 Keith Ingold, an English friend of mine, climbed Mount Louis near Banff with me, and then we went down the Kananaskis to climb what we thought was going to be Mount Blane. In fact, we climbed Mount Brock, which is immediately north of it. Keith and I unwittingly climbed the wrong mountain and found ourselves on a summit that had never been visited. So we were rather tickled with that.

The next year I arranged a climbing trip with Dave Kennedy, Frank Karsh and Jerry Johnston. I am afraid there is some tragedy in all of this. We went down to climb Mount Blane and Jerry and Frank went on one rope, while Dave and I went on another. We had a Grade IV climb—that's what we'd call it in those days, using ropes if necessary, and Dave and I got up there and were starting to come down when Jerry came up and said, 'I couldn't climb behind Frank because he was knocking rocks down on me.' We went looking for Frank and to make a long story short, we couldn't find him, so we went back to Banff and immediately called

Ruthie at Wasootch Slabs, 1973. Photo: Ruth Oltmann collection.

Walter Perren, a dear friend, and Walter said, 'You get ready to leave at one o'clock in the morning.' We went back and looked all over the mountain. It didn't take long until Walter found my friend who had died—struck by falling rock. It was a windy day and there was the odd pebble and rock coming down.

Not to be too sentimental about this, but I am very much reminded of Earle Birney's poem *David*. It is a beautiful narrative poem and it ends up saying, after there had been a tragedy of some kind, 'It was the last day of the summer and the last day of my youth.' That's what an accident like that means.

Mount McDougall (2726 m), across the valley to the east from the Kananaskis Village, was named after Rev. George Millward McDougall and his sons, Rev. John McDougall and David George McDougall, who were Methodist missionaries to the Stoney Indians. This mountain was first climbed in 1952 by an Alpine Club of Canada party. The long, bald ridge in front has locally been known as Old Baldy since at least the 1960s. A gentleman who made friends with Gordon Matthews, the former ranger, would hike up once a year via the big gully that faces the highway. I used to look at it out of my window at the hostel until it, too, beckoned me. I've since been up it eight times.

Driving to Kananaskis Village gives one a panoramic view of Ribbon Peak and Mount Bogart, located between Mounts Allan and Kidd. Mount Bogart (3144 m) was named after Dr. D. Bogart Dowling, the geologist, and was first climbed in 1930 by Katie Gardiner and her guide W. Feuz via the southeast ridge from the south fork of Ribbon Creek. Ribbon Peak (2880 m) appears to be part of Mount Bogart, but is classed as a separate peak. The peak is sometimes referred to as "The Perch." It was first climbed in June 1957 by F. W. Crickard, R. Higgins and Hans Gmoser (the famous heli-ski guide). They approached the mountain from the forks on Ribbon Creek via the large avalanche slide that Ida Matthews said looks like a map of Alberta backwards.

Rock climbing really came into its own with the creation of Kananaskis Country. Wasootch Slabs and the King Creek cliffs were pioneered by the British and Canadian armies, then the hostel association started using Wasootch Slabs for their rock schools in the 1970s. It wasn't long before climbing clubs were doing the same. Barrier Bluffs became extremely popular with the publication of *Barrier Bluffs* in 1987 by Kelly Tobey. John Martin opened up new climbing areas through his guidebook *Kananaskis Rock*, which was published in 1989. This book was followed by *Sport Climbs in the Canadian Rockies* (which includes the Kananaskis Valley) by

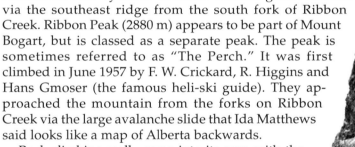

Ed Peyer during first ascent of Mt. Wintour.
Photo: Glen Boles.

213

John Martin and Jon Jones. Allan Kane's book *Scrambles in the Canadian Rockies*, which came out in 1992 and turned the scrambling world upside down, has many peaks in the Kananaskis Valley described. Scrambling is now a very popular sport throughout the valley and the Canadian Rockies as a whole.

Glen Boles

The first time I actually tried to climb something in the Kananaskis Valley was in June 1961 with Brian Greenwood. We wanted to do The Blade, the separate peak on the south side of Mount Blane. We went up in the afternoon and bivied in the saddle and tried it early in the morning, but the rock was terrible, so we backed off. I almost got the chop that time. In those days equipment wasn't that good and I had an old war surplus rucksack with a metal frame that curved around the side of the waist. We didn't have one of these descenders like we have now, so we did a body rappel using a dulfer sling. I went down first and I got the rope underneath the metal pack frame. I was part way down when the rope started to pull my rucksack up over my shoulders. Because I had to let go with my lower hand, I started to skid down the rope. I was hugging it with my neck and finally I bit the rope, doing everything I could to arrest my descent because I couldn't grab the bottom section of the rope again. Finally I did get hold of it and stopped myself. I rope burned my neck very badly.

Since then I've climbed just about everything in the Opal Range. I remember the first ascent of Mount Wintour. The north ridge had been climbed to the north summit quite a few times. Ken Pawson was after me to go up and have a look at the main summit so we went up and it looked really difficult. In 1966 I went back with Bob Geber and Walter Batzhuber and had a closer look. There was a gendarme to the right of the notch and we went in behind that but it looked difficult, and we were feeling a little lazy, so we climbed the north peak. I went back in September 1967 with another Swiss guy named Ed Peyer. It was a good climb. We were on the summit and there was a storm coming in, so we came down the west ridge a little bit and then went south into one of those big gullies. Ed always carried a 200 foot rappel rope and we had the climbing rope, so we tied the two together, and rappelled one slab that was just like a baby's bottom. We couldn't see the rope at first and didn't know where it went, but finally I saw one tip and knew it had touched the ground, so we got off that way.

On another occasion we were going to climb the peak just north of Mount Evan-Thomas, which had no record of anybody climbing it. We got part way up and got hit by a snow storm, so we came out. Three weeks later Don Forest and I and Mike Simpson went up that same creek and crossed the height of land into Rocky Creek. We camped in there and went straight up two peaks to the east from where we camped. They were unclimbed. Then we went south and did the other peak just north of Mount Evan-Thomas, but the funny part is when we got to the top there was a canister with Jim Tarrant's name and all the ones who had made the first ascent of Evan-Thomas. They thought this peak was Evan-Thomas! That same day there was a party who had made what they thought was the first ascent of Packenham. Everything was clouded in and they had no map. Both parties had actually climbed one peak farther north than the one they were after. Jim Tarrant's group didn't climb Evan-Thomas, they climbed the one to the north and this other party climbed Evan-Thomas, and they both left records! Anyway, we climbed three peaks that day and the peak north of Evan-Thomas we named Potts. I think it was the year of the RCMP centennial, 1974. The other we named Denny after the RCMP gentleman who, I think, was under Colonel Macleod when they settled in Calgary at Fort Calgary.

Also in the seventies Don Forest and I and Gordon Scruggs and Mike Simpson climbed what we later named Mount Schlee after a member of the Alpine Club *(Gerry Schlee)* who drowned in the Bow River trying to save somebody about that time.

In 1962 during a Calgary Mountain Club weekend in the Kananaskis we climbed the buttress on Mount Kidd, above where the hotel is now. We just got the buttress done, although we were thinking of doing the whole peak, but we ran out of time, so we came down the easy slope on the back side to Ribbon Creek. It was very difficult. I remember sitting on several ledges with my feet hanging over the edge.

Another really good climb is the south ridge of Mount Lougheed. Brian Greenwood and I were always wanting to do a complete traverse of all four peaks of Lougheed, but it never seemed to happen and then all of a sudden Donnie Gardner and Neil Liske did it from south to north, so Don Forest, Al Cole, John Atkinson and myself went into Spray Lakes and did it from north to south. We had bivy equipment, but it was such a beautiful day that by four o'clock we were on the fourth peak. I think we did it the best way, because the south slopes on all those peaks had scree we could just run down. That was 1970. Gardner beat us to it in '67.

Golfing

The Kananaskis Country Golf Course, situated along the Kananaskis River below Mount Kidd, provides golfers with dramatic mountain views in all directions, as well as a world-class golf course. The course was opened on July 22, 1983 by Premier Peter Lougheed, and has two 18-hole courses: Mount Kidd and Mount Lorette. It was designed by the world-renowned golf course architect, Robert Trent Jones, who said this was the epitome of his career and was the finest location he had ever seen for a golf course. Utilizing the many tributaries, backchannels and main channel of the Kananaskis River, the two 18-hole courses are of championship calibre and draws people from all over the world. Owing to the elevation (1477 metres), the ball goes 10 per cent farther than is usually the case.

Top soil for the golf course was acquired from various locations, including Wedge Pond, which was drained and excavated for its soil. Previously, because the pond could not be seen from the old Forestry Trunk Road, the fire suppression crew used it for a bath tub. The ranger station where the crew was located did not have a good water source, but as the pond was shallow and warm it was ideal for baths on hot days.

The golf course has been managed since its inception by two brothers, Brian and Wayne Bygrave, for Kan-Alta Golf Management Ltd. James O'Connor was the first course superintendent, from the time the course opened until June 1993.

As the popularity of the golf course grew, the pro shop moved from the main clubhouse to a new building. The Robert Trent Jones Pavilion was built and opened in July 1988 as a tournament and banquet centre. Special tournaments can take place annually, every two years or on a periodic basis. The Alberta Inter Club Tournament in July has become an annual event since 1983. The Roger Southworth Memorial Tournament has also taken place annually in July

Peter Lougheed and Robert Trent Jones at the opening ceremonies of the Kananaskis Country Golf Course in 1983. Photo: Gillean Daffern.

since 1983. Southworth worked with Robert Trent Jones in the golfing business and was killed in a plane crash. Each year a junior golf camp is held for boys and girls from Alberta. The Alberta Golf Association and the Alberta Ladies Golf Association make the selection from among the best juniors in the province. This is an elite camp held every May.

Over the first 14 years the golf course operated it gained an enviable position in the international golf world. In 1996 the Golf Digest, which has a worldwide distribution, selected the Kananaskis Country Golf Course as "the best 36-hole public golf facility in North America."

Param Sekhon

My involvement with the golf course was with the construction of the clubhouse. I think we started in late '81 and the clubhouse was finished in mid-'83. We had the opening in July of '83.

Winds in Kananaskis can be something at times. During construction of the clubhouse we had this roof erection going on, and one time the contractor finished his work on Friday and left it for the weekend. He came back on Monday and the roof was gone! The wind just blew it off.

The clubhouse was originally called a family recreation centre. We had a little difficulty in meeting the needs of the average public who were not interested in golfing, but who also wanted to come and enjoy the facilities at the clubhouse, and at the same time taking care of the golfers. I think in the long run it all worked out well. In fact, the golf course operators, I believe, like the idea of the public coming to the golf course because they have a meal there and purchase stuff from the pro shop, so it adds to their revenue. I think it was a neat concept in that sense—that the golf course not be limited to golfers, but be open to everyone.

Snowmobiling

The Kananaskis Lakes region of the valley became a mecca for snowmobile traffic in the sixties and early seventies. More popular were the old (1936) forestry road along Pocaterra Creek, the Smith-Dorrien/Smuts Creek four-wheel drive road (the present Smith-Dorrien/Spray Trail road) and the Elk Pass powerline service road (now Elk Pass Trail and Hydroline Trail).

Once Kananaskis Provincial Park was created, snowmobiling was banned as it was not within provincial park legislation to have this activity in parks. Other provisions were made for snowmobiling outside of the valley in Kananaskis Country.

Cross-Country Skiing

Ribbon Creek. As Ribbon Creek Hostel became more popular, the Canadian Youth Hostel Association applied and received permission from the government of Alberta to cut a two kilometre novice cross-country ski trail. In 1973 the CYHA hired Don Gardner, who was a cross-country ski racer with experience in trail cutting. He commenced cutting a trail that began at the hostel and ended at a waterfall on Marmot Creek, which he named Troll Falls.

Troll Falls Trail was only the beginning of trailblazing in the Ribbon Creek area in the 1970s. A reconnaissance uncovered a large number of disused logging roads that were ideal. The Marmot Basin experimental project had a number of narrow roads that were also used. Don Gardner made a big poster-board map of all the trails he had discovered, and posted it in the Ribbon Creek Hostel. After Gardner finished that project, I skied and hiked the trails and added to the map. Eventually a hand-map was made by Gardner for use by hostellers.

Word soon spread about the great cross-country ski trails. I would organize work parties to clear the trails of deadfall, and the outings ended up being happy social events with potluck dinners and cozy evenings around the fireplace.

Once Kananaskis Country was created, the trails in the Ribbon Creek area were marked and maintained by the government trail crew. Some names were changed, and when Nakiska ski resort was built a few disappeared. The trails are now groomed and trackset regularly.

When I was working as a cook at the Kananaskis Field Station in the late seventies, I remember going to Ribbon Creek after work one evening to walk to Troll Falls, a favourite haunt. I guess I arrived at the wrong moment, because I discovered the Troll Falls trail had been widened for cross-country ski traffic. I had arrived before the trail work was completed, right when it looked its worse, and I got very upset. I subsequently wrote a nasty letter to Premier Peter Lougheed. Later, Don Gardner, who was involved in trail development for the government, talked to me about what they were doing. A few years later, after I had been working in the Barrier Lake Visitor Information Centre for a while and learned how much visitors enjoyed the ski trails, I didn't mind at all. There are now about 60 kilometres of maintained trails in the Ribbon Creek trail system.

Ski trail names at Ribbon Creek have an interesting history:

Skogan Pass and Skogan Pass Trail were named by Don Gardner in 1973. Skogan was originally spelled Skogen, a Norwegian name for a forest of elves and dwarfs. When Kananaskis Country took over the maintenance and development of the trails, the spelling somehow got changed to Skogan. Originally Skogan Pass

Trail started from the Ribbon Creek parking lot and followed the old mining road for a few kilometres. When the Nakiska road was built over it a new lower section was cut that turned out to be more picturesque than the section it replaced. The lovely views of the Kananaskis Valley along the trail add much to its allure, and a hill very exciting to ski down in the winter is a special bonus. The trail crew for Kananaskis Country call this hill "The Screamer."

Skogan Pass Trail does not go over Skogan Pass proper, but runs above it on the south side of the actual pass. Parts of the original telephone line trail, which went over the pass to Canmore, were still visible in the 1970s. I spent a lot of time scouting it out and found all the sections in the forest above the 1936 forest fire line. The rest was completely gone. The telephone line was strung in 1936, and may have been maintained after the forest fire that year. The present Skogan Pass Trail uses former research roads, logging roads and the powerline service road. It passes through forest that escaped the 1936 forest fire, so consequently there are trees 200-300 years old. Dennis Jaques did tree core samples in the 1970s and determined the age.

In 1973 when Don Gardner was working on Troll Falls Trail and training for cross-country ski races, he would take time out to ski up Skogan Pass Trail, over the top, and down the other side to Dead Man's Flats (about 18 kilometres) and back again—in two hours return!

Ruthie's Trail is another trail named by Gardner in 1973. I discovered this trail was part of the original telephone line running from Canmore to the ranger's Boundary Cabin. Some of the telephone line was still on the trees in 1973. I loved to ski the fast downhill on the trail and would often refer to it as "my trail" and to Troll Falls Trail as "your trail" to Gardner. In the end, when Gardner put the trails on a map, he also named this one.

When Nakiska was built, about half of the original trail was taken out by downhill ski runs. Hobbit Hill, where I used to go for afternoon tea, is indiscernible, but the best ski run of all remains—the hill down to the junction of Troll Falls Trail. The trail name was originally Ruthie's Run, but some time after Kananaskis Country took over trail maintenance the name was changed. The trail crew also cut down the tree that was on the hill in the middle of the trail, eliminating one of the challenges!

Hay Meadow Trail was named by Gardner as well. During the life of the coal mine on Mount Allan, the meadow was used for grazing horses that were employed in the early days of the mine. South of the main meadow there was a smaller one on the edge of the river. Woody Crites and Heather McLaurin (a former Ribbon Creek Hostel manager) were married there on July 14, 1984.

The Doctor's Trail no longer exists. During the 1970s Dr. David Gill found the remains of a trail off Ruthie's Trail. He convinced some of the hostellers to help him clear it and found a route around a side hill to the small powerline that provided power to the research sites on Mount Allan, and accessed Skogan Pass Trail. The powerline is gone but its clearing is still partially visible. The trail came by its name naturally. It was pretty scary because you needed a doctor if you skied it!

Stump Meadow Trail crossed the lower slopes of Mount Allan, above the present Nakiska ski lodge, and connected Mount Allan Trail with Skogan Pass Trail. This trail is no longer used, as much of it is obliterated by ski runs. I have

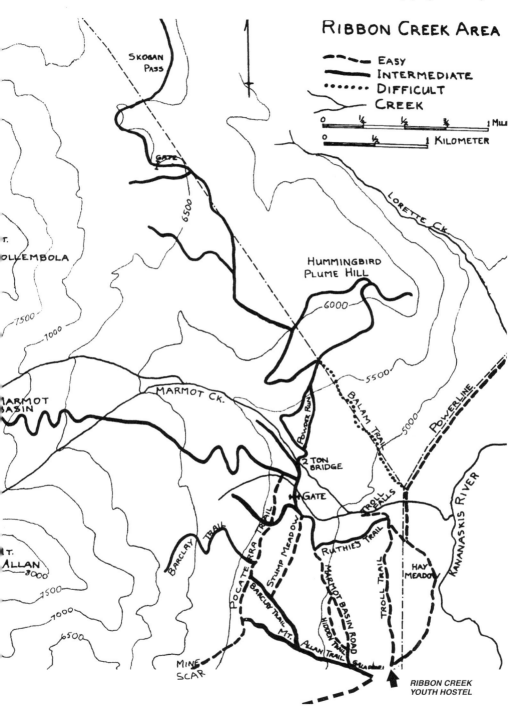

RIBBON CREEK AREA

— — — EASY
———— INTERMEDIATE
••••••• DIFFICULT
———— CREEK

Drawn by Don Gardner c. 1973 for the Canadian Youth Hostel Association.

Ruthie at Troll Falls, 1974. Photo: Merlene Sparks.

seen lynx track on this trail for the past 20 years, even since Nakiska was built. The name of the trail resulted from an open area with previously logged tree stumps. The section that is close to Coal Mine Trail still exists. Watch for a slight opening on the right after rounding the second corner. A terrific view of the valley is the reward for those who venture into the Stump Meadow. I named this one; it was one of my favourite places for a tea break.

Coal Mine Trail was originally called Pocaterra Trail after George Pocaterra with whom Gardner felt a special affinity. When Kananaskis Country took over maintenance they renamed it Coal Mine Trail because the upper section of this trail was the coal mine road during the life of the mine. The lower section was called Mount Allan Trail prior to the Nakiska development, but in 1995 the trail crew combined the name to be less confusing.

Marmot Basin Trail has seen a few changes as well. The original Marmot Basin Trail was located south of the present one. It is now used by the Nakiska crew to access their mid-mountain lodge with snowmobiles. The present trail used to be called Cabin Trail because of a little cabin, used by the Marmot Basin research people, that was located along the trail close to Marmot Creek. Today you can access Nakiska's mid-mountain lodge via this trail. In the old days you could access Marmot Basin via this trail. Where the old, wide trail stops, there was a narrow trail (wide enough for Denny Fisera's wide-track snowmobile) that made 16 switchbacks into the cirque.

Sunburst Trail is a pretty name for a trail. It was first called Hummingbird Plume Hill, but that may have been too long for the Kananaskis Country trail crew, because its name was changed. It was originally named by Gardner when he first discovered it in 1973. Some of the old-timers still use the original name for the hill at the top, including Gillean Daffern in her trail guide. The trail follows an old road that went to a fire lookout. The remains of the lookout are still there, but the trees have grown up on the edge of the bluff so you don't get the same view unless you stand on the edge.

Kovach Trail was named after Joe Kovach, the ranger in the valley from 1940-1953. Kovach Pond picnic site and this trail commemorate him. The northern section of the trail, the part facing Ribbon Creek, was a logging road dating back to the Second World War. Some time after the Kananaskis Village was built the trail was extended to the south, along with Aspen, Terrace Link and Link Trails.

Kananaskis Lakes. The ski trails in Peter Lougheed Provincial Park were built as a result of the development of the park. Bob Reynolds, the director of operations for Kananaskis Country, and Don Gardner scouted the area for places where they could interlink trails that would be out of avalanche hazardous terrain and that would be suitable for all levels of expertise. The result was approximately 90 kilometres of trails that are very popular today. Some of the trails have historic names such as Pocaterra, Amos, Wheeler, Sinclair, Woolley and Patterson. Stroil Trail is a bit of Don Gardner himself, as Stroil was a nickname he gave himself.

Kayakers on the Kananaskis River. Photo: Gillean Daffern.

Ice fishing on Upper Kananaskis Lake. Photo: Gillean Daffern.

These trails are close to the Continental Divide and thus receive much more snow than the Ribbon Creek area. For example, Elk Pass Trail has a long ski season. On May 14, 1991, when I skied it there was still over a metre of snow on the pass!

In 1977 this trail system was the site of the first Kananaskis Ski Marathon, also known as The Great Cookie Race. It has been running in February every year since. Organized by the Foothills Nordic Ski Club of Calgary, it was a 45-kilometre race initially, but as it gained popularity this changed. Today there are courses of varying distances: 42, 24, 15, five and three kilometres and one kilometre. It started out as a classic-style race, changed to free technique, and has gone in a full circle back to classic style only. It starts and ends at the Pocaterra Ski Hut, where the prizes are awarded at the end of the day. The feeding stations set up at points throughout the courses offer fabulous homemade cookies and juice to the participants, hence the alternate name.

Ice Climbing
Ice Climbing started to become popular in the valley in the 1980s. The guide-book *Waterfall Ice* by Albi Sole, later updated by Joe Josephson, contributed to its popularity. Chantilly Falls along Evan-Thomas Creek was one of the first frozen waterfalls to attract ice climbers. Of late, frozen waterfalls on Mount Kidd have become increasingly popular. My brother, Phill Oltmann, did the first ascent of Troll Falls—not a major climb, but a bit of interesting trivia.

Ice Fishing
Ice fishing has been popular for many years on the Kananaskis Lakes and Barrier Lake. The most popular fishing spots on Lower Kananaskis Lake are: near Canyon day-use area where people walk on to the ice, and near Panorama day-use area where they fish in open water below the powerhouse. On Upper Kananaskis Lake the most popular spot is accessed from Upper Lake day-use area, which has picnic facilities. The beaver ponds along the old road just south of the Wasootch day-use site are another popular spot, but it is a 10-15 minute walk to reach them. The south end of Barrier Lake traditionally has good fishing both summer and winter. Unfortunately, fishermen are notorious for keeping the best fishing spots to themselves!

Once, while taking pictures of ice fishermen on Lower Kananaskis Lake I observed that a fellow with just a fishing rod had the most fish, while those with fancy equipment such as stools or fishing tents had none!

Water Sports
Canoeing, kayaking and rafting are very popular activities on the stretch of the Kananaskis River below Barrier Dam. Most people put in their craft at the Widowmaker, a unique rock outcrop in the river, and either take-out at Canoe Meadows or the Bow River at Seebe. Commercial raft trips go all the way to the Bow River. The section of river at Canoe Meadows has a kayak slalom course, the result of a modification of the original riverbed. Many national and international kayak races are held here and members of the Canadian teams come to practise throughout the year. The keeners will be out in just about any weather, until the temperature drops below -15 degrees Celsius.

Many hours of negotiation have taken place with TransAlta Utilities in working out compromise solutions for water levels in the river for these recreationists. The Barrier Lake Visitor Centre has provided information on river running hours for several years. When Sasha (I don't know her last name) was on a major racing team, her mother would call me every Friday from Sundre to get the "dam times," so Sasha could plan her weekend training program.

Cycling

The paved bike trails in Peter Lougheed Park and the Evan-Thomas bike path from Kananaskis Village to Wedge Pond are well used throughout the summer.

Param Sekhon
One of the projects I really enjoyed working on was the bike trail from Kananaskis Village to Wedge Pond (Evan-Thomas). When we finished that project there was concern expressed for the safety of the bike riders, especially for keeping the uphill traffic separate from the downhill traffic. They asked me about the possibility of separating the uphill and downhill traffic in spots. I suggested, 'Why don't we paint a yellow line on critical spots to separate the traffic?'
'Oh, it will not work.'
'If you say it will not work, then you don't understand Canadian people. In Canada we follow rules.'
So we tried that, and amazingly people stuck to their side and there never was any problem. Right after we tried this approach on Kananaskis trails I noticed the city of Calgary started painting a yellow line on their bike trails. I don't know if they got the idea from us or not.

In the spring when the section of Highway #40 over Highwood Pass is still closed, hundreds of cyclists can be found on the road as soon as the snow melts. The road parallels the Continental Divide and is the highest road in Canada. The summit of Highwood Pass is 2206.3 metres (7,239 ft.).

The Alberta Lung Association has held their annual cycling "trek" in the valley since 1990. The trek starts at the Kananaskis Inn in Kananaskis Village. On the first day they bike to the top of Highwood Pass and back, and on the second day they bike to Highway #1 and back. The Association organizes the trek as a money-raising activity. Participants must raise $350 if they ride for both days and $175 if they ride for one day. Over the years the ride route has changed for safety reasons and the number of days has changed from one to two.

Mountain Biking

Mountain biking in the valley has mushroomed in recent years. Many trails that were once narrow dirt roads are ideal. However, lots of young people enjoy the challenge of steep, narrow trails where they have to carry their bikes. Kananaskis Country staff have adapted to this development by producing trail maps that separate out biking and hiking trails.

In the summer of 1996 a young woman went on a bike ride from Mount Kidd R.V. Park planning to end at the Little Elbow Recreation Area at the west end of Highway #66 where her boyfriend was waiting. Unfortunately, the route wasn't as easy as she thought. She followed the Evan-Thomas backcountry trail over Evan-Thomas Pass, a feat in itself, but when she arrived at Little

Evan-Thomas bike path. Photo: Gillean Daffern.

Elbow Trail she made the mistake of turning right instead of left and ended up on the Sheep Trail, which took her to Bluerock Campground at the west end of Highway #546. This was a much longer ride and she was not where she was supposed to be. Subsequently, her boyfriend frantically phoned all over Kananaskis Country trying to find her. The rangers were notified and were preparing for a possible search when a ranger in the Sheep Valley found her and drove her to the Elbow Valley Visitor Information Centre where her boyfriend was waiting.

Mountain biking can be dangerous in the mountains, not only because of routefinding problems, but because of rough terrain. Rangers are periodically called in to rescue people who have had bad spills. But it can also be a lot of fun. One of the more popular trails for ambitious riders is Prairie View Trail at Barrier Lake. It requires a bike carry, but rewards the effort with spectacular views and challenging hills.

Running

The K100 road race is a popular event. This 100 mile road race is hosted by Hostelling International Canada-Southern Alberta Region and runs from Highwood House, at the junction of Highways #40 and #541, north along Highway #40 to Barrier Lake, across Barrier Dam and south along Stoney Trail to its end at either Nakiska Ski Resort or Kananaskis Village. This is a relay race drawing about 180 teams and 10 racers per team. The race is "a fundraiser that supports Hostelling International in the development and enhancement of new and existing hostels in southern Alberta." The race first started in 1987 and takes place annually in the middle of June.

Hunting

The Kananaskis Valley has been open to hunting since game preserve restrictions were lifted in 1957. When Gordon Matthews left the valley in 1974, he said there was a noticeable decrease in the number of animals since his arrival. In order to maintain the wildlife numbers, limitations on the number of animals hunted are set. There is no hunting in the specified recreation areas and in Peter Lougheed Provincial Park. Hunting permits are distributed by a draw system for certain animals.

Eagle Watching

Eagle watching has become a favourite pastime of many people ever since Peter Sherrington discovered the eagles' migration route over the Rocky Mountains. Sherrington's cherished spot is in Hay Meadow below Nakiska, where he sets up his telescope and counts eagles and other raptors every spring and fall. The prime viewing time is late March for the spring migration, as they fly over the Kananaskis Valley and Mount Lorette.

Endnotes

1. *Tim Horton Children's Foundation, A Summer to Remember, brochure, Oakville, Ontario, no date.*

The Romance of the Kananaskis

8

ᵂeddings

So many people have become endeared to the Kananaskis Valley it is now a favourite place where couples come to get married. Kananaskis Village, which has four major viewpoints on the Village Rim Trail overlooking the valley, is one of the most popular locations for weddings—so popular that it has to be booked far in advance!

John Johanson was a forerunner of this romantic spirit when he proposed to his mail-order bride by letter from Ribbon Creek Village. Heather and Woody Crites were another of the early couples who turned the valley into a cathedral when they married in Hay Meadow at Ribbon Creek.

I remember one young couple returning from a backpack hike to Ribbon Lake in June of 1994 who became part of this romantic atmosphere when they stopped for a rest at Ribbon Falls. Sitting on the bench, overlooking the waterfall, he proposed. The proposal was a complete surprise to the young lady, but it didn't stop her from saying yes! By the time they arrived at the Barrier Lake Visitor Centre to return their backcountry registration slip, they were so excited they put the wrong date on the registration, and just had to tell me their romantic story.

Tessy Bray, John Dupuis
When we were thinking of where to get married we naturally considered Kananaskis Country because we use it and like it so much, and we both have lots of connections with it.

The advantage of the Kananaskis Valley was it was developed and people could stay in one of the hotels nearby or go to the hostel. Most of our friends were outdoor-type people who would be happy camping. We looked for a group campsite we could book and where we would have a nice spot to get married. We looked at Porcupine, which wasn't big enough, at Pocaterra, which was fairly ideal, at Lower Kananaskis Lake and the Interlakes, but they were too overused, and at Pine Grove, which wasn't bad, but it wasn't great. So we focused our attention on Pocaterra. When we inquired we found out we had to book a date and that it wasn't guaranteed because it was decided by a draw.

We decided to get married in early July, so we picked a couple of weekends and tried for these campgrounds and, of course, we didn't get any of them. We got Porcupine, but because it didn't have a shelter and there was no nice place to have a ceremony, we were left trying to resolve these concerns at places that weren't too far from Porcupine. One place was the Barrier Lake knoll. We saw it in February and thought it was a nice place with a nice view, even though the highway was right there. We didn't know if it was nice in summer because neither of us had been there before. In case of rain we thought we could use the Charlie Beil room in the Kananaskis Village Centre. If it was nice we wanted to have the reception outside. John's paddling friends suggested Canoe Meadows, so we booked it for the reception.

Heather and Woody Crites. Hay Meadow, July 1984. Photo: Ruth Oltmann.

Our wedding invitation had a picture of us paddling together. The invitation said, 'To work the wave together you have to be working together.'

We sent out the invitations before the campground was confirmed, and as we didn't get Pocaterra, we had to send another invitation. It said we were still going to take the plunge, and included a picture of us going over a ledge in a canoe, with the wording, 'Please note the changes.' We included a map showing the campgrounds and the Kananaskis Village Resort.

As things hadn't worked out with Pocaterra, we had our backup and everything was arranged. Our friends were hauling canoes all the way out to Canoe Meadows, the keg was prepared before the ceremony, and they had already set up the banners on the signs.

The whole idea behind the timing of the wedding was we wanted people to include it in their weekend recreational plans. Some people drove out for the wedding only and wore nicer clothes, but we had people who cycled from Calgary that day, and some people came from Canmore after hiking. We had 10 dogs, 10 kids, and people in dresses to people in their lycra shorts and tank tops.

A large banner, which said Dupuis/Bray Wedding, had been done on a computer and was hand coloured. It was put up on the Barrier Lake Trail interpretive sign. As well, another banner was put up over the big green sign on the road where the sign for the boat launch and day-use area is.

We got married on the knoll overlooking Barrier Lake, on July 11, 1992. I wore a cream-coloured dress, with a brocade pattern, an old-fashioned lace collar, puffy three-quarter length sleeves and little pleats. I wore nice shoes, but I hiked up in flat shoes and instead of a flower girl I had shoe girls! John had long hair then, pulled back into a pony tail, and a collar, flowing shirt and casual dress pants.

John: All the way up Mom said Grandmother was complaining, 'Why does John have to get married up here?' Mom said she got up there and looked around and said, 'Oh, now I know why they want to be up here.'

Tessy: Once our friends were gathered on top of the hill, John and I walked holding hands up the trail through a cathedral-like hallway formed by the aspens, which we hadn't known about in February, and then we came to the top and all the flowers were in bloom. It was perfectly lovely. It had rained all of June—there might have been one sunny day, and the first 10 days of July had rained until we thought for sure we would be having it in the Charlie Beil Room. We started to gear our plans for doing that and then on the morning of July 11th it was beautiful and clear.

The Justice of the Peace, Sarah Segstro, wore a traditional judicial gown, which has pleats all the way down, with a large lace collar. Usually these things are black, but Sarah had a blue one for our friends' wedding and she wore a gold one for ours. I thought it was wonderful.

After the ceremony this unplanned thing happened where people started lining up and coming up to us, and then they went down to the parking lot and off to Canoe Meadows for the reception. By the time we finished with the last people everyone else was already gone, so we went up last and came down last.

At Canoe Meadows we set up a canoe with ice in it, and put a keg of beer and kegs of wine in it for the reception. For the buffet we lined up some of the picnic tables in a row and covered them with red and white checkered cloth. The caterer did an outdoor buffet dinner with roast beef, homemade pies and salads. The caterer's parents were in the catering business, too, and felt the amount of food she had prepared was way too much. We had 100 people at the wedding and they said that the amount she had would feed at least 125. It was all eaten, because it was mostly outdoors people.

Camp fires were lit in both firepits, and became focal points for people. Some people had guitars and harmonicas, which made the atmosphere nice. This all happened spontaneously.

John and I stayed the night at the Kananaskis Hotel in an executive suite with a jacuzzi in it. We had the buffet breakfast the next morning, then went back to Canoe Meadows.

Looking in my dictionary, I find one description of romance that says, "The character of that which appears strange and fascinating, heroic, chivalrous, and the like; delight in what is chivalrous, adventurous, fanciful or mysterious."

I believe the Kananaskis Valley fits this description. After all, the weather in the valley can be strange; it's certainly pictorially fascinating; heroic adventures have taken place, not only by the people mentioned in this book, but by many others; when the sun shines it is like a chivalrous cloak draped over one's shoulders; one can fancy oneself, for example, a great mountaineer, or great golfer. And it is also mysterious; there is always a new place to find adventure.

Visitors continue to enjoy the valley's awesome beauty and its wonderful facilities. It continues to be a place of spiritual renewal both to the Stoney Indian and to the non-native person.

For me the valley will always be a big part of my life; after all, a long time ago I married the Kananaskis!

Tessy Bray and
John Dupuis, July 1992,
Sarah Segstro J.T.
Photo: Wayne Spivak.

References

Alberta, June 15, 1976, A coal development policy for Alberta, Dept. of Energy and Natural Resources: Govt. of Alberta, Edmonton, Legislative Bldg.

Alberta, Dept. of Lands and Forests and Environment Canada, 1973, The foothills resource allocation study, Phase One, Kananaskis-Spray Drainage District: Canada Lands Inventory Program.

Albertan, The, June 1961, Seventy of 300 applicants draw Kananaskis lots: Calgary, The Albertan (newspaper) (Canadian Press).

Albertan, The, April 7, 1967, New ski resort to open in fall: Calgary, The Albertan (newspaper) (Canadian Press).

Albertan, The, September 2, 1970, Firm loses Kananaskis lease: Calgary, The Albertan (newspaper) (Canadian Press).

Anderson, Dr. P. K., 1976, personal communication.

Bearns, Chris and George, 1975, personal communication.

Berton, Pierre, 1971, The last spike: Toronto, McClelland and Stewart.

Berton, Pierre, 1975, Hollywood's Canada: Toronto, McClelland and Stewart.

Boles, Glen W., 1996, interview, Cochrane, AB.

Bowen, Lynne, 1994, interview, Nanaimo, BC.

Brace, Lorne, 1975, personal communication.

Bray, Tessy, 1995, interview, Calgary, AB.

Bygrave, Brian, 1996, personal communication.

Byrne, A. R., 1968, Man and landscape change in Banff National Park before 1911; National Park Ser. No. 1, studies in land use history and landscape change, J. G. Nelson, ed.: London, Univ. of Western Ontario.

Calgary Power Ltd., 1971, Power for progress; some facts about Calgary Power Ltd., sixtieth anniversary edition: Calgary, Calgary Power Ltd. (pamphlet).

Calgary Power Ltd., ca. 1971, Power for progress, thermal and hydro plants: Calgary, Calgary Power Ltd.

Calgary Power Ltd., 1975, Some facts 1974: Calgary, Calgary Power Ltd. (pamphlet).

Campbell, P., December 19, 1936, unpublished report.

CanPac Minerals Ltd., 1973, Industry and Environment: Calgary, CanPac Minerals Ltd. (pamphlet).

Chamney, Ronald, 1996, personal communication.

Charlesworth, Jack S., 1975, personal communication.

Chevalier, Michel, 1975, personal communication.

Christensen, Joel, 1996, personal communication.

Coats, Douglas, 1974, The economy of Calgary, 1875-1911: Calgary, Univ. of Calgary (mimeographed report).

Cochand III, Emile, 1996, personal communication

Cole, Joyce, 1974, personal communication.

Copithorne, Clarence, 1976, personal communication.

Crag and Canyon, September 24, 1975, Wilders take over Fortress Mountain: Banff, The Crag and Canyon (newspaper) (Canadian Press).

Cragg, Dr. J. B., 1976, personal communication.

Crockford, M. B. B., 1949, Geology of Ribbon Creek area Alberta, Report No. 52, Research Council of Alberta, Univ. of Alberta: Edmonton, King's Printer.

Crossley, Desmond, 1985, unpublished interview with Peter J. Murphy and James M. Parker (courtesy of Lynne Bowen).

Donelon, Steve, 1996, interview, Canmore, AB.

Dowling, D. B., 1915, Coal fields and coal resources of Canada, Canada Dept. of Mines, Geological Survey, Memoir 59, No. 55 Geological Series: Ottawa, Govt. Printing Bureau, No. 1388.

Duffy, Dr. Patrick, 1994, interview, Vancouver, BC.

Dupuis, John, 1995, interview, Calgary, AB.

Engler, Bruno, 1975, personal communication.

Ernst, Bruce, 1994, interview, Exshaw, AB.

Feldberg, Beverly, 1976, personal communication.

Field, George, 1996, personal communication.

Final Progress Report, December 1969-December 1970; NRC Negotiated Development Grant awarded for a three-year period April 1, 1968-March 31, 1971: Univ. of Calgary, Environmental Sciences Centre (Kananaskis).

Fraser, Esther, 1978, Wheeler: Banff, Summerthought.

Gardner, Donald, 1973, personal communication.

Getty, Ian A. L., 1974 and 1996, personal communications.

Giggs, Dennis, 1976, Dept. of Fish and Wildlife, Province of Alberta, personal communication.

Goodman, David, 1976, Federal Business Development Bank, personal communication.

Goodwin, Joanne, 1974, personal communication.

Gray, Mary, 1972, A preliminary survey of the history of the Kananaskis Valley: Calgary, Univ. of Calgary, Environmental Sciences Centre (Kananaskis), (unpub. ms.).

Green, Sheryl, 1996, personal communication.

Guinn, Denise and Rick, 1996, personal communication.

Haddin, J. A. Papers 1910-1961, November 1912, Glenbow-Alberta Institute Archives: Calgary.

Hanna, David, 1996, interview, Bow Valley Provincial Park, AB.

Hanna, Earl J., 1995, personal communication.

Hanson, W. R., ca. 1974, History of the Eastern Rockies Forest Conservation Board 1947-1973: Calgary, University of Calgary, Kananaskis Field Stations, (unpub. ms.).

Harrington, Lyn, 1954, Eastern Rockies forest conservation project: Canadian Geographical Journal, v. 48.

Hawkes, Brad C., 1978, A fire history and fuel appraisal study of Kananaskis Provincial Park, unpublished report.

Hendry, M. C., 1914, Bow River power and storage investigations, Dept. of the Interior, Canada, Water Power Branch, Water Resources paper No. 2: Ottawa, Govt. Printing Bureau.

Herald, The Calgary, October 9, 1970, Greyhound acquires Snowridge Ski Resort: Calgary, The Calgary Herald (newspaper) (Canadian Press).

Hodgson, Dr. G. W., 1976 and 1995, Calgary, AB, personal communications.

Holmgren, Eric J., 1983, Prisoner-of-war and internment camps in Alberta, photocopied manuscript, Edmonton.

Holmgren, Eric J. and Patricia M., 1976, third edition, Over 2000 place names of Alberta: Saskatoon, Sask., Western Producer Prairie Books.

Hostelling International—Canada—Ribbon Creek Hostel files.

Horton, Tim Children's Foundation, A Summer to Remember, brochure, Oakville, Ontario, no date.

Jackson, Dr. Lionel, 1995, interview, Calgary, AB.

Jaques, Dennis, 1974 and 1994, personal communication and interview, Vancouver, BC.

Jaques, Virginia, 1994, interview, Vancouver, BC.

Jenness, S. E., 1965, Geological Survey of Canada, Report 65-1, Report of activities field 1964.

Johnsrud, Sgt. John, 1995, interview, Exshaw, AB.

Kennedy, Fred, 1975, Alberta was my beat: Calgary, The Albertan (newspaper) (Canadian Press).

Kirby, C. L., 1973, The Kananaskis Forest Experiment Station, Alberta (history, physical features and forest inventory): Edmonton, Northern Forest Research Centre, Inf. Rept. No. NOR-X-51.

Kovach, Joe, Alberta Forest Service diaries, 1940-1953, copies held by Univ. of Calgary, Environmental Sciences Centre (Kananaskis).

Krowchuk, Art, 1975, personal communication.

Langille, Eileen, 1974, personal communication.

Leader, Canmore, July 1995, Locke acquires Nakiska: Canmore, Canmore Leader (newspaper).

Leader, Canmore, June 11, 1996, Mountains hold their secrets: Canmore, Canmore Leader (newspaper).

Legge, Dr. Allan, 1995, interview, Calgary, AB.

Longair, Art, 1995, interview, Chestermere Lake, AB.

Lonsdale, Rev. T. H., 1974, personal communication.

MacEwan, J. W. Grant and Foran, Maxwell, 1968, A short history of western Canada: Toronto, McGraw-Hill Ryerson Limited.

MacGregor, J. G., 1974, Paddle wheels to bucket wheels on the Athabasca: Toronto, McClelland and Stewart Limited.

Mackie, Richard, 1974, personal communication.

Marriner, Ray, 1974, personal communication.

Marsh, Janet, 1975, personal communication.

Matthews, Gordon and Ida, 1975, personal communication, 1996 interview, Cochrane, AB.

Matthews, Gordon, 1974, personal communication from his records as District Forest Officer, Kananaskis Ranger Station.

McAffer, Verda, 1995, interview, Canmore, AB.

McDonald, Captain H. B., 1974, personal communication.

McGuffin, W. C., 1975, personal communication.

McLaws, Donald, 1976, personal communication.

Mutch, Dr. Robert and Dr. Cynthia, 1995, interview, Medicine Hat, AB.

Nakamura, Toby and Staythe, Hugh, 1976, personal communication.

Natural Resources Conservation Board Hearing, Application 9104, June 5, 1992, Volume IV.

Nielsen, Dave, 1996, personal communication.

Nordegg, Martin, 1971, The possibilities of Canada are truly great, T. D. Regehr, ed.: Toronto, Macmillan.

O'Shaughnessy, John, 1975, personal communication.

Patterson, R. M., 1961, The buffalo head: Toronto, Macmillan Co. of Canada Limited.

Petrov, Peter, 1975, personal communication.

Piper, Norma was the daughter of Dr. W. A. Piper of Calgary; Glenbow Alberta Institute Archives: Calgary. Mrs. Pocaterra taught music in Calgary in her Pocaterra Studio.

Pocaterra, G. W., 1963, Among the Nomadic Stoneys: Alberta Historical Review, v. 11, No. 3, summer.

Pocaterra, George W., Information has been taken from the Pocaterra Papers: Calgary, Glenbow-Alberta Institute Archives.

Quinn, Alvin, 1976, personal communication.

Reeves, B. O. K., 1974, Archaeological reconnaissance, Kananaskis Highway, Stoney Indian Reserve, Rocky Creek: Calgary, Lifeways of Canada Ltd., (unpub. reports for the Alberta Minister of Highways and Transport, Edmonton).

Reeves, B. O. K., 1975, personal communication, 1996, interview, Calgary, AB.

Reynolds, Robert, 1994, interview, Canmore, AB.

Riebenstein, Ernst, 1976, personal communication.

Riley, Dan, Primrose, Tom and Dempsey, Hugh, 1968, The greatest mystery of the Canadian Rockies, The lost lemon mine: Frontier Book No. 4.

Roxburgh, Peter and Lucille, 1995, interview, Calgary, AB.

Rummel, Elizabeth, 1974, personal communication.

Sadler, Thomas and Grey, Mary, 1973, A history of the Kananaskis Valley: Calgary, Univ. of Calgary, Environmental Sciences Centre (Kananaskis), (unpub. ms.).

Sage, Clarence and Jenny, 1975, personal communication.

Schmidt, Walter, 1972, personal communication to Mary Gray.

Schulte, Theodore, 1976, personal communication.

Sekhon, Param, 1995, interview, Calgary, AB.

Sibbald, A., 1920, Alberta Historical Review, Winter 1971, v. 19, no. 1.

Skrastins, Alf, 1996, interview, Calgary, AB.

Smith, Donald, 1986, November 9, Majestic Monuments: The Calgary Herald: Herald Magazine.

Smith, Floyd, 1974, personal communication.

Smithers, Dr. L. A. (Bud), 1994, interview, Westbank, BC.

Smythe, Hugh, 1976, personal communication.

Smythe, Sandra, 1996, personal communication.

Snyder, Dr. Floyd, 1994, interview, Calgary, AB.

Spry, Irene M., 1963, Routes through the Rockies, Beaver Magazine Autumn, 02.6, Sp. 8, PAM.

Stalker, A. MacS., 1973, Surficial geology of the Kananaskis Research Forest and Marmot Creek Basin region of Alberta: Geological Survey of Canada, Department of Energy Mines and Resources, paper 72-51.

Stephenson, H. G., 1974, personal communication.

Stomp, James, 1996, interview, Bow Valley Provincial Park, AB.

Strom, Theodore, Reminiscences re. Eau Claire Lumber Company 1886 ca. 1912, (23.1.): Calgary, Glenbow-Alberta Institute Archives (unpub. ms.).

Swanson, Dr. Robert W., 1995, interview and personal communication, Canmore, AB.

Tietjen, Dr. Cord, 1976, personal communication.

Township plans and memorandum of applications and grants for timber and grazing lands registers, 1903, 1904: Edmonton, Provincial Archives of Alberta.

Trailblazer, Summer 1996, Calgary: Hostelling International—Canada-Southern Alberta Region.

Van Sant, Vernon, 1975, personal communication and information gleaned from the files of the Kananaskis Exploration and Development Company: Calgary.

Verbicky, Elaine, 1970, A pilgrimage: former prisoner of war returns to camp at Seebe: Calgary, The Calgary Herald (newspaper) (Canadian Press).

Von Darl, Ingrid, 1996, interview, Calgary, AB.

Wallis, Dr. Peter and Marcia, 1995, interview, Medicine Hat, AB.

Wilcox, W.D., 1902, The National Geographic journal, Vol. XIII, No. 5 May 1902 and Vol. XIII, No. 6 June 1902.

Wilcox, W. D., 1909, The Rockies of Canada: Banff, Archives of the Canadian Rockies.

Wise, S. F., 1970, Director, Directorate of History, Canadian Forces Headquarters, Ottawa; personal communication to Mary Grey.

Further Reading

Boles, Glen W., Kruszyna, Robert, Putnam, William L., 1966, 1973, 1979, *The Rocky Mountains of Canada South*: The American Alpine Club, New York, and The Alpine Club of Canada, Banff.

Cameron, Ward, 1996, *Kananaskis*: Canmore, Altitude Publishing.

Daffern, Gillean, 1992, *Kananaskis Country Ski Trails*: Calgary, Rocky Mountain Books.

Daffern, Gillean, 1994, *Canmore & Kananaskis Country: Short Walks for Inquiring Minds 1*: Calgary, Rocky Mountain Books.

Daffern, Gillean, 1996 and 1997, *Kananaskis Country Trail Guide, 2 vols.*: Calgary, Rocky Mountain Books.

Dougherty, Sean, 1996, *Selected Alpine Climbs in the Canadian Rockies*: Calgary, Rocky Mountain Books.

Eastcott, Doug and Lepp, Gerhardt, 2nd edition 1993, *Backcountry Biking in the Canadian Rockies*: Calgary, Rocky Mountain Books.

Hanisch, Ernst, 1996, *Kananaskis Ram: a story from Kananaskis Country*: Calgary, Rocky Mountain Books.

Josephson, Joe, 1995, *Waterfall Ice Climbs in the Canadian Rockies*: Calgary, Rocky Mountain Books.

Kane, Alan, 2nd edition 1995, *Scrambles in the Canadian Rockies*: Calgary, Rocky Mountain Books.

Karamitsanas, Aphrodite, 1991, *Place Names of Alberta, Volume 1*: Calgary, University of Calgary Press.

Lent, D. Geneva, 1963, *West of the Mountains, James Sinclair and the Hudson's Bay Company*: Seattle, Univ. of Washington Press.

Luxton, Eleanor, G., 1975, *Banff: Canada's First National Park, a History and a Memory of Rocky Mountains Park*: Banff, Summerthought.

Martin, John and Jones, Jon, 1996, *Sport Climbs in the Canadian Rockies*: Calgary, Rocky Mountain Books.

Oltmann, Ruth, 1978, *The Valley of Rumours … the Kananaskis*: Exshaw, Ribbon Creek Publishing Company.

Oltmann, Ruth, 1983, *Lizzie Rummel: Baroness of the Canadian Rockies*: Calgary, Rocky Mountain Books.

Schmaltz, Ken, 1996, *Rocky Mountain Retreats*: Calgary, Points West Publishing.

Spry, Irene M., ed., 1968, *The Papers of the Palliser Expedition 1857-1860*: Toronto, The Champlain Society, v. 44.

Tobey, Kelly, 1987, *Barrier Bluffs, The Guide*: Calgary.

Index